THE DOLLARS AND SENSE OF DIVORCE

Judith Briles, Ph.D.
Edwin C. Schilling III, JD, CFP
Carol Ann Wilson, CFP, CDP

Dearborn
Financial Publishing, Inc.®

Dedication

For my daughters, so they never have to repeat mistakes.

> —Judith Briles

To Lanell, my wife of 34 years, who inspires and encourages me, and challenges me to grow.

> —Edwin C. Schilling III

For those struggling with divorce—may this book give you hope and make the process easier.

> —Carol Ann Wilson

Editorial Director: Cynthia A. Zigmund
Managing Editor: Jack Kiburz
Interior Design: Lucy Jenkins
Cover Design: Design Alliance, Inc.
Typesetting: the dotted i

Published by Dearborn Financial Publishing, Inc.®

Library of Congress Cataloging-in-Publication Data

Briles, Judith.
    The dollars and sense of divorce / Judith Briles, Edwin Schilling
III, Carol Ann Wilson.
        p.   cm.
    Includes index.
    ISBN 0-7931-2763-7
    1. Divorce—Economic aspects—United States.   I. Schilling,
Edwin.   II. Wilson, Carol Ann, 1937– .   III. Title.
HQ834.B75   1998
306.89—dc21   98-7416
                                                      CIP

Contents

Preface

Congratulations! In your hands you have the most complete and up-to-date book on divorce today. Many other books on divorce are full of legal mumbo jumbo. Unless you are a true devotee of the legal word, you could end up a zombie! This book is different. *The Dollars and Sense of Divorce* provides answers to just about any question you can come up with—and is entertaining at the same time. Even though divorce is something most people would not choose to go through as a source of amusement, a little humor can bring clarity to a difficult situation.

Your authors have written more than 20 books among themselves. We have financially advised, served as expert witnesses, and represented men and women for a combined total of more than 60 years. Each of us has laughed and cried, felt the misery and, believe it or not, the joy our clients have experienced. And from their (and sometimes our own) mistakes and mishaps, we are able to present the ultimate book on divorce.

The Dollars and Sense of Divorce works for anyone who is thinking about a divorce. This book talks about the before, during, and after of divorce, and addresses the emotional, legal, and financial issues you are facing. If you have kids, there's a special section to guide you, and them, through this traumatic time. And we've also included an "anger plan" for when conflicts hit the big time. Chapters end with our *baker's dozen*—13 tips, techniques, and ideas to make your life better—and to make you wiser.

We have distilled information from the experts—those who have walked in your path as well as those who have advised them along the way. We've analyzed and probed from the inside out. The result—a real and practical book.

Why You Need This Book

Why a book called *The Dollars and Sense of Divorce*? Divorce is not a simple process. You probably don't know what questions to ask or when to speak up. It's time you learned. You are in new territory—lawyers, summons, temporary orders, and judges, all components of a "friendly" divorce. (Imagine the "unfriendly" one . . . the one that is just shy of World War III!) It's not uncommon to sense your brain is turning to mush. Getting incomplete or wrong advice from others (sometimes well-meaning friends and family, not to mention some of the "professionals" you may erroneously engage) can greatly impact the final outcome of your divorce.

Would this book have helped us? You bet. For Ed, the mega-hours he has spent within his law practice guiding and advising clients on the divorce highway would have been more productive and efficient if he could have placed *The Dollars and Sense of Divorce* in their hands and assigned homework. It certainly would have saved his clients some money—answers would have been available in simple English for approximately $20. Beats spending $150 an hour.

For Carol Ann and Judith, *The Dollars and Sense of Divorce* would have been a great solution for the thousands of women and men who have routinely sought their financial advice and recommendations before, during, and after their divorces. On a personal side, Carol Ann confesses that it could easily have made the difference between starting over in poverty when she divorced or having a solid financial foundation. For Judith, it would have exposed the myth and realities of divorce. She once believed that all courtrooms were like Perry Mason—the bad guy (or gal) always confesses and pays the penalty. Instead, she learned that people lie—including lawyers, in-laws, and ex-husbands and wives.

Knowledge is power—and this book is packed with information that can help you "muscle up" for the challenges you face. Divorce can be like a dance, with moves and countermoves. Our goal is to teach you the steps and nuances and reduce the number of times that your toes are stepped on—by others, by the system, or by yourself.

How to Use This Book

We know, this is a big book. Not just in its amazing breadth of information, how-tos, and zany stories! The time you spend reading this book could be an excellent investment in your future. You might even want to plan a grand holiday with all the money you are going to save by becoming a divorce planning–savvy dude or dudette. Here are two ways to use (and profit from) *The Dollars and Sense of Divorce:*

1. Flip to the chapter that identifies your current concerns and devour everything within it. Since behaviorists tell us that in order for information to stick, we need to redo, reread, or rethink whatever we are trying to do and learn, plan to reread the chapter a few times. Then move on to the next chapter of interest.
2. Read everything from cover to cover. You can use the information or you can pass it on to one of your friends who is contemplating a divorce.

The Dollars and Sense of Divorce is ideal for any person who has had a broken relationship. In fact, it would be an excellent primer for anyone who is considering *marriage.* Not to scare them, but to make each spouse aware of the things that they should know financially, legally, and emotionally before embarking on this journey. This book contains many examples of couples we have worked with throughout the years. Their names have been changed, but their circumstances and outcomes are real.

—Judith Briles, Edwin C. Schilling III, and Carol Ann Wilson

Acknowledgments

Acknowledgments are always the last thing that an author does. The people who are behind the scenes are the critical components in bringing an author's words to life.

The book you are holding would not have happened without the vision and quickness of Cynthia Zigmund, our editor. She saw our idea, understood its immediate need, and said "yes" without hesitating. Her right hand, Sandy Holzbach, was terrific to work with, and Jack Kiburz did wonders in the art of copyediting. We thank them all.

Our staffs have been supporting and fun as we dug into the book, counting on them (yes, and praying for them!) to cover when we needed to be underground writing.

Judith thanks Dolores Hall, the Lukemeister, and hubby John Maling, her best cheerleader.

Edwin sends grand bouquets to Dr. Lanell Schilling, his partner in life and one savvy therapist.

Carol Ann thanks Nan Coursey, the general manager of the Institute for Certified Divorce Planners, for all her help and encouragement, and Carolyn Madden, CFP, CDP, and Barbara Stark, JD—two terrific trainers for the Institute for Certified Divorce Planners—for providing constant updates on legal and financial information on divorce.

1

What If I Don't Want a Divorce?

Let's face it—divorce is not a lot of fun. It can be the real pits. For most, it's a very painful journey, one that would rarely make the "top ten list of great activities that make my day."

Because of the negativity and agony so often associated with divorce, millions stay in unhappy marriages. Not surprisingly, postponing divorce has positives and negatives to it. On the plus side, the postponement allows time for smoothing out the bumps in a marriage. If there are kids, studies show that they would do just about anything to keep their parents together. On the downside, men and women in unhappy marriages often do and say things to their partners that would have been unthinkable during the days of courtship. If there is verbal and physical abuse, the cons start outweighing the pros.

We Can Make It Work

The marriage stats aren't wonderful. According to the U.S. Census Bureau, 50 percent of marriages end in divorce. The average marriage lasts 11 years. Pretty grim, especially when you consider all the guilt and devastation brought about by the failure of a relationship that was supposed to last a lifetime.

Most men and women don't throw in the towel easily. Few marriages are created from a moment of frivolity; neither is the decision to divorce. Usually a lot of thought and planning go in both processes.

So, what if you really don't want a divorce? Friends may be telling you to split. Your parents may be saying, "I told you so." Your kids may even be saying, "We would be better off without _____ here all the time." What do you do when you still (or think you still) love your spouse? Do you listen and act on everyone else's advice? Or, do you try one more time to make it work?

For what seems a zillion years, women's magazines have carried columns on relationships and marriage. You can bet you won't find a "can this marriage be saved" column in *Popular Mechanics* or *Esquire*. No, these are usually found in magazines like *Ladies Home Journal*. Does that mean that men aren't so into saving a marriage? We don't think so.

Well then, what can you do for a last-chance effort before declaring your marriage over? Experts in marriage issues will tell you that poor communication is at the top of the "what's wrong" list. It is not easy to put a marriage back together. It's hard work and cannot be done by only one of the partners. It takes two. If there are kids in the picture, it's no longer between the two of you.

The Window Is Still Open

This could be the last time you and your spouse are open and willing to entertain a continuation of the marriage. The window is open, but most likely, not for long. Start with getting help. There are plenty of counselors out there—you just have to find the right one. (We will go into more detail on this subject in the next chapter.)

Our experiences are that the right therapist will be someone who has a sense of humor, has been in practice for at least five years, and is married, a good communicator, skilled in conflict resolution, interactive, and able and willing to confront either of you with your garbage and baggage. Yes, you've got it, and so does your spouse.

When a marriage is on the outs, conflict is everywhere. Minor things like parking the car in the garage or major things like not showing up for dinner can erupt into World War III. A counselor who is savvy in conflict resolution, even teaching you how to "fight fair," is a major player in pulling a marriage out of the drain.

It takes more than looking up marriage counselors in the yellow pages. Start by asking friends who have successfully pursued this route. Don't be afraid to ask if they have worked with someone who wasn't good—duds, rejects, or mistakes in their pasts. Your rabbi or clergyperson can be helpful. Many are quite skilled in counseling and should be among the first sources to turn to. Ask at your place of worship if there is a couples' group (many offer programs such as couple week-ends and marriage encounters). Some have small groups that focus on couple accountability and support during turbulent times.

For some couples, it doesn't matter if they work with a man or woman. For others, it makes a big difference. If either of you has a bias against one or the other, select someone with whom you both can work. If you don't agree on the therapist, you or your partner will sabotage, consciously or unconsciously, the therapist's suggestions, strategies, advice, and recommendations. If you are serious about not divorcing, then you both need to be present—mentally and physically.

When interviewing therapists check out your comfort level. Is he or she easy to communicate with? Do you feel that you are being patronized or placated? Your comfort level should be high—after all, some nitty-gritty stuff is going to come out, stuff that you wouldn't like e-mailed to the rest of the world. You definitely want to be able to speak and have your issues heard clearly. The last thing you want, or need, is to have someone looking down his or her nose at you.

> • • • • •
>
> If, at any time, you or your spouse feel that the therapist is not helping you, stop going. If you are still committed to trying to save your marriage, get another therapist pronto. It is important to work with someone that you respect and trust. No exceptions.
>
> • • • • •

How Did We Get to This Point?

The mere fact that you have bought this book, or that someone has given it to you, says that you are not having a lot of fun right now. There are plenty of reasons why you are at this stage. It could be that you and your spouse are just different from the two you were when you first got together. There could have been a significant event in your lives—a failed business; death of a child, parent, or other loved one; increasing age; or an illness. For whatever the reason, life is just not the same.

Warning Signs

At some time, you will ask, "Where did it all begin?" or muse, "If only I/we hadn't done or said _____, we wouldn't have these problems." Rarely is that thinking going to help you or remove you from the spot you are presently in. Most marriages fall apart over a period of time. Here are a few of the classic signs that it's over or almost over:

- Your spouse ropes you in (or vice versa). Any type of personal growth and development is forbidden or strongly discouraged.
- Respect is missing—either individually or mutually.
- Your lifestyle and values are no longer in sync.
- Having a root canal is preferable to having sex with your spouse.
- You fight over anything and everything.
- One of you has outgrown the other.
- You rarely communicate.
- Your spouse is never home or available to you.
- You would rather spend time with others than with your spouse.
- You believe that you would be better off alone (or dead).

If you respond, "That sounds like me/us," no wonder you aren't happy. We would vote that you are downright miserable.

Should I Just Leave?

You can just walk out the door, but you definitely should talk to a lawyer before you decide to do this, outside of any abuse, of course. If a litigated divorce seems likely, you must consider the impact leaving can have on a variety of strategic moves. For example, if a husband seeking custody of the children leaves home without the children, he may be at a substantial disadvantage when custody proceedings begin.

A physical separation also may affect the timing of the divorce. For example, if the wife wants the husband out of the house but is reluctant to agree to a divorce, it may be a strategic error for the husband to leave. Once he is out, the wife's desire to separate has been met and she may feel there is no need to speed along the divorce proceedings. Time is then on her side. She may stall and make unreasonable settlement demands to delay resolution of your case. The more the delay irritates one party, the more leverage the

> • • • • •
> If you believe that physical harm may come to you or the children, leave immediately regardless of the legal consequences or potential loss of some strategic advantage.
> • • • • •

other one has, and the irritated party may be willing to concede certain crucial issues just to end the case.

On the other hand, refusing to leave the house when your spouse wants you out reverses the leverage. The more the desire to have you out, the greater the leverage that can be employed to obtain concessions in other areas of negotiation.

Warning: In so-called "fault states," marital misconduct must be proved before divorce can be granted. In these states, leaving the marital home can be considered desertion if the legal period of separation is met. Only when the departing spouse can prove a valid basis for leaving can the separation be construed as "constructive" desertion and provide grounds for divorce for the departing spouse. No-fault states are listed in the Appendix.

In considering leaving the house it is important to consider that the longer you are gone, the more difficult it may be to be able to move back in if your spouse opposes it. Courts are sometimes reluctant to even enforce agreements permitting the spouse to move back in if the separation has been a long one and the spouse in the house opposes it.

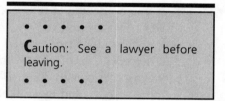

Caution: See a lawyer before leaving.

Separation—The End, or a New Beginning?

Let's say nothing is working. Your spouse refuses counseling (or decides it's a waste) and has declared, "Enough." What do you do—throw in the towel or try to come back for another round? There is a third choice—you could call a "time-out" by filing for a legal separation.

There are three primary reasons why you might want to consider a legal separation: your health—you may need surgery, are currently undergoing some type of treatment or therapy, or you just don't want additional stress that the divorcing process can bring about; your religion may not condone divorce; or you are still not totally sure you want one.

Not all separations result in a divorce. Some couples actually separate to create a cooling-off period and do hope to save their marriage. Sometimes it works; most times, it doesn't.

Separation is usually the second stage to divorce. All the disagreements, fighting, and the like are the first stage. It enables each party to find out what it is like to truly live alone—to have separate finances, accounts, and responsibilities.

If yours is a legal separation, it will be formalized with a legal document. This is different from one of the parties saying, "I'm out of here. I'll pick up my things later." A separation agreement usually sets forth each of your positions and views of rights relating to such things as the marital property, support, and custody. It becomes a guideline if a final dissolution comes about. Each of you contributes your thoughts and wants to it.

One of the pluses of a separation is that it can enhance self-esteem. You may ask how a separation can be a confidence-builder when pain and hurt is everywhere. By separating, you may find out how strong you, alone, really are. We know it's not an easy street, but it is a street that you can navigate with an open mind and willingness to stretch. Sometimes a brief separation, regardless of whether it is formalized with a legal document, can open new horizons. It delivers a preview of what tomorrow may look like to you as an unmarried person. Another plus is that if you do decide to divorce, a legal separation has formatted most of the groundwork; it goes quicker.

Emotions run a broad spectrum during a separation and the initial stages of a divorce. One of our favorite bumper stickers reads, "The road to success is always under construction." The road that you take during this process will have detours, curves, and most likely, a few dead ends.

To help you along your journey, your communication skills need to be finetuned. Whether you and your spouse get back together or you end your marriage, talk and listen. Most couples find that the range of emotions are at their highest during the first year after a decision to separate or divorce. This is the time when our brain can turn to mush.

If you are the initiator of the separation, you are a few steps ahead of your spouse. You have thought about being alone, on your own. If you are not the initiator, there is usually a higher level of fear. And pain. And anger.

Separate, but Still under the Same Roof

It's expensive to maintain two households. For that reason alone, many couples separate emotionally but continue to live under the same roof. Reasons for this arrangement are many: money; family or child care obligations; appearances; timing; or health or religious reasons. Whatever the reason, don't allow your home to become a war zone.

If you maintain a one-roof policy lay out some ground rules for the two of you

> If you have kids, do not, do not, do not use them as your messengers or weapons.

and stick to them. Divvy up sections and rooms. Because of the trapeze of emotions, trespassing can become treacherous. Move and keep your personal things in your room, your safe zone. Your spouse should do the same.

You Are the Winner

Think of separation as a cleaning and clearing-out stage. Start literally with your own closet. If you are the one who separates physically from your joint residence, you are not going to be keeping or taking things that you don't really want, that don't give you any type of pleasure, and that you no longer use. It puts you in a win-win spot. If, for whatever reason, you reunite and the marriage gets better, you both win. If you proceed with a divorce and the marriage ends, you prosper with your newfound knowledge. You are a survivor and can go it solo. You discover, if you didn't already know, that you have developed phenomenal endurance skills, all necessary for the years ahead.

13 Movies to Rent, Watch, and Learn From

· · · · ·

1. *The War of the Roses:* Michael Douglas, Kathleen Turner, Danny DeVito
   The granddaddy of divorce movies—the underlying theme is that success breeds contempt and that whatever looks like "ours" is really "mine." The spouses don't communicate, don't value each other, and are out for revenge. Dark humor brings out the ugliness of shattered relationships. If you are considering revenge, see this flick, and then think again.

2. *Kramer vs. Kramer:* Dustin Hoffman, Meryl Streep
   Mom decides that there is another life to be led and leaves the kids with an awkward dad, who learns how to become a terrific parent.

(continued)

The movie features communication issues, value of self, and the impact of divorce on kids. It's sure to stir up your emotions in a divorce where kids are involved.

3. *Liar, Liar:* Jim Carey
At his fifth birthday party, a boy wishes his divorced dad would just show up for visits and stop lying to him, to his mom, to everyone. His wish comes true, forcing his lawyer dad to tell the truth for a whole day. The movie tackles issues of old, new, and unfinished relationships. A funny and thoughtful movie.

4. *Mrs. Doubtfire:* Robin Williams, Sally Field, Pierce Brosnan
Estranged from his kids, goofy dad finally gets his parenting act together (there's more to parenting than being a buddy to the kids) through a series of events around child care, new relationships, self-evaluation, and redirecting misdirected talents. Robin Williams' schtick will leave you laughing out loud.

5. *The First Wives' Club:* Goldie Hawn, Diane Keaton, Bette Midler
The underlying theme of *FWC* is, don't get mad—get even. Laced with humor, this movie starts with the three women's drive to turn a former schoolmate's suicide into a statement of value, and along the way tackles trophy wives, hidden assets, kids, and getting back on track for self. Women howl at and many men shrink from this movie.

6. *Scenes from a Mall:* Woody Allen, Bette Midler
Couple spends the day at the mall on their anniversary and look back at what should have been and wasn't; and what is, and they don't like. Relationships look in the mirror and reveal aspects that aren't so nice.

7. *Three Men and a Baby:* Tom Selleck, Ted Danson, Steve Guttenberg
Three bachelors end up with a baby at their doorstep. One of them is the father. They attempt to care for the baby (and fall into some stereotypical problems with infant care and responsibility) and all comes out well.

8. *The Truth about Cats and Dogs:* Janeane Garofalo, Uma Thurman, Ben Chaplin
On-air radio veterinarian talks listeners through problems and relationships with their pets. From pets, they move on to people and their miscommunications and misconceptions about themselves and others. Dialogue is sharp, fun, and realistic.

9. *Dead Poet's Society:* Robin Williams
Ideal for parents who think their kids should be or have a specific occupation as an adult. Focuses on two themes: "To your own self be true" and "Seize the day"—strong messages for adults to heed, and share with their kids and themselves.

10. *The Doctor:* William Hurt, Elizabeth Perkins
Regarding Henry: Harrison Ford, Annette Bening
You may wonder why these two movies are included in a book about divorce. Both Hurt and Ford have marriages that aren't so hot; both treat other people like they are paper boxes—kept around just in case you might need them, then discarded when falling apart or no longer needed. Only a personal crisis delivers a wake-up call.

11. *Not Without My Daughter:* Sally Field
Based on a true story, Sally Field's character goes through a divorce. The catch is that she has moved to her physician husband's homeland in the Middle East. The culture is not female-friendly. Field fights for her life, and for her daughter's, as they try to escape.

12. *Starting Over:* Burt Reynolds, Jill Clayburgh, Candice Bergen
Not letting go before diving into another emotional relationship is the theme delivered in this fun probe of a divorced man's confusion over falling in love.

13. *The Full Monty:* Robert Carlyle, Tom Wilkinson, Mark Addy, Steve Huison
The Full Monty is one of the wackiest English movies of 1997. Out of work, down and out, and trying to raise back child support funds, six

(continued)

men decide to overcome their obstacles and become England's answer to the Chippendale dancers. This fun flick is full of belly laughs—
the perfect antidote for just about anything.

14. *Make-another-batch-of-popcorn bonus!*
    As Good As It Gets: Jack Nicholson, Helen Hunt, Greg Kinnear, Cuba
    Gooding, Jr.
    Multiple awards were delivered for this sharp, poignant, and witty
    romp through an unlikely trio (plus a neat dog) that get thrown to-
    gether. From obsessive-compulsive disorders, to downward-spiraling
    self-worths, to distrust and disbelief, this movie is as good as it gets!

• • • • •

13 Most Frequently Asked Questions about Divorce

• • • • •

1. **Will I be able to receive alimony?**
   There are several tests for alimony:
   • Need (Can you support yourself with earned income plus invest-
     ment income?)
   • Ability to pay (Does the payer of alimony have sufficient funds to
     pay?)
   • Length of marriage (A long-term marriage—ten years or more—is
     more likely to have longer alimony paid to the lower-earning
     spouse.)
   • Age and health of both parties

2. **Do I have to share my pension?**
   Most pensions and retirement plans are considered marital assets in
   most states. Depending on the state where you file for divorce, the

portion earned before your marriage could also be considered a marital asset.

3. **Should the wife get the house?**
   It depends on several things:
   - If the wife has custody of the children, you may want to keep change to a minimum.
   - She should not depend on alimony to make high house payments.
   - If the payments are low, she probably should keep the house.
   - If the equity in the house is all she receives, she may need some liquid funds (cash).

4. **What if I bring a house into the marriage that is in my name only, and I add my spouse's name to the deed?**
   Then the whole house is considered to be marital property. You have made a "presumptive gift" to the marriage. In other words, it is assumed you gave your spouse a gift of half the value of the property.

5. **Is my IRA considered marital property? It's in my name only.**
   Everything acquired during the marriage, no matter whose name it's in, is considered marital property. In some states, the increase in value of separate property is considered marital.

6. **I have never worked. Can I get Social Security?**
   If your spouse has worked and is eligible for Social Security and if you have been married for ten years or more, then you are entitled to one-half of your spouse's Social Security or your own, whichever is higher. It does not lower your spouse's benefit.

7. **How do we figure how much child support should be paid?**
   All states now have child support guidelines. You can get a copy by asking your attorney or by contacting the local bar association.

8. **Do we have to go to court?**
   Only if you can't reach an agreement. Then, a court date is set and a judge hears the case.

(continued)

9. Can we use just one attorney?

It is not recommended. If you do use your spouse's attorney, remember that this attorney represents your spouse, not you, if the going gets rough.

10. Where can we find financial help?

Certified Divorce Planners are trained to help people through the financial maze of divorce. They sift through the financial issues including incomes, expenses, assets, tax issues, pensions, and division of property to help you reach a financially equitable settlement that is fair to both parties. Call the Institute for Certified Divorce Planners at 800-875-1760 for a list of Certified Divorce Planners in your area.

11. Who will pay the attorneys' fees?

Today, the most likely answer is that each pays his or her own attorney fees. There are always exceptions, with a significant disparity in financial positions. Unless the couple agrees that one will pay the other's attorney bills, the judge will decide.

12. Who will pay our debts?

It is imperative that you be specific about what is your debt and what is not. Part of your responsibility is to create a plan for repayment of debt that is yours.

13. What child custody arrangements will we have?

It's a good idea to explore alternatives to your situation. Some holidays are more important to one parent than to the other. Sometimes joint custody works well, sometimes it doesn't. Some parents stay within the same neighborhood or school district for their school-age kids. Some even rotate who lives in the old family residence as the custodial parent so the kids stay put—it's the parent who packs his or her bags.

• • • • •

2

The Five Stages of Divorce

"**B**eing widowed would have been more desirable," said one of our clients. "When you are widowed, everyone is sympathetic. There is support from men and women alike. When you are divorced, it's different. There are times when I felt as if I had a contagious, life-threatening disease—I felt like an outcast."

The decision has been made—a divorce. You can read all the latest statistics and intellectually understand that a whole lot of other people out there are going through the same ordeal. It doesn't lessen the frustration, anger, even fear that you may be experiencing. Right now, you and your soon-to-be-ex are the only statistics that count. Not millions, just the two of you.

The Dance

When a relationship begins, it is similar to a dance. When a marriage is ending, it resembles a different kind of dance. There are moves and countermoves that a couple goes through. Sometimes they are original, one of a kind, other times they mirror moves from the past or those we've seen others do. You are no different. There are times when you will be in a parallel movement with your spouse, and there will be times when you both will be moving in different directions. Your relationship was like that even when times were good. Now that the differences far outweigh the similarities, you may be wondering how you ever got on the dance floor in the first place.

Jean Hollands is a therapist, consultant, author, and founder of the GLC Clinic based in the heart of Northern California's Silicon Valley. For several decades, she has observed and counseled individuals, couples, and companies throughout the various stages of divorce. Companies? Yes, when principals in a company disagree, even break off, the process is similar to the one divorcing couples experience. Hollands is brought in as the corporate therapist to ask, Can this company be saved?

One of the exercises she asks each client to complete within the first session has two parts:

1. Imagine the divorce is over. Two years have passed. What does your life look like? What are you doing and feeling? Who are your friends? What do you think your ex is doing and feeling? If you have kids, what are they like? How are they feeling? How do they spend their days? How are they doing in school? Where is everyone living now, including you?
2. Imagine the divorce didn't occur; you stay together. Two years have passed. What does your life look like? What are you doing and feeling? Who are your friends? What do you think your spouse is doing and feeling? If you have kids, what are they like? How are they feeling? How do they spend their days? How are they doing in school? Where is everyone living?

Although this exercise seems simple, it requires work to delve into your fears of the future and imagine your new life as a single or your continuing existence as a couple. By going through Hollands' process, you begin to erode the fear factor. Some couples even decide that with some tuning—both minor and major—they are willing to try to work things out.

The Five Stages of Divorce

In 1969, Elizabeth Kubler-Ross published her classic book, *On Death and Dying* (Macmillan, 1969). Within it, she identified the five phases that most people go through when dealing with the death process: denial, anger, bargaining, letting go, and acceptance. When there is a divorce, a type of death is occurring—the death of your hopes and dreams regarding this relationship. A relationship that came together with optimism and great intentions has gone sour.

1. Denial

During the denial stage, you don't want to accept that anything serious is wrong with your marriage. You (and your spouse) are very unhappy. It's one of the worst stages of all because you feel that it will never end. How do you know when the end is near or has passed you by? It happens when one of you decides to take the lead and file for a legal separation or divorce—or when you go into counseling to rectify the situation.

For some, the denial stage stays with them throughout the entire divorce process—the feeling that this can't be happening.

But once one of you files the first set of papers, it often brings a sense of relief. It also can introduce the next stage—anger.

2. Anger

With the official filing, all your pent-up feelings and emotions regarding the relationship surface. If your spouse files against you, you may find yourself reluctant to go along with the process (even if you want the divorce), and may even feel angry at *yourself* because you dragged your feet.

During this stage, a lot of hatred comes out. If anyone comes within earshot, you may be ready to blast him or her for the slightest infraction. You unload every nuance you can image. It doesn't matter that it qualifies for a round of trivial pursuit. At this point, nothing feels like it is trivial. Your attitude, and reactions, are usually maxed to their limits.

This stage is full of reactions and feelings. On one hand, you can't figure out how this person, your about-to-be-ex partner, had any qualities that you, the sane rational person you know you are, could ever have fallen in love with in the first place. On the other hand, if you choose to maintain that he or she was a nice person, it is difficult to express and acknowledge the anger you are feeling.

3. Bargaining

It's common for any anger you feel to overlap into the bargaining period, a stage where you didn't want the marriage to end and you may concede anything to keep it together. Don't. This is the time you need to start building your own strengths, even power. The powerful person in a divorce will ultimately use it to create a better settlement. That, in turn, could create better conditions for terminating the marriage.

4. Letting Go

This is a critical stage. During the letting-go stage, revisiting the scenario of where you will be in two years is a good idea. A few months may have gone by.

Where you thought you wanted to be may be totally different from where you are going or where you think you want to be at this point in time.

5. *Acceptance*

The day you accept a divorce is a red-letter day. With acceptance, you drop the burden you have been carrying around on your shoulders for months, even years. You will learn there is no need to continue to invest in a relationship that is dead.

• • • • •

A word of caution: Letting go and acceptance may not happen until long after your divorce is final. Don't give up hope!

• • • • •

The Divorce Cycle

The five stages of denial, anger, bargaining, acceptance, and letting go usually flow in a cycle. Sometimes stages overlap; sometimes they are repeated. We have found that the illustration in Figure 2.1 represents the most common behaviors and emotions experienced within each cycle.

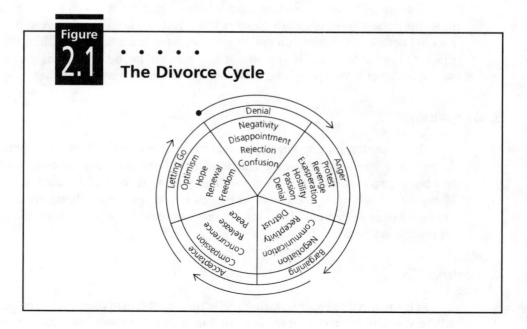

Figure 2.1 • • • • •
The Divorce Cycle

You will note that the anger section includes more behaviors. Anger can be very scary. Sometimes good can come from it, if you move off the dime and take action. The question is, what kind of action? Because anger is so common throughout, before, and after divorce, we have created a special chapter dealing with it, "When Love Takes a Back Seat." If you feel that anger may be getting the best of you (or your ex), turn to Chapter 11 now and learn a few techniques that can be lifesavers for you, your family, and your friends.

It Takes Two to Tangle

Now, what happens during these stages? Hollands identifies what she calls "the separation dance." It is a series of forward and backward steps that couples use when one may make a move toward reconciliation. The other responds by taking a step toward it and then backing away. Then, each makes a negative move followed by one making another conciliatory dance move. The process repeats itself many times.

The steps could involve little gestures such as calling and saying, "It is our anniversary and I feel like going out with you anyway, even though we are getting a divorce. How about dinner?" That query creates a move for the continuation of the marriage. If the other spouse says, "OK, let's meet at 6:30 P.M.," or "I'll pick you up," the next step is taken.

One partner may be excited about the prospect of getting back together. Over dinner, she is hopeful, finding all kinds of things about her estranged spouse to fall in love with again. On the other hand, the spouse whose idea was to go to dinner might be thinking, "Boy, am I glad we are getting a divorce." So, he is done with it.

Now, he has pulled back and she makes a move and she may make another move toward him and he may think, "I had better be good or she is going to change the settlement on me." This dance could go on for months, even years.

Understanding this separation dance may yield great rewards to you in the planning stage of your divorce, especially if it goes on for several years. Don't be surprised if you find yourself skipping stages only to go through them later. Life isn't in perfect order; most likely, your separation and divorce will not occur in an orderly fashion. Psychologists report that most of the anger has been vented within the first year of the decision to divorce. At that time, conflicts, hostilities, and angers subside. That's a good sign.

13 Ways to Survive the Divorce

· · · · ·

1. Laugh. It heals and cures incredible pain.

2. Read *How to Survive the Loss of a Love* by Melba Colgrove, Ph.D., Harold H. Bloomfield, MD, and Peter McWilliams (Prelude Press, 1993).

3. Get a therapist who specializes in divorce and join a divorce recovery group. This usually is a short-term engagement.

4. Treat your friends with kindness. It's easy to abuse those close to you, especially in the beginning stages of a divorce. Remember why they are your friends.

5. Get smart—educate yourself about divorce. Talk to people who have gone through it. Ask, "If I could roll back the clock, would I have done anything differently?"

6. Stay busy. Volunteer within the community if you are not working for pay.

7. Keep communications open with your ex-to-be and definitely with your kids, if you have them.

8. Surround yourself with positive people. It's common to want to hang out with others who are in the same boat. That works for a short while. After that, the ship begins to sink. Negative people beget negative people.

9. Be assertive and clear about what you want. If you feel weak in this area, there are classes that you can take that will assist you in speaking up for yourself. Remember, if you have kids and are going to be the custodial parent, you are speaking for them too.

10. Keep track of the hours you put into gathering data for your attorney. Then figure out how much she would have charged if she had had to do the sleuthing. Do the math and determine just how much money you saved.

11. Make a list identifying the top four things that are important to you personally and professionally. Next, turn down activities and projects for the next month that don't tie in with your top four. Instead, pour your energy into your big four—you will feel terrific.

12. Watch our top 13 (actually 15) movies (see Chapter 1).

13. Plan a celebration when it is over. A celebration of a divorce? Yes. You have been through a lot—a pat on the back is in order for not following through with some of the nasty thoughts you had along the way. It could be dinner out with a friend, a movie, even a trip.

• • • • •

3

Therapy—Avoid World War III during Your Divorce

We have referred to therapists in previous chapters. The type of therapist we are referring to is a specific therapist—one who specializes in divorce. This is not every therapist. In fact, only a small portion of licensed therapists have true expertise in working with their clients through divorce. Oh, they have clients who are in various stages of divorce. The difference is that the divorce therapist understands divorce—the stages, the dance, the emotions, and their impact—and ties the process in with the real world.

The term *divorce therapist* may be new to you. A divorce therapist is very different from a marriage counselor, whose primary thrust is to reunite you as a couple. The "let's put it back together" counselor isn't very helpful when everything is falling apart, when your world is shattering (or at least one of you feels as if your world is falling apart). Working with someone who is well-versed in the stages of divorce, a therapist who can deal with the intensity of those five stages of divorce and the divorce dance, is important.

Outside of a child or spouse dying, divorce is one of the top three stress factors. It is a huge psychological crisis in an individual's life. So, why not get help in this area? There are plenty of excuses why you shouldn't: having friends to talk to, rationalizing that you can't afford it, preferring to call your attorney, or (even) ego issues. Let's look at a few of them.

Who *Not* to Call

- Your Friends
  Friends are critical in helping you through the stages of divorce. But it's easy to misuse friends. Sure, they will support your decision and lend an ear and shoulder when the going gets rough. They also have their own lives and families. You may wear them out.
- Your Attorney
  You may think about using your attorney as the one to bounce ideas off or to grumble and complain. Hear this loudly and clearly: Your attorney is *not* your therapist. Attorneys don't have the psychology skills that a trained therapist does. On top of that, they cost a lot more. Remember, they will charge you by the hour and *none* of it will be reimbursed through your health insurance coverage.
- Your Ego
  Egos are funny things. Women are far more likely to seek counseling than men. It's an ego thing. Somehow, engaging a therapist is interpreted as a sign of weakness by many men. We disagree and believe that it is a good antidote for pushing through the thorns you meet along the divorce course. Thorns come in all shapes, sizes and genders, including you.

> • • • • •
>
> If you and your spouse are willing to see a counselor as a couple who is uncoupling, it can remove many of the emotional roadblocks that spring up in the divorce process.
>
> • • • • •

Who Are You Going to Call?

Your pastor, priest, rabbi, or other religious counselor can be helpful. But it is important for you to discern where they are coming from before agreeing to their counseling. If you are in a brutal marriage and your counselor's attitude is that all marriages are meant to be permanent no matter what, you will be short-changed. If your counselor is compassionate, realistic, and primarily interested in getting you back on your feet, then you are headed in the right direction. Let's face it; mistakes get made. People get married for the wrong reasons and do well; people get married for the right reasons and do well; people get married for the wrong reasons and do miserably; and people get married for the right reasons, and still create disaster.

One of the therapist's goals should be to help you become more independent: to rebuild or even find your self-esteem. Go to a therapist with this goal in mind: to become stronger. Often, a divorcing person will come to the therapist with no agenda, saying "Well, my lawyer said to come. Why am I here?" This person has put himself or herself immediately in the dependent, student, child position. The work starts right away with, "Tell me what you think? What would you like to get out of talking with me?" Unless the therapist can really get that person motivated to look at how he or she can use the therapist's and lawyer's help, that person will always be dependent.

Fear Factors in Men and Women

There are differences in the fear levels of men and women in divorce. Women are more inclined to fear economic issues. Men rarely voice those issues in therapy—at least not the issue of whether he will have enough money to cover expenses. In working with men, we have found that they express a high level of concern about "their" money—pensions and just how much they are going to shell out for alimony. Data has consistently shown that men usually fare better financially after divorce. The work done in divorce therapy shows that both women and men can have fulfilled lives if they feel strong enough about themselves and are involved in their work and other outside activities.

For women, three fears surface repeatedly in divorces and the break-up of a long-term relationship:

1. Many fear being broke, even a bag lady.
2. Some fear they will never find anyone else. They're not so worried about being alone, but of not finding the "right" person.
3. She may fear the "shame" of being unmarried. For the woman who has been married for a long time, it often takes time, lots of it, to get past the cultural message (yes, it is still out there) that it isn't right to be unmarried. When the relationship finally breaks up, she may feel that her whole world has collapsed.

In the psychological sense, depending upon the woman, her life experiences and upbringing often will direct how she responds and feels. There may be very little self-esteem because of the way women in general have been socialized for centuries as the caretaker, as the homemaker. When that primary identity is taken away, everything becomes mush. The woman literally has to start over again. As independent as many women are today, undercurrents of the past are still present.

Here's the good news for most women: Once in the process, most women find that they are strong—very strong. Women are more inclined to willingly enter into therapy, moving the emotional process along.

Men are different. It is quite common for men to jump into another relationship, even before the divorce is over. Men often remarry soon after the divorce papers are signed. Why? They fear being alone. In couplehood, the majority of women take care of household necessities—cooking, cleaning, and the like—and serve as the family nurturers. When the couple breaks up, often the man looks for someone else to serve these functions.

On the surface, the monetary issue is usually okay for men; the undercurrent of emotions isn't. Getting therapy is not high on their list. Men usually don't gain their identities from who they are within marriage. If there are kids, a man's primary fear is that he will be prevented from seeing his kids.

Enlightenment May Not Be Enough

We once worked with a photographer named Kate who was in the process of a divorce from a man who traveled a great deal. They had four sons. Her husband would take a great deal of pleasure in mentioning her work to his business acquaintances when it appeared in national magazines. But he would become upset and angry when he came home to find a note that she was on a shoot and that she hadn't made dinner.

When the divorce finally hit, Kate felt that she was a total failure, unsuccessful as the nurturer of the young, the old, and most of all, her husband. It didn't matter how enlightened she felt herself to be. Her religious upbringing told her that because she filed for the divorce, she was a sinner with a capital *S*.

The divorce is over and she is still shooting pictures. In fact, she has accomplished a great deal. Her kids are in college, her work has been nationally acclaimed and she has a new relationship with a man she loves. Still, deep down, she has that feeling that she was a failure in some basic, womanly way. She is pleased with her professional accomplishments but she feels that somehow it should all have been different.

We have said it before. Going through a divorce is not the cat's meow. At times, it will be painful, hurtful, hateful, and even harmful. You may think you are doing well. Are you? Friends, colleagues, coworkers, and bosses may tell you differently.

Seek and You Shall Find

How do you go about finding a therapist? First of all, if your state licenses therapists, we believe you should choose among licensed therapists.

Therapists work under a variety of degrees and licenses. There is a marriage and family counseling license, a clinical social worker license, a PhD or PsyD in psychology, and an MD, who would be a psychiatrist. There are also licensed nurses and practitioners who specialize in psychiatric work. Some have multiple licenses in different disciplines.

The next step is to find someone you can relate to, trust, and feel comfortable with. Your best resource will probably be a friend in the area who has benefited from therapy. You may decide to go see that therapist, or you may feel it is inappropriate if your friend is seeing the therapist. A phone call or visit to that therapist will allow you to determine if you stay or seek another recommendation.

Cost will likely be a major concern. If you go to a psychiatrist or psychologist in private practice, it is more than likely that you are going to be paying at the upper end of the fee range, approximately $60 to $170 per hour. If you go to someone who is involved with a training institution, the fees will be more moderate, perhaps as low as $30 or $35 an hour. Many therapists work with some individuals at the lower end of the scale, even though their normal fees are higher. If they have an open hour, they are sometimes willing to charge less. Some also are willing to see people who can't normally afford their regular fee. Many have a rule that if they have seen someone in the past, they would be willing to see them again, regardless of their financial circumstances. You also can go to someone who is affiliated with the state or a local mental health clinic; there might be no fees or fees might be based on your income.

If you elect to go to a clinic, more than likely you will have no choice as to who handles your case. Whoever is there to take your information assigns you. If you don't like the person to whom you are assigned, you can usually ask to see someone else. In a training institution, you sometimes have the opportunity of requesting a specific person. If you go to a private practice, you will be dealing with the person with whom you made the appointment, unless you mutually agree to switch to someone else.

What happens if a therapist is booked solid? You can still get help—therapists refer to other therapists. If money is a problem, they will refer either to a good training institute or to someone else who would be willing to take on or had an opening for a client at a lower fee.

Full Disclosure

Some state laws require therapists to reveal certain facts to clients. In our home state of Colorado, in most cases therapists are required to provide the following information, in writing, at the initial interview:

1. A listing of degrees, credentials, and licenses
2. A statement about the state regulation of therapists and the address and phone number of the state grievance board
3. A statement indicating that
   - a client is entitled to receive information about the methods of therapy, the techniques used, the duration of therapy, if known, and the fee schedule.
   - the client may seek a second opinion from another therapist or may terminate therapy at any time.
   - in a professional relationship, sexual intimacy is never appropriate and should be reported to the grievance board.

In addition, the therapist must explain the circumstances in which information provided by the client during therapy sessions is and is not legally confidential. This is very important in a divorce.

While your state may not have such a requirement, this information can help give you a road map of the topics you need to raise in your initial interview.

> • • • • •
> Sexual intimacy is *never* appropriate between a therapist and patient. *NEVER.*
> • • • • •

Why Not Refer?

In talking with a number of attorneys, we found that many, after some hesitation, admit that their clients would have benefited from some type of therapy during the divorce process. In speaking with thousands of men and women who underwent therapy during their divorces, we found that almost all said it was helpful. Some would say it was lifesaving. Those who hadn't sought therapy wished that they had or that someone would have suggested it. Those who didn't seek it felt that somehow their attorneys would take care of whatever support was needed.

Do attorneys refer clients to therapists? Sure, but they are in the minority. They usually refer if they see extreme behavior or if the client is blatantly difficult to work with. They want to get all the emotional stuff out of the office.

Granted, many attorneys who specialize in family law have some skills in counseling—not degrees in counseling as therapists have, but are skilled enough to recognize warning and danger signals that could indicate the need for a specialist to be brought in. Our question is, Why wait until there is an urgent need? Instead, it makes sense to have a therapist as part of the team. Why, then, don't attorneys refer their clients to counseling? Could it be that they feel they might lose control? Or that dollars are going in a different direction—away from their wallets? Or, they just don't realize the need for therapy.

One More Thought

We couldn't leave this section without reminding you: If you are dealing with physical violence, contact your local domestic violence hot line immediately. *We also strongly believe that you should leave.*

Once physical violence starts, it rarely stops. Telephone information operators will know the local numbers of domestic violence hotlines as well as your local police and fire departments. Law enforcement organizations have become more sensitive to the seriousness of domestic violence over the past few years.

> • • • • •
> If there is child abuse, take the kids and leave—now. As an adult, you may choose to take the abuse, but a child does not have a choice.
> • • • • •

In the right case, a "peace bond" may be sought from the criminal court with the assistance of your local police as a substitute for a divorce court injunction. If you can prove that your spouse has been physically abusive, the court will require the posting of a cash bond that will be forfeited if the abuse is repeated. If it is regularly necessary to obtain law enforcement assistance for domestic disturbances, you may need psychiatric intervention in addition to separation, or divorce, or all three.

> • • • • •
> If you want to short-circuit the stress on your life and that of others around you, consider therapy as part of your solution.
> • • • • •

13 Questions to Ask a Therapist

· · · · ·

1. **What is your educational background and training?**
   The therapist may have a doctorate or a master's degree in marriage and family therapy or in a field such as psychiatry, clinical social work, psychiatric nursing, or the ministry. If the professional's degree is not in marriage and family therapy, ask about what additional postgraduate training the therapist has completed in marriage and family therapy.

2. **Do you have a state license? What is it in?**
   In most states, you do not have to have a state license to hold yourself out as a "therapist." We believe that a therapist should be licensed if the state has a licensing program.

3. **Are you a Clinical Member of the American Association for Marriage and Family Therapy (AAMFT)?**
   A therapist who has clinical membership in the AAMFT must have met the educational supervision and training standards of the association. These standards meet or surpass the training and experience requirements for the states that license marriage and family therapists.

4. **Do you have experience treating or dealing with my kind of problem?**
   The therapist must understand your problem and should have experience dealing with that type of problem.

5. **How much do you charge? Are your fees negotiable?**
   Many therapists will work with you even when you have minimal dollars. The important thing to do is to ask. Fees will range from $60 to $170 an hour.

(continued)

6. What insurance or managed care plans do you participate in?
Most insurance providers have an allowance for mental health coverage. Check with your employer and your policy. If still in doubt, call your insurance provider's customer service department.

7. Do you use psychological testing?
Tests can help diagnose a problem, determine the course of treatment, and reduce the number of sessions needed.

8. How long do sessions last?
The usual session is 50 minutes. Group sessions may average two hours.

9. How often are sessions held?
Most therapists will see you once a week, but will see you less frequently once there is improvement.

10. Based on what I have told you, do you have an idea of how many sessions my therapy may take?
Some therapists have a minimum number of sessions they want to work with; others don't. Ask.

11. Do you set goals for treatment at the beginning of my therapy?
The therapist should set goals and should be actively involved in the course of your treatment. You do not want a therapist who is passive and merely reflects what you have said.

12. Do you give your patients assignments?
Some therapists may ask you to keep a journal, read certain books, or complete other types of activities. The objective is to enhance your self-resilience and confidence.

13. How will you know when I do not need any more therapy?
When you begin to ask this kind of question, you are on your way to recovery. When you begin therapy, this is a good question to throw on the table. Ask the therapist to identify various benchmarks that you can check as you go through the process.

• • • • •

4

Sherlock Homes, Move Over
The Critical Role of Keeping Good Records

During your divorce, you may harbor suspicions, right or wrong, that your spouse is hiding assets. And you may very well be right.

Assets are traditionally hidden in one of four ways:

1. By denying the existence of an asset
2. By transferring it to a third party
3. By "claim offset" (which means the asset exists but was diverted)
4. By claiming the asset was lost or dissipated

In addition to these, there is a new way to hide assets: by creating false debt. This means that loans and other obligations may suddenly appear. Your spouse claims that his or her father is owed $10,000. You had thought it was a gift; now it's not.

A Surprised Service

What happens if out of the wild blue yonder you get served with divorce papers? First of all, don't panic. In most states, you have 30 days in which to respond. If you haven't done so already, now is the time to go shopping for an attorney. (Chapter 7 will give you tips on questions to ask, what should be expected, even the kinds of fees involved.) At this time, you need to scramble (and we mean *scramble*) to gather information.

Rally Back

Even if your spouse has planned to leave you for quite a while, as a rule his or her mailing address hasn't been changed yet. Copy everything in sight. You are on shaky ground if you open mail that is identified as separate property, even if you steam it or rip it open and claim it was an accident. Instead, write down the date that you received it and copy the envelope.

The IRS has a special form that will allow you to obtain past tax returns. It could take a couple of months, so the sooner you get going, the better. Note bank statements and bank account numbers. Accounts have probably been moved, but if you had a joint account, you've got the number. Ask for copies from the bank for the last five years. Expect a charge—after all, they are not going to do anything for free.

Ask your attorney about changing the door locks and the garage door opener code. You don't want to risk anything else leaving your home after you are on notice. It is amazing how objects, artwork, and the like suddenly disappear after a divorce has been filed. Find out if any large sums have been withdrawn from your bank accounts. Ditto for any stock or other investment-related accounts.

As you obtain bank statements, bills, and any correspondence that refers to assets and income, you begin the next critical step—sitting down and starting to reconstruct your financial life. Determine whether you normally spend $1,000 a month, or if you spend $7,000 a month. How much cash do you personally use? How much walking-around money does your spouse have? In the past, did cash tend to come home in the evening? If a business is owned and there is always cash around, it is *important* to register this in your mind. Carry around a small note pad and start taking notes. It is amazing what can jump into your mind at the oddest moments and, if not written down, is forgotten.

Do everything you can to put aside anything emotional. Right now, you are gathering facts. If your spouse has business partners or colleagues, go see them right away. More than likely, they are not going to be terribly positive about you and probably won't want to talk to you. Don't expect much warmth. Your intent is to put them on notice that you just want them to know that you certainly don't want to cause any harm, but that you want the truth to come out about your financial affairs. You are glad to allow the divorce (assuming they know about it), but you want to make sure that whatever the two of you own is going to get split equally.

In other words, the business partners and colleagues are now on notice that there could be an investigation into assets and income. If they are thinking of any hanky-panky in terms of helping hide some assets, they'll now know that it is totally unacceptable. By doing this you let them know you are not a dummy, and that you are aware that they can be contributing factors.

The issue here is not for you to know the law. Instead, you are stanching the flow of money very quickly. You want information and assets retained. It is not legal to go around stripping all your assets, but you need to know that this is a possibility.

> • • • • •
>
> *Discovery* is the process during which both sides in the case share documents and financial information before the case goes to court. Throughout the divorce process, you will discover a variety of things—not all of a monetary nature.
>
> • • • • •

Roll up Your Sleeves

The sooner you learn about you and your spouse's assets, the better.

First, you must evaluate your expenses. Try not to guess. Ideally, it makes sense to know where monies were spent for an entire year. If you don't have access to all your records, three months usually gives a good snapshot. If you have no records, your last resort is to "guesstimate."

Gather up canceled checks, charge receipts, and cash receipts if you have them. Allocate them to specific areas: housing, utilities, automotive, insurance (auto, medical, dental, life, disability, homeowners, fire, etc.), retirement funds, entertainment, education, contributions, charge accounts, wardrobe, cleaning, pets, dues, subscriptions, education (yours and the kids'), food, dining out, medical, dental, prescriptions, vacations, gifts, travel related to business, taxis, tips, and rentals. Don't forget ATM receipts—what did you do with the money after you withdrew it?

This probably seems overwhelming, but it has to be done. If you don't have computer access, get a multicolumn spreadsheet (all stationery stores carry them)—or you divide a sheet of paper into columns headed "auto, housing," etc. For charged

> • • • • •
>
> If you have access to a computer, you can save mega, mega hours. Purchase a personal accounting program such as Quicken (approximately $50). With an investment of a few hours of your time, your financial life can take on incredible order, at least the tracking of it. And you don't need a PhD to use it.
>
> • • • • •

items, make sure you put the entire amount charged, not the minimum amount to pay per month on a greater balance. Remember, you are identifying exactly how much you spend each month.

Did you enter the marriage with any separate property or did you receive any gifts during your marriage—money, jewelry, houses, apartments, stocks, bonds, artwork, bicycles, furniture, etc.? Any item that you owned prior to your marriage or were given during your marriage may still be separate property. In other words, it is yours and is not included when joint assets are divvied up.

What to Gather

We encourage you to copy any account numbers and make copies of the statements; it makes tracking and verification easier. Refer to Chapter 8 for the list of documents you want to gather up before the first strategy meeting with your attorney. In addition to those, do yourself (and your attorney) an enormous favor by assembling the following before your initial appointment:

- *Your check registers for the past few years*—If you have your financial information or your check register on a computer program like Quicken, make a copy onto a disk and hold it for safekeeping.
- *Any prenuptial or postnuptial agreements*—Gather up any agreements that were drawn up prior to your marriage, or even during your marriage that might designate how assets were to be split or identified, or which designate proportions on earnings for either one of you. If you and your spouse signed a prenuptial agreement, this is a critical document. Its terms will affect many of the issues you must face. In fact, it may mean that there is little, if anything, left to resolve.
- *A complete household inventory*—Take pictures. If you have a video camera (you can rent one), don't forget to open up closet doors and take sweeping shots of your living room, dining room, wall hangings, floor coverings, even your outdoor patio. When in doubt, aim the camera and push the button.
- *Tax returns that show depreciation schedules as well as gross revenues*—Ask the accountant or bookkeeper for copies of their work papers. The IRS has a form that you can sign to acquire past tax returns if you don't have them. Make sure that you have at least five years' returns.
- *Partnership tax returns*—If you have invested in any partnerships, contact the general partner and get a full copy of the partnership tax return. Ask the person who sold you the investment for an updated evaluation.

- *Annual bank, savings, and investment statements*—Most recap additions and withdrawals at the end of the year. Don't forget business-type credit cards. Diners Club and American Express send out year-end statements summarizing charges into various categories.
- *A copy of the corporate tax return for any family businesses/corporations*— If the business is filed on a Schedule C within your own tax return, make sure that you know, or better yet, obtain copies of the work papers that consisted of the expenses and revenues that constituted the entire schedule. Your accountant can be helpful here. If you feel some resistance in getting the information you request, just say you are getting ready to spread expenses for next year and you would like to have some guidelines on what was done the previous year.
- *Financial statements to banks*—These reveal a lot of information, often most optimistic. Few business owners hide how well their businesses are doing; rather, they brag about what they own. If you need to, call the bank and tell them that you are doing updated financial statements and you have lost copies of previous ones. Ask them to send you a copy so that you could make sure that you do not exclude anything.
- *Warranty deeds, contracts, title insurance, and other documents that establish ownership to investments and real estate other than your residence*
- *Any preliminary title searches showing other ownership*
- *Title certificates and registration statements for boats, cars, recreational vehicles, trucks, etc.*
- *List of all current debts, monthly payments, and reason for the debt*
- *Any notes payable to you or payable by you*
- *Any deeds (first, second, even third trust deeds) or sales contracts on real estate*
- *Any retirement, pension, or profit-sharing plans; IRAs; Keoghs; and brokerage, bank and money market fund statements*—Financial institutions and employers who have pension and profit-sharing programs send out annual statements. Get copies when possible.
- *Copies of all personal and business insurance policies*
- *An estimate of the value of your automobiles*—In evaluating cars, call the local bank and say that you are interested in purchasing whatever the car is that you and your spouse currently own. Ask for the high and low *Kelley Blue Book* values. Ask if they would be receptive to financing the car. If that feels uncomfortable, call the bank and say that you are completing a net-worth statement and you don't know what value to put on your car. Could they look it up in their *Blue Book?* Or, visit the library or go online to find

the *Kelley Blue Book* (www.autoweb.com). If your car is older and not carried, check the classified ads in your newspaper. You may own a classic!

- *For owners of a small business, copies of all journals and general ledgers*— Don't overlook any accounts receivable, works in progress, inventory, or bank statements. Payroll and sales tax returns give a lot of information. Some attorneys will recommend that you get the corporate minutes book and the stock books. Our experience has been that many small businesses ignore these and fill these in after the fact, often several years down the road, if they are needed for an audit. Not that they are supposed to do it this way; it's just one of those "I'll get to it" projects.

- *A copy of your spouse's previous month's payroll stub (preferably at least three months' worth)*—Why? Because not all items are deducted from each paycheck. Sometimes it is every other paycheck, other times, it's once a month. Call the payroll department where your spouse works and ask them to explain it to you.

  We once had a client call and merely state that she was getting more involved in the finances and that she needed to have her husband's payroll stub explained to her. By the time she was done, besides the normal deductions for federal and state taxes and Social Security, she discovered that her husband was setting aside $500 a month in a tax-sheltered annuity, was paying one of the car loans, and had an extra savings account, as well as excess contributions based on a percentage formula in retirement programs. If she hadn't done that, she very well could have missed out on thousands of dollars in hidden assets.

- *All W-2 statements that were filed with the last tax return*—Note if there is any difference in the amount from which federal taxes are withheld and the amount on which Social Security is based. If the Social Security wage base number is higher than the reportable W-2 earnings for tax purposes, you know that funds are being placed in either a tax-sheltered annuity or a 401(k) program where federal and state taxes are deferred until they are withdrawn. Social Security tax, though, is not deferred, and is calculated on earnings on an ongoing basis. Both annuities and 401(k) plans offer the ability to defer taxes on current income.

- *Copies of any records relating to savings and credit union accounts, bank statements, and any royalty payments*—If your spouse is an author or artist, you do own a portion of what is completed, regardless of whether the work has been sold.

- *Any certificates that show values of gems, antiques, artwork—anything collectible*
- *Monies that are placed in tax-exempt investments*—These are often difficult to track. It is imperative for you to get at least the past five years of statements and tax returns if this is one of the possible areas in which investments are placed.
- *Interest earned from Treasury bills and municipal bonds*—If you or your spouse have invested in Treasury bills, the interest received is nontaxable on your state return but is fully taxable on your federal return. If you live in one state and own a municipal bond that was originated in another, the interest is tax exempt on your federal return but taxable on your state return—the opposite of a Treasury bill or bond. This is why you want both federal and state tax returns—to cross-check income that is reported.
- *Documentation of any investment*—Anything in which monies have been placed for creating income investment growth needs to be checked and tracked down.
- *Patent applications, license rights, or royalty agreements if your spouse is an inventor*
- *An estimate of your spouse's salary (if you don't know)*—If you are unclear as to what your spouse makes (this assumes you don't have W2s or payroll stubs), check publications such as *Fortune, Forbes,* and *Working Woman,* or trade publications for his or her profession. They publish annual surveys of what various positions and industries pay. If you have access to the Internet (most libraries now have computers available to the public), go to "key word" and then type in various words that fit your spouse's job title and query for salary range. If you know anyone who works in the executive-search field or in a job placement agency, they could estimate your spouse's earning power. If you don't, call one and say that you are doing some research on career opportunities and ask if they could give you some guidelines on what to expect.
- *A copy of any employment contracts*—They should state clearly not only initial salary, but bonus formulas and stock options.
- *Any data that can show that personal expenses or quasi-personal expenses are run through a family business as expenses*—This could be a potential jackpot. Most self-employed taxpayers who are not incorporated report income on Schedule C within their regular tax return. Usually, they report as much as they possibly can as business expenses.

Many of these expenses may be personal. Examples would include travel and entertainment—a huge area that absorbs a lot of personal pleasures both of you may have enjoyed in the past year. Professional services could have included having your will drawn up; the new painting that hangs in your living room could have been expensed under office furniture; the car that you drive may very well be identified as the company car. The list goes on and on.

This is not the time to go about refinancing your home unless you can control the extra funds that come out of it. Nor should you enter into any investments that might demand future payments, or even cosign a loan. Your objective is to become less liable for things as you move through this stage of your divorce.

We know this seems overwhelming, but take a deep breath—a lot of this is merely detail and paperwork. If you would rather pay an attorney big bucks to do it for you, you can. We recommend you don't. Today, judges are reluctant to award any legal fees. You are on your own.

Planning Leads to Survival—Yours

In your planning phase, you need to determine what should be valued and if there are fluctuating prices on the open market. It is not uncommon for one spouse to pay all the bills. Whoever does has a better fix on what it costs to operate the household. Part of your planning is making sure you know those ongoing costs. If you haven't been the payer, get involved. It could lead to more money to be divvied up at a later date. Who knows? Since money is the number-one problem in divorces, your overall active involvement, awareness, and participation could put the marriage in a different perspective.

Granted, we know that some spouses will be suspicious. Before you start sleuthing, we suggest you start to talk about money and assets when together. You might say something along the lines that you saw a segment on one of the daily TV shows, heard an author on the radio talking about couples who don't communicate about money, are looking forward to attending a program on money offered by the bank or community college, or even that your friends are talking about money (they could be starting an investment club) and you realized that you aren't so savvy.

Don't Be Penny-Wise and Pound-Foolish

Becky and James decided to divorce after 35 years of marriage. James owned a heavy construction business. He agreed to split the business assets 50-50. The CPA at work had placed a value on it at $300,000. At first, this seemed fair enough—then Becky started thinking. She told her attorney, "I used to keep the books for the business. I can remember taking in more than a million dollars each year. I think the company CPA has purposely lowballed the value. Do you think the business is only worth $300,000?"

Not likely. Becky's attorney insisted that she have the business appraised. The appraisal cost her $4,300, an amount that seemed huge to her and made her nervous. What if the business was only worth $300,000? She would have kissed off the $4,300! The appraisal opened her eyes—it valued the company at $850,000! Her investment of $4,300 netted her $275,000 more than she would have received with the $300,000 valuation!

When looking at an offer for settlement of a business, ask yourself the following three key questions:

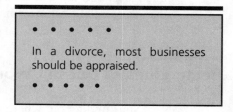

In a divorce, most businesses should be appraised.

1. Is there something that you don't know about that you are leaving on the table? In many states there have been cases where, if the husband defrauded the wife by not revealing information, she was able to go back to the court to have the settlement adjusted.
2. Are you being given truthful information when you look at what's on the table? Are you getting bad data on values?
3. Are you making up a wish list for things that don't really exist?

When looking at a cash-and-carry-type business, you need to determine a range of values. Some of the ways to determine these values include rule-of-thumb multipliers, capitalization rates, defined ratios within the industry, book value, adjusted book value, net book value, replacement value, depreciated value, stock market value, liquidation value, and fair market value. Who knows? There could even be a toss-of-the-coin value.

Usually, good will should be included, especially if the business has been a going concern for a number of years. What is good will? A dictionary defines it as the value of a business in patronage, reputation, and established popularity over and beyond its tangible assets—in other words, the perceived public value in excess of cash and equipment and other material items.

Whatever the acceptable value ranges, it's important that you determine whether you are dealing with smaller amounts of money such as in a range of $5,000 to $40,000 or larger amounts that can run in the hundreds of thousands of dollars. Once you know an estimated value range, you can then determine how much money you are willing to spend to go after the business. Remember, Becky was antsy about spending $4,300 on a business that was worth hundreds of thousands of dollars. On the other hand, it's crazy to spend thousands of dollars when the business may only be worth a few thousand.

A complication rears its head. You need to determine whether data you receive is valid. This could come partly from your own intuition and practical observation about what kind of lifestyle you have been living. Talk to employees, colleagues, and associates, and use your direct information—things that you had a hands-on relationship with.

Being Clueless Doesn't Work

Start finding out where things are, how much money you have, what kind of debt you are liable for, and where the life insurance papers and wills are. When it comes to investments of any type, determining your tax cost (basis) is important. Basis is the number the IRS likes. When something is sold, taxes are computed from the basis, which could be actually less than what you originally paid. How so? Various tax write-offs and deductions over the years can alter the initial cost. So can infused money, as in improvements.

The Scavenger Hunt

The scavenger hunt should be an integral part of your planning phase. Once one of you moves out, so do many of the marriage assets, especially when it comes to personal items.

By now you may have learned of assets you previously didn't know were assets. Most marriages have hidden loot. In many cases, each partner has a different perception of its value. The obvious ones include whole life insurance policies, especially old policies with face values of $1,000, $5,000, and $10,000. They often contain many thousands of dollars in cash value that have been earning a very low interest rate.

If you know of any that are in your spouse's name (or yours, for that matter), write the representative or the insurance company, indicate the policy number, and state that you are completing updated financial statements and need to include their value for the bank's purposes. You should expect a reply within a few weeks. This doesn't mean that you are going to cash the policies out—although you certainly can if your name is on them—it's merely for your own information.

Today's computers can cross-search names as well as addresses. Don't forget to check for liens or loans against your own house.

Check your homeowner's insurance policy to see if there are addenda to cover extra items, including your jewelry, artwork, and furs if you have any. A client whose husband collected trains was elated when she discovered a $30,000 addendum to cover their value. That was the key that led to our valuation. Not wanting to part with his toys, he gave her the house as a trade-off.

If you have to play coy in getting some of the information you need, then by all means go ahead. Make sure you check out any magazines that may be lying around, a wallet or purse that's left open, keys that are unfamiliar to you, correspondence from a club that you haven't seen in the past. Work on getting your name on anything that is in your household, is jointly owned, or was ever a gift to your spouse. Of course, the advice is the opposite if it relates to you. You don't want your spouse on anything.

Never Underestimate the Value of Junk

If you or your spouse is a pack rat, you may be sitting on a gold mine of goodies. Some are highly visible, while others may be buried in boxes, forgotten, at least by most.

According to a study done a few years ago by the advertising agency of Foote, Cone and Belding, 20 percent of all Americans collect things. Men lean toward coins, cars, and stamps, while women are more interested in antiques, gemstones, and books.

Do you have a valued collection of toys or old radios? How about stamps or buttons? Old beer cans? Does anyone in your household collect figurines? One client had more than 100 Hummel figurines—thousands and thousands of dollars of them were displayed on every ledge and table. Another coveted license plates, even keeping a very detailed book as to their origins, how much they had cost, and their estimated market value—clearly, a serious collector.

What kind of collector are you? Better yet, what kind of collector is your spouse? The things that are accumulating that you thought were junk may indeed have significant value, especially now.

You want to get a valuation if you are going to keep the items, based on what you would receive in a sale on the open market within a fairly short period of time. If your spouse is going to take them, then you want the appraisal at top dollar. If you leave it up to the court, you may be in for a big surprise. Many courts will accept the "garage sale" value—great news if you are trying to get something at bargain prices; not so great if you are trying to trade assets worth a lot.

For antique buffs, the best time to get those items evaluated is during a time of inflation. Traditionally, they decline in value when deflation is in effect. On the other hand, if it's something that you love and you are in a period that is more deflationary, by all means, it is worth your while to get another appraisal. An important thing to keep in mind is that there are different kinds of appraisals. There is an insurance replacement appraisal and there is a market value appraisal.

Figure 4.1 represents only a partial list of what's available. Anything can be classed as a collectible if you have enough of them. There are books and clubs throughout the country that track values and trading sources. Use them as a valuable reference guide. Check with your local library for one near you.

You will note that a lot of these things are not huge and are easily portable. That means that they can freely exit the house.

Great Gifts Come in Small Boxes

Gold coins, stamps, diamonds, and gems are often stashed in a safe-deposit box. These could be a source of cash for you, or at least a negotiating tool. Make sure you take pictures of the contents, even if you don't remove anything.

You want to be on the lookout for any hidden accounts. Although most people don't have secret bank accounts in foreign countries, this is always a possibility, especially if your spouse deals with large sums of cash, travels a great deal, and is thought of as being wealthy or well-to-do.

Summing Up

A variety of professionals other than attorneys and accountants can help you determine value of your marital assets. Don't forget professional organizations and

Figure
4.1

Figure
4.1 • • • • •

Antiques (Furniture,
carpets, fountain
pens, banknotes,
dolls, hat pins,
stock certificates,
toys, cookie cutters,
kitchenware, china,
glassware, games,
currency, linens,
and quilts)
Beer cans
Bottles
Bubblegum cards
Cameras
Cards (baseball,
children's games,
and playing)
Cartoons
Catalogs
Ceramics

Clocks
Coins
Comics
Dolls (Shirley Temple,
Storybook, Barbie,
Beanie Babies)
Drawings
Election memorabilia
Elvis memorabilia
First editions and rare
books
Figurines
Gems
Guns
Jukeboxes
License plates
Magazines
Movie memorabilia
Music boxes

Newspapers
Photographs
Pinball machines
Pipes
Plates
Political memorabilia
Postcards
Posters
Radios
Records
Science fiction books
Slot machines
Stamps
Tickets to historic
events
Toys (all types)
Trains
War memorabilia
Watches

how-to books. Use the telephone to track down appraisers, handymen, or others who can help. The yellow pages and ad sections of your newspaper always include service people in specific areas. Believe it or not, they usually can give you a good thumbnail appraisal of what your car, antiques, or that odd collection in the back of the garage is worth. If you have real works of art, a museum curator or art dealer could become your right hand.

All it takes to discover buried treasure is focused attention. Primarily, yours.

13 Ways to Be a Super Sleuther

• • • • •

1. Make copies of all financial statements.

2. Obtain copies of tax returns.

3. Make duplicate copies of any computer files that relate to ownership and financial matters.

4. Obtain copies of current insurance policies.

5. Obtain copies of any wills and trusts.

6. Make an inventory of contents in safety deposit boxes. Take someone with you to witness. Take photos.

7. Contact the county assessor to get a copy of any deeds and titles for real estate owned.

8. If you own a small business, get copies of financial journals, ledgers, payroll, sales tax returns, and expense account disbursements.

9. Obtain copies of any appraisals for artwork, antiques, jewelry, and other collectibles.

10. Videotape your entire house, including contents of closets.

11. Obtain information on pensions for both you and your spouse.

12. Obtain copies of at least three of your spouse's recent pay stubs.

13. Obtain a current report of earnings from your local Social Security office for both of you.

• • • • •

5

Plan ahead Now
So You Don't Pay Later

Strategy and planning will make or break your divorce. Our experience shows that men usually don't file the initial papers for a divorce. They do, though, plot and plan once it is officially set in motion. Women tend to think that the system will sort itself out and be fair in the end. While women are talking with their friends, men are gathering financial documents.

The Unraveling of a Marriage

There are, of course, exceptions. Sarah was one. She had been married for almost 30 years. At the time of her divorce, she was 50 and had three grown children. She had met her husband, Tim, at college, married, and eventually moved to the West Coast. Eventually, they became a cornerstone in the development of a small town that was later to become a prominent city. They were the unofficial "first couple."

Unfortunately, the first couple did not have a first-rate marriage, at least behind closed doors. Sarah had an artistic flair and developed a nationwide reputation in the field of art jewelry, designing and obtaining exquisite pieces for a very select clientele. For years, she had covered up many of the business blunders Tim had gotten them into. Tim, always looking forward to deals, had gotten them involved in activities that Sarah scrambled to unravel with the help of attorneys and

43

bankers. Over the years, he had freely loaned money to friends, even new acquaintances, without bothering to keep track. Finally, at some point, Sarah said, "No more."

Then Tim began to make a variety of threats, including not paying their bills, and saying that it was his house, his money, his store, and his jewelry. They lived in a community property state and he was borrowing several hundreds of thousands of dollars at a time from the bank and signing his name, which automatically involved her because of the community-property status.

Sarah had seen so many women pass through the jewelry store—Women like herself, all socially prominent with beautiful homes and nice things. Many later divorced and were left with virtually nothing—no money, no prestige, no real skills to produce the lifestyle to which they had been accustomed and in which they had been trained for many, many years.

They had not been prepared for what could happen and had trusted their husbands or their husbands' attorneys to take care of them. Nor did they have the vaguest idea of what their assets were. She was determined that it would not happen to her.

The couple had started counseling but Tim refused to continue it, claiming that there was nothing wrong with him—the problems were Sarah's. Three years before the marriage collapsed, Sarah sought the counsel of their attorney at the suggestion of the marriage counselor.

Seeing their joint attorney sounds warning lights. Conflicts of interest rise quickly to the surface. Their attorney friend was putting his neck on the line in speaking to her without Tim present on this type of matter.

After she told the attorney what Tim had been doing, he said, "Look, I'm going to have to suggest some things. If the divorce doesn't happen, then no problem. And if it does, at least you will be a lot better off."

First of all, he advised her to get a post office box in her name alone. He told her to make sure it was not at a post office close to where she lived. Second, he told her to open checking and savings accounts, at a bank where she did not ordinarily bank—again, not close to where she lived.

Sarah was still doing the books for the store and she began to siphon off a little money at a time—a few dollars here, a hundred dollars there. If any insurance refunds came in, she would stick those in her secret account. Initially, Sarah said she was shocked when their attorney and friend suggested she do this. Looking back five years later, she realizes that it made all the sense in the world.

Her husband had spent a huge amount of money on himself. Over the years, he hunted and fished, expensive hobbies when you consider the cost of guns, ammunition, and all the fishing paraphernalia. Tim always had the top of the line and newest gear. Sarah was sure that over the 30 years they had been married he had spent in excess of $100,000 on these hobbies alone. Now, it wasn't that she didn't spend money on herself; she wore designer clothes and her jewelry was spectacular. She viewed her apparel as part of the business. Her appearance was part of their product.

For the next few years, every time Tim went on a hunting trip or spent money on ammunition, she would figure out how much he spent and would take an equal amount and sock it away—a new definition of matching funds!

For the first time in years, Sarah didn't feel guilty about spending money on herself, and even if her marriage had worked out, she still wouldn't have. Over a period of time, whenever she had accumulated $1,000, she would take that lump sum, go to a second bank in the area, open an account and invest in a certificate of deposit. At a third bank was her safe-deposit box, where she kept information on her other two bank accounts and her post office box key, as well as other items relative to her personal assets. A friend was named on both the savings accounts, the safe deposit box, and the post office box, and of course knew everything that was going on. Sarah never had bank statements mailed to her home or to the business—they went to her friend's home.

Sarah also applied for a Visa and MasterCard at her new banks, using her post office box as the billing address. Sarah made sure that every month she charged a few items on both cards, then paid them off in full at the end of the month. This way she created a credit profile.

The next thing she did was start to build her "divorce documentation." At the time that she started setting funds aside, she estimated the value of their community assets at $5 million. When you deal with jewelry and other items that are portable, such as art, it is easy to move assets around. Sarah was sure that Tim could pick out the most expensive stones and pieces and walk away with them at any time. If that happened, Sarah felt that she would be up a creek without a paddle.

She found out that Tim was lying more and more. He told her that they didn't have money to pay their bills. Then when she would look at their books, she would find that he had given a friend $15,000 that same month. When she returned from a trip, she went to the bank and discovered that Tim had closed a joint account— which the bank shouldn't have allowed without both signatures— and opened a new one in his name alone. The deposit was $200,000.

Sarah began to track Tim's spending, pulling receipts for every dollar that was spent on guns, on hunting trips, on money being given away or loaned, even clothes that he was buying—spending $2,000 for one suit! All of these records were put in her safe-deposit box. In addition, she began to have things repaired, and not just household items. She had all her teeth fixed, including caps. Her piano was refinished. She fixed household things that she would take if and when the divorce happened. Often, the repairs ranged from $100 to $400, all things that she would have to pay out of her pocket if she were to have them done later.

"When I needed new glasses, I didn't buy just one pair, I got eight pairs. When hose were on sale, I bought 100 pairs. During the last year, I began to buy personal items—nightgowns, robes, lingerie, sheets, towels, and bedding—and put them away for the future. During the last six months before the final break-up, I bought enough dishes, silverware, and small appliances to start up a new house." Everything was stored at her friend's.

During those three years prior to the final break-up, she checked in every three months or so with the attorney just to let him know what was going on. She let him know where the bank accounts were and how much she had set aside in each of them. She also told him how much should go to each of her children if she were to die.

Now, while Sarah was in her shopping mode, she also did something else that was crucial. She made an inventory of every single item in the house under the pretense of reappraising their insurance. It began with photographs of every painting, the crystal, dishes, jewelry, silver, even expensive pieces of clothing such as coats and boots. The task took her months to complete. She put a label on the back of each painting with the size, the artist, where it was obtained, and the cost. She did the same for her jewelry and other tangible assets.

Actually, this was something she had wanted to do for years, as she and Tim had collected some beautiful pieces and she wanted their children to have an idea of where the pieces were bought, how much was paid for them, and their appraised value. Some of the items had been gifts from famous people or had been purchased in Europe.

Sarah was almost Machiavellian in her planning. Under the auspices of acquiring new insurance, she got Tim to sit down with her and give her a price on every single item. Finally, just before their separation, she had completed the inventory. She had it typed out listing every penny, every piece of jewelry, every collectible, all their bank accounts, even a valuation of the business. She had all the receipts, so she knew what had been paid for everything. The only thing that she had in excess value was her jewelry, and she used that as an offset against his items, primarily the hunting and fishing gear. She had categories labeled as "his" and "hers."

Every time Tim went out of town to negotiate a deal or pick up gems, she went through the books, papers, and notes—everything on and in his desk. It was here that she found a handful of scribbled notes showing he had loaned out over $100,000—$5,000 here, $10,000 there—to different friends. Nothing like that had ever showed on any of their financial statements.

Just prior to the actual divorce, Sarah discovered that their personal debt exceeded $750,000. Thinking that she could be responsible for half of it, she was stunned when her attorney told her that because of the community-property laws, she was responsible for *all* of it.

With her marriage disintegrating in a free-fall, she wanted out. Her health was deteriorating. The stress and pressure of denial and the magnitude of the deals that Tim was getting into were far beyond anything that she had anticipated or planned for.

Sarah got through the Christmas holidays. She approached Tim once more to go to counseling. Tim refused. A week before, she had made arrangements with her attorney and their counselor that if he stated that he would do nothing, then she would, in turn, feign a meeting with their attorney, get Tim to meet her, and have the attorney present Tim with arbitration.

On the same day as Sarah approached Tim about counseling, a check for three major jewelry pieces totaling $250,000 came in. Sarah told Tim that she would take it down to the bank and deposit it, which she did. But she then wrote a check for that amount to their attorney to hold in his trust account on behalf of both of them to prevent either one of them from raiding the account.

When the check came through, a bank teller happened to mention it to the manager, who in turn called Tim. Tim immediately went down and canceled the check. The banker then "froze" the money to pay off one of the unsecured loans, a loan that wasn't in default and on which regular payments were being made. He told Sarah later that he was "covering his ass"—and if she didn't like the way he operated, she could sue him. Needless to say, Sarah was irate. She believed that a portion of that money was hers and it could have been her down payment on a new home and the beginning of her new life.

At this point, Tim knew that the end was near. He had agreed to meet with their attorney and Sarah on a Sunday to commence arbitration and go over the inventory list that she had put together. Sarah said that she will never forget that Saturday night. They all went through the charade of a family dinner. She said it was almost a farce. Tim went off to change his clothes to go to a baseball game with friends. Shortly after he left, the phone rang and it was their attorney. He told her that Tim had just called to cancel the meeting the next day, stating that he was getting his own attorney on Monday.

The attorney warned Sarah that when Tim got another attorney, that new attorney would look at the estimated $5 million valuation of the business and their assets and not only would he get a percentage, it would become a motivating factor to prolong the proceedings. When she asked if she should remove some of the art and jewelry, the attorney said he couldn't advise her on that, but that if she did, she should not take one penny more than $2.5 million worth.

Sarah sent her daughter home and set to work. She packed up some of her most valuable things, including antique silver, her jewelry, and some clothes. Sarah called her friend across town, saying that she would be bringing over a lot of stuff for safekeeping. Frightened, she rushed to the store. She knew that if she looked suspicious, the police might think she was a burglar and her plan would be ruined. The store had an elaborate alarm system. In her nervousness, she was sure she would set it off. She fantasized that she would have an accident when she left, spilling jewelry, precious antiques, and artwork all over the highway.

Sarah didn't have an accident, but she did set off the alarm. The police who came knew her and she explained that she was working late. (Well, she was.) With her assets on wheels, she headed for her friend's. After unloading, she then went to her daughter's to spend the night, knowing that Tim carried a gun and could become violent when he returned home and saw what she had done. Her son-in-law called and left a message on their answering machine at home for Tim explaining that Sarah was with them.

When Tim called, he said, "Well, at last you got my attention. I never believed that you were serious until now when I walked in and saw things missing." Sarah told him that she was indeed serious and had been for a long time. She also informed him that she had been to the store and had taken the most expensive items as collateral and they were in safekeeping. Sarah now had leverage, a critical ingredient. She firmly believes that if she had not taken and safely put those things aside, she never would have gotten her fair share. In looking back, she felt it was the smartest thing she had ever done. Leverage made Tim communicate.

In the end, Tim underestimated the value of his gun collection and personal items and overestimated the value of Sarah's jewelry. All in all, she was glad to be out—she didn't feel it was worth her energy or time anymore. He could have the house. The cost of maintenance and mortgage was over $5,000 a month and, without a steady income, she could not afford it. She took jewelry and other collectibles that could be sold over time to help support her as she went back to school to learn new skills and complete her degrees.

Shortly after the first of the year, she planned on moving to start her new life. She had done the profit-and-loss statements for the business, had gotten all the material together to complete the taxes by the first week in January, and had turned it over to the accountant. All personal bills had been paid, even fees for the accountant who was to do their income taxes. The financial slate was clean when she walked through the door that final time. Tim would owe nothing but the house payments.

The final cost, excluding her time and emotions, was $5,000 in attorney fees. If a regular divorce had gone through with $5 million to be divvied up, it would not be surprising to see attorneys' fees of $100,000 or more. Sarah's planning paid off for her. And, that's why you should plan.

A Plan Can Lead to Hope

Not many couples divide up millions of dollars—some spouses feel fortunate to leave with their name and sanity as their only assets. But we can learn from Sarah's story. She was methodical and very detail-oriented. If she hadn't been, she could have lost it all as she saw some of her friends do over the years.

Sarah took responsibility. If we were to change anything in her set-up and strategy, we would have suggested she do two more things: Obtain a line of credit and apply for a Diners Club or American Express card. A line of credit is a specific amount, such as $5,000, that a bank allows you to use whenever you want to, usually by writing a check. MasterCard and Visa have limits on what you can charge. Business cards, like Diners Club or American Express, do not. You want both types.

This is also the time to contact a credit-reporting bureau and obtain a copy of your credit report. If you plan to rent (or buy) a property, rental agencies do a preliminary credit check on an applicant. You need to determine if there are any blotches within your file that need to be fixed. The three main reporting agencies are Experian, Equifax, and Trans Union. You can get a copy of your credit report by contacting each bureau:

Experian	800-392-1122
Equifax	800-685-1111
Trans Union	800-922-5490

These companies usually charge a small fee when you request a copy of your credit report. Definitely get a copy, because you may find a high percentage of errors. It is one of those "to do" things that is wise to do on an annual basis, regardless of whether you are planning a divorce.

If you live in a community-property state, take advantage of the fact that joint credit evaluations are still available. You could have had a credit account in your own name based on the joint earnings even if you are not the primary breadwinner. You don't have to tell them you are contemplating a divorce; all you have to do is apply based on your previous taxable year's income.

Over the past few years, the weekly mail brings applications from different institutions for open lines of credit. Now, this type of money usually carries a very high interest rate, but think of it as rainy-day funds. What happens if you have no extra cash, or your spouse ties everything up and you can't come up with a first and last month's rent if you find that you want to move? It is there for you, for emergencies.

Evaluating Your Expenses

When you file for divorce, you are going to have to put in a detailed expense statement. Don't guess. You should be gathering up canceled checks and allocating them to specific areas such as mortgage or rental costs, utilities, automotive, insurance (dental, medical, life, home, and disability), retirement funds, entertainment, doctors, education, contributions, charge accounts, wardrobe, cleaning, even your pets. This is a time to scan your various charge accounts to see if you charge anything such as dues, subscriptions, business or educational tapes, and the like on the account.

Again, don't take the minimal monthly payment as your expense, even if you don't pay off the entire balance. Instead, include the entire amount. Your objective is to determine the total expenses per month. Other areas that get forgotten include special treats, lessons, movies, dinners out, even a favorite food.

If you are a sports enthusiast, either as a participant or a viewer, monies spent add up quickly—dedicated joggers replace shoes frequently. Any therapy, planned surgery, or an ongoing medical need should be included—allocate the amount that your insurance doesn't cover.

When the divorce is over, you may not be able to afford your present lifestyle. For this purpose, add in those expenses if you have in the past. Don't forget to include the maintenance, cleaning, and repair of "luxury items"—those amounts add up.

If you give gifts to others, including greeting cards (today, most cost a dollar plus), include a monthly average of what you spend on these items each month. Your newspaper, health food store, dry cleaning, travel related to your job including taxis and tips—all should be included. And don't forget all the "cash" expenditures, especially if you have an ATM card that lets you withdraw funds via bank machines.

Gathering this information makes you a winner. When you begin to get involved in the daily, weekly, and monthly expenditures of the family, as well as of the family business, you get an inside track of what is going on, as well as an overview of what your spouse does with his and your money. Learn about investments, an area that has some complexities—where your money is, how it is doing, what the yields are, and whether there are gains or losses occurring. It lets you look at what your lifestyle really is. You may be surprised to find that you could live a little better than you actually are.

Hanging in There

There are times when waiting is on your side. If you have been married nine years, it makes absolute sense, unless you are physically threatened, to stick in there for the tenth year. At that point, you become entitled to half of the Social Security benefits your spouse has accumulated. If your own benefits will yield more than half your spouse's, forget about waiting to qualify for your spouse's benefits.

Lawsuits are another area where it also pays to pay close attention to timing. If your spouse is a plaintiff, the person who sues another in an action for any injuries where money could come from gets the money. Your strategy may be to not file for divorce until after the suit is completed. That way, you can share a portion of the proceeds. On the other hand, if there is no way that you can hang in there, make sure that you include in your settlement agreement reimbursement for any monies that were expended from the marital side in caring for the injured party, as in the case of an accident. When you are the plaintiff, then by all means get going as soon as possible. Monies that you receive after the divorce are yours. That is, unless your divorce agreement states otherwise.

Again, if there is a physical threat, you do not have time to gather everything up before you leave. What is more important is to preserve your sanity, your health, and possibly your life.

Summing Up

Gathering information, compiling facts, and determining your priorities will be key components as you go through this process. Keep Sarah's story in the back of your mind. You may not have the amount of money that she was working with, but her strategy and her success can become part of your plan.

Don't feel that you need to rewrite divorce law in these initial steps—keep it simple. First of all, the assets of your marriage need to be identified and known. Do a balance sheet of what property is held jointly and what is separate. If that is unknown, try to do an income-and-expense statement on either a monthly basis or a yearly basis. What comes in, and what goes out—your checkbook can be a guide here. Tax returns are essential. They aren't perfect sources, but they tell a lot about your assets. Ideally, obtain them before leaving or moving out, if that is what your intention is.

We know that the strategizing and planning sides of a divorce take time and require extra doses of patience. If you put energy into planning, you'll find that you've opened the door to your future instead of having it pushed at you.

13 Mistakes Even Smart People Make

· · · · ·

1. Signing papers without understanding what they mean.

2. Canceling or changing insurance policies without thinking through the consequences.

3. Withholding information from their lawyers because they now think what they did or said might have been a big mistake.

4. Going into denial about the process, withdrawing, or taking it too lightly.

5. Forgetting about the tax consequences of certain matters in the divorce.

6. Relying more on the advice of family and friends than on their lawyer's.

7. Not having enough life and disability insurance to protect an income stream they will depend on.

8. Waiting too long to take action to enforce child and spousal support that has stopped.

9. Not seeking the advice of psychological and financial professionals.

10. Not planning far enough ahead for health coverage after the divorce.

11. Thinking that all participants are "fair."

12. Dumping the case in the lawyer's lap and expecting good results.

13. Letting emotions run away from the facts.

· · · · ·

Putting Together Your Divorce Advisory Team

By now, you probably have made contacts with a few of the many advisers that you may come in contact with over the next several months—or years. The most common are the attorney, accountant, and financial adviser (usually a stockbroker or financial planner).

Outside of the death of a loved one, divorce ranks at the top as a stress inducer. Your advisory team's function is to reduce your stress levels and help pave the way to your new beginning. We have seen individuals go through a divorce successfully, orchestrating all the moves and hiring only an attorney to do the necessary paperwork. We also have observed and worked within divorces that took on a life of their own. Years—and in one case a decade—can go by before the divorce is finally resolved and dissolved.

There will be times when one member of your advisory team carries a larger load and has a louder voice than at other times. Remember the couple's divorce dance referred to earlier? The advisers have their own version. Throughout the divorce process, one will lead and dictate certain types of strategy, and at other times, will be led. With that in mind, let's start with the beginning leader—the attorney.

The Attorney

Besides you and your spouse, this is the primary player. As a rule, the attorney will be the conductor, orchestrating various sections of the team as the divorce moves along. Several chapters of this book are dedicated to the attorney—covering costs, questions to ask, even divorcing (i.e., firing) the attorney. Unless your situation is simple (you have no assets and no children are involved), you need an attorney. Yours should dedicate a minimum of 50 percent of his or her practice to divorce. If not, take a pass.

One of the important things to find out when you make an appointment with an attorney is whether he or she will charge you for the initial interview. But you had better be serious about working with that attorney. If he or she doesn't charge for the initial interview and it becomes clear that you are really there to obtain free information, the interview will probably be ended.

The Therapist

A therapist, someone who is an expert in the divorce process, helps you to get a handle on the emotional gyrations that occur before the filing and during proceedings, as well as after the divorce is final. Not every therapist, counselor, psychologist, or psychiatrist is an expert in divorce matters. For tips on selecting a divorce therapist, see Chapter 3.

Therapists work with you on an hourly basis, with fees ranging from $60 to $170. Many will request a minimum commitment of a specific number of sessions.

Financial Consultants

We have grouped several professionals under the financial consultant category. They include accountants (CPAs), Certified Financial Planners (CFPs), Certified Divorce Planners (CDPs), employment counselors, and employment evaluators. Some of these will be referred to you from friends and associates; some your attorney will directly recommend; and some you may actually see or hear on the radio or TV, or read about in a book or magazine or newspaper article.

CPAs

Not all CPAs (or professionals who identify themselves as accountants) are alike. You want a CPA who is experienced in divorce taxation issues. Most of us assume that attorneys and CPAs know all that is necessary to either comply with present tax law, to take advantage of it, or to avoid monetary penalties. But horror stories abound—of assets being distributed without consideration of tax ramifications.

When assets are to be sold or pensions distributed, alternative minimum taxes, loss carry forwards (personal and business), and other tax consequences must be planned out before any action is taken. It is not uncommon for couples to lose the documentation that will verify the original cost of all the homes that were owned during their marriage. CPAs can recreate the basis in the primary residence if it is to be sold so that it is satisfactory for the IRS.

CPAs take ongoing continuing education courses for tax planning updates. CPAs who are knowledgeable in the divorce area are used in the courtroom as expert witnesses. CPAs will charge you on an hourly basis with a cost range of $65 to $200 per hour.

The Certified Financial Planner

The CFP designation is granted by the College of Financial Planning in Denver, Colorado. CFPs have met educational requirements in a variety of financial areas and must take continuing education courses to retain the CFP designation.

A CFP can project your net worth and earnings in future years based on the financial data you provide. A CFP can provide evaluations and recommendations on investments and insurance, and tax planning. Check out how they are compensated. Some will charge you a flat fee to develop a financial plan, some will charge you on an hourly basis, some will receive commissions on products and investments they sell to you; some do a combination of all three.

If you've used a financial planner is the past, most likely, he or she has information about the cost basis of investments you are presently holding, their yields, and the overall status for each. If you own any limited partnerships, a financial planner can be helpful in determining their values, as well as the tax consequences when they mature or fail.

Caution—if the financial planner you use was your planner when you were a couple, he or she can't take sides and must talk to both of you, giving the same information at the same time. If your spouse was given information that caused him or her to allocate shares to you and the deal fails, the financial planner risks a lawsuit.

The Certified Divorce Planner

The CDP designation is granted by the Institute for Certified Divorce Planners in Boulder, Colorado. Anyone with a CDP has extensive background in financial planning, and probably will be a CFP or CPA specializing in the financial complications of divorce. CDPs must participate in continuing educational courses. They are skilled in expert courtroom testimony and charge between $75 to $200 per hour.

The CDP is trained in the financial issues of divorce and provides data that creates equitable distribution of assets. Areas covered include the tax consequences of property divisions, payment and receipt of alimony and household support, personal versus marital property, pension and retirement accounts (value and division), and the results of selling the house versus keeping it. CDPs often create a powerful presentation that encourages settlement instead of a courtroom battle.

Employment Evaluator (or Counselor)

The employment evaluator projects the amount of increased earnings you could receive with additional training and expanded skills, as well as the cost to obtain them. If you believe an employment evaluator could be an asset to your team, ask your attorney to refer you to a few. Employment evaluators are commonly used in personal injury cases. Their services will be based on an hourly fee, ranging from $50 to $150 per hour plus costs for testing.

Your local community college usually has a resource center that is available to both men and women seeking employment counseling. It will assist you in résumé writing, aptitude testing and skills evaluation, and possibly refer you to a potential employer. In many states, a portion of your divorce court filing fee funds a local center. The cost to you is minimal.

Insurance Agents

You may need to obtain information about a variety of forms of insurance, such as automobile, life, and property. Some agents offer all types of insurance, while others only offer a particular type; some represent many companies and others sell products only from one company.

After asking your friends or family for referrals, look in the yellow pages for listings. We suggest that you seek an agent who has some professional designation such as: CFP (Certified Financial Planner), CLU (Certified Life Underwriter), ChFC (Chartered Financial Consultant), or LUTCF (Life Underwriter Training Council Fellowship). These designations represent varying levels of training and testing, but overall reflect a person who is serious about his or her profession. Too often you will find insurance salespeople who are not insurance professionals—they may have been selling appliances, real estate, or cars a few months ago.

When it comes to purchasing an insurance product, it pays to shop around. You do not always get more coverage for more money. Check the most recent *Consumer Reports* ratings on insurance companies.

If you are knowledgeable about your life insurance needs, then there are many companies that offer you a service comparing several companies and policies when it is time to purchase additional or new coverage. This is painless, and you can save lots of money. It's all done over the phone. No sales personnel will call you in an attempt to sell you anything. Here are a few that we have used with success: TermQuote (800-444-8376); Master-Quote (800-337-5433); and OmniQuote (800-966-6641).

> • • • • •
>
> All insurance companies are not equal in service and coverage.
>
> • • • • •

Also, if you are purchasing an annuity or cash-value policy, check with Veritas (800-929-4970). Veritas is a direct consumer service division of Ameritas Life, an insurance company that specializes in low-cost life insurance for both term and cash-value policies.

Insurance professionals rarely charge an hourly fee. Their compensation comes from new sales—commissions. If you do purchase any insurance, don't be shy about asking what the agent or broker is making. After all, it is your money too.

Asset Evaluators

If you have "things," they have some value. The key is to determine just how much value your possessions are worth. This is where asset evaluators come in; they usually have a single function—to evaluate assets and prepare a report (usually written) that will be used for settlement purposes. With the exception of the real estate agent, they will be paid on a per-hour basis or at a flat rate.

Real Estate Appraisers

If you own a house or other type of real property, its value must be determined. If your spouse gets an appraisal, you should get one too. You can then agree to use one or the other, compromise between the two evaluations, or have the court decide. An appraiser will work up an appraisal based on comparable properties that have sold within the past year and on current construction costs. Real estate appraisers are certified for work in specific areas, such as residential, commercial, or agricultural. Fees are usually $200 to $500, depending on the size of the property and location.

Real Estate Market Analysis

Some people use a local real estate agent to get an estimate of their home's value. Real estate agents will often bring several agents in to preview your home and assess its value to potential buyers. After all, there is a listing possibility, so helping you now may earn them big bucks down the road. That's why there is no cost. If you go this route, ask for two listing figures—the first for a regular sale that could take several months and the other for a quick sale. You can call your local Board of REALTORS® and ask for the average sale period in your area and price range to help guide you.

Personal Property Appraisers

If you have antiques, gems, artwork, any type of collections, pedigreed animals, anything of value, you need to know what they are worth. Some items, such as Dept. 56 ceramic villages and accessories, have guidebooks and newsletters that list values; some hobby stores carry books and lists of hundreds of collectibles, even phone numbers that you can call for trading. Or check out the Internet—all kinds of stuff is traded in cyberspace.

Your nearest museum is an excellent resource for a referral for art, antiques, and other collectibles. Some art galleries are able to locate prices for you. When it comes to the "my stuff is valuable" area, be aware that there are two prices circulating. The first is what you will wait to receive for a valued item. This is the price at which you should carry your insurance coverage. The other price is what you will accept just to get rid of it. There is usually a wide gap between the two.

Pension Plan Evaluators

If you don't have a pension or any retirement accounts set aside, you can pass on this professional. But if you do, you may need to know the present value of the future income stream. If your pension is from the federal government or military, there are specialists who deal with the rules and regulations that are specific to that specific area.

Evaluators usually charge a flat fee, anywhere from $200 to $3,000. Your attorney is usually the best source for referrals here.

Business Appraiser

A business appraiser will look at the revenues, expenses, type of industry, equipment and other asset values, even economic impact on the local, state, or national economies. Factors are taken into consideration that involve many items outside of the net worth or book value of the business. *Never* use any value that is provided by the business's accountant or CPA. There are many ways to value a business.

Business appraisers sometimes have to do their own sleuthing. For small businesses, especially cash businesses (restaurants, cafés, bars, salons, a store where one of the spouses is a partner), individuals or investigators are hired to actually sit in the business, use its services, and buy its products. Why? To help determine how much cash is flowing through. The accountant can then verify if those purchases appear on reported gross receipts. If they don't, you have confirmation that skimming or nonreporting of income is occurring. The next step is to determine what percentage or amount is involved.

You want someone who specializes in evaluating businesses or, better yet, to evaluating your type of business. Most likely, your appraiser will be a member of the American Society of Appraisers (ASA), the International Society of Appraisers (ISA), the American Association of Appraisers (AAA), Institute of Business Appraisers (IBA), and is a Certified Business Appraiser (CBA). CBAs must pass a rigorous exam and submit their appraisals for review by a committee of experienced peers. The cost for an appraisal of a small business can range from $2,000 on up; for larger business, it's not unusual to see several thousands of dollars charged.

Child Advocates

If you have kids and want to explore different custody options and living arrangements, or if it looks as though there will be a dispute with custody arrangements, your kids need a rational voice on their team.

Psychologist

In some cases a psychologist can be useful in building a case for you to have custody of the children by presenting a formal psychological evaluation of your fitness to have custody. Fees can be based on a case basis or an hourly amount.

These evaluations frequently are based upon the results of certain psychological tests, such as the MMPI and the MMPI-2—the Minnesota Multiphasic Personality Inventory. This is a very complex area, because different evaluators may give the same test results different "spins." Psychological evaluation is an art, not all science. If your attorney is not familiar with the use of a psychological evaluator, he or she needs to become familiar with the selection and use of this resource-person, as well as how to present your evaluation and challenge that of the opposing party.

An excellent primer is Marc J. Ackerman's article, "The MMPI-2 in Child Custody Evaluations," found in the *1996 Wiley Family Law Update* (John Wiley and Sons, Inc., One Wiley Drive, Somerset, New Jersey 08875, 800-225-5945).

Custody Mediation Specialist

Deep down, most parents want what's best for their kids. But a divorce can often cloud "the best" with anger. A custody mediation specialist forces parents to focus on their kids' needs and step out of the power struggles that custody issues create. A custody mediation specialist works to settle custody issues outside of the courtroom.

Most are proponents of using contracts that are parental agreements, signed by both, that include a breakdown of parental responsibilities, how information is exchanged, which decisions will be allocated directly to the mother and father, who pays for what, what happens in the case of an illness or injury, participation in school and outside activities, and if there is an impasse, an agreement to submit to a third party (already identified within the agreement) to arbitrate.

Your attorney is usually the best resource for referrals—or you can call the local bar association and ask for specialists in this area. Custody mediation specialists are paid on an hourly basis with fees ranging from $50 to $150 per hour.

Guardian ad litem

If custody is a mess and you don't have a custody mediation specialist to work with, the court may appoint a GAL who will represent your children's interests, especially if they are contrary to yours.

The guardian *ad litem* is, in essence, an attorney appointed by the court to protect a child and to advise the court as to the best interests of the child (which could be contrary to yours). In some jurisdictions, the GAL can go beyond this role and actually become an advocate for the child to express the child's desires in custody matters. These attorneys are paid according to the order of the court, which will vary from one location to another. Expect to pay in the range of $125 to $175 an hour.

Other things that you can do for your kids include getting books on divorce, talking to the school psychologist about your situation, seeing how the kids are doing during the school day, having your kids participate in a divorce recovery group (your place of worship and therapists are resources here), or hiring a therapist or attorney exclusively for the kids. (This last option is an extreme measure, to take when nothing else works).

Summing Up

Not all divorces require a gaggle of experts. In fact, most don't. Before you rush off to hire each and every type of expert, we suggest you sharpen your pencil. Will the potential financial outcome exceed what you will have to put out to get an expert's opinion or report? How much energy and input will you be required to make? Is their use in your (or your children's) best interests? If your answers are yes, then jump in. But first, do them, and yourself, a huge favor by gathering whatever data is necessary from your own files.

13 Tips on Building an Advisory Team

· · · · ·

1. A properly assembled advisory team can reduce your stress and improve your outcome.

2. Since you may need their testimony in trial, each team member (except your attorney) should have experience in testifying as an expert witness.

(continued)

3. Be realistic about how you use your money, and carefully evaluate the need for each team member.

4. Your attorney is the conductor. The size of the orchestra depends on your case.

5. Your attorney should have a lot of experience in divorces. Don't use an amateur.

6. Much of the divorce process is tied to emotions, so a good therapist can be a tremendous help.

7. Money is at the heart of most divorce issues, so well-trained financial assistants may be a necessity.

8. A good CPA (not just a bookkeeper) can help organize financial information and find the money trail.

9. A Certified Divorce Planner has special training and skills in solving many of the money problems you will face during and after the divorce.

10. You may need to change automobile insurance policies, so now is a good time to shop around for what you will need after the divorce.

11. You may need professionals to answer the question of what marital assets are worth.

12. Not all real estate agents are qualified to give an appraisal for use in court.

13. Pensions are usually the most valuable assets in a marriage, so make sure you have an expert on your team unless your lawyer is one of the few who really understands how to evaluate, divide, and value pensions.

• • • • •

7

Choosing and Working with Your Attorney

Do you need an attorney? In a nutshell, we say yes. But there are exceptions. In most states you can get a divorce without a lawyer. If you choose to go this route, be aware that handling a divorce without a lawyer requires the existence of certain key emotional and legal conditions. You can consider *not using* a lawyer if:

- You and your spouse have approximately equal emotional power and stability in the relationship.
- You both will (and do) stand up for your rights.
- You both have a track record of being fair and honest.
- No complications (children, property, etc.) are involved.
- Both of you can agree on every issue.
- You have no significant property to divide, such as a house, business, or pension plan.
- You have no children to provide for.
- There will be no alimony for either party.

If this above sounds like you, then congratulate yourselves on saving money on legal fees. There are several do-it-yourself books available to assist you through the process.

> • • • • •
>
> Beware if the decision to not use a lawyer is driven by the spouse with power in the relationship to destroy the weaker partner.
>
> • • • • •

If this list doesn't describe your situation, continue through the rest of this chapter. How you hire, and manage, an attorney will have a substantial impact on your checkbook.

Good Legal Advice Is Hard to Find

Legal representation is critical in any divorce that involves assets.

In most cases, it is insane to use the same attorney for both of you. One of our clients was able to pick up an extra $15,000 during an hour-long appointment and one phone call made to the couple's "joint" attorney, who was the client's friend. It was discovered through our standard questioning that the equity in the home had been determined by the difference between the original cost of the house and the current market value. All wrong: Equity is determined by the difference between present mortgage(s) and current market value.

Fifteen thousand dollars is small change, compared to another client who left more than $1 million on the table because her attorney (and good friend) said he wouldn't handle the divorce if there was any bickering over assets. Whether it is $15,000, $1 million, or just a couple of hundred dollars, you are strongly advised to have your own advocate. Not necessarily one who is adversarial, but one who only owes allegiance to you.

Understand that one lawyer can never really represent both you and your spouse. But it is not always necessary to have two lawyers. If the matter is simple and there are no contested issues, one of the parties can appear *pro se,* that is, represent himself or herself. The one lawyer draws all the necessary documents and proceeds with the dissolution without the necessity of a second lawyer. If you are going to "share" a lawyer, make it clear who that lawyer's client is.

A word of caution: If your divorce involves regular support payments; questions over custody or visitation of children; or division of property is involved, you should at least have a second lawyer to look over the agreement before you sign it. A small change in the weekly support rate can mean thousands of dollars over an extended period. A misunderstanding about your interest in marital property could result and create an unexpected tax obligation, and so on. Only in the most basic cases should you consider going it alone—and perhaps not even then.

> • • • • •
>
> Remember, the lawyer can only represent *one* of you.
>
> • • • • •

Who's the One?

Rarely will you find the right attorney by simply calling the local bar association for the recommended list of the month. A referral from a close friend who went through a divorce is better.

Unfortunately, that doesn't always happen. Oh, there are plenty of referrals, but usually they come from friends who dealt with attorneys on real estate deals or in drawing up wills. Family law and divorce are highly specialized fields. Choose someone in that field and who has been doing mostly family law for at least five years.

There is a lot to be learned and plenty of mistakes that can be made. Open your ears—you will be surprised what your friends, next-door neighbors, and co-workers share about their catastrophes as well as successes. Pay close attention to the catastrophes—they can shorten your learning curve.

> • • • • •
>
> Experience *does* matter. Let the new lawyer learn the ropes at someone else's expense, not yours.
>
> • • • • •

We are adamant about your need for a top-notch attorney. There are horror stories about attorneys being interviewed, passing all the client's questions with flying colors and then being rejected because the client felt they were too expensive. Three or four years later they hobble back to the original attorney to straighten out the mess that was generated by the less-experienced and less-sophisticated counsel. A common statement is, "Oh, I wish I had kept you in the beginning. You were right. I didn't follow your advice and went to a cheap lawyer and got cheap work done." Does the original attorney take the case back? Most likely, not. It's not a punishment, but a factor of the law of diminishing return. Most of the damage has already been cast in concrete and is unchangeable.

Specialist versus Generalist

A lawyer does not necessarily have to be a divorce specialist, but we believe that you should strongly consider using one if you have a choice. At a minimum, the lawyer must be familiar with the rules of procedure and practice used in the court where your case will be heard. Your choice is similar to that offered in choosing a doctor—if you have a complex medical problem, you more likely will go to a specialist than a general practitioner. If your case is simple and on the borderline between not needing a lawyer at all, then you have less of a need for a specialist than if your case is potentially complex or contested. Even in simple cases, your lawyer can give you perspective about possible results in your case.

If you are seeking alimony (or are going to pay it) or if you have children who will require financial support, your lawyer must be familiar with the support ranges and property divisions customarily granted in your court. Changing laws and changing judges result in changing applications of the law. A novice or someone who doesn't keep up with family law changes can easily sabotage this area.

Your choice of an attorney may be influenced by your spouse's decision. If you suspect that your spouse has hired or will hire a lawyer with considerable experience who carries a great deal of weight in the court where your case will be heard, you need a lawyer with equal influence. The consideration your case and your lawyer will receive is very often related to the respect your lawyer can command from the court and the opposing lawyer.

One woman said that her husband decided to settle the case when he saw the car his wife's lawyer was driving. He told her, "I thought you were going to have a beat-up, used-car lawyer, but when you showed up with a Ferrari lawyer, I figure I was beaten already." Although this woman's lawyer had an impact on her spouse, don't choose a lawyer based upon your assumption of how your spouse will react. Choose one who will have a positive impact on your spouse's *lawyer.* There will be little if any interaction between your lawyer and your spouse if your spouse has a lawyer.

> A knowledge of tax law is a must where property transfers and support payments are involved. You need a divorce lawyer who can foresee potential problems and make their resolution part of the settlement. Outside tax expertise can be called upon to assist in the resolution if necessary.

Where Not to Look

There are a number of ways *not* to choose a lawyer.

- Do not ask a lawyer to handle your case if that person is not a divorce lawyer.
- Do not choose the lawyer who handled your parent's estate, who helped you prepare your wills, who handles the business law issues you or your spouse face, or who handled the real estate closing on your house to handle the divorce.

- Do not ask an attorney friend to take your case—you'll both end up regretting it. If you ask a friend to take your case, he or she may do so only because of your friendship. Don't put your friend in this position.
- Do not call an attorney who has handled things for your spouse in the past.

Where to Look

Your best sources of attorneys will be from personal referrals:

- Ask an attorney you have used—and liked—for a recommendation.
- Ask friends and relatives who have dealt with divorce lawyers. (Since no one ever feels like a winner in a divorce, they may even refer you to their spouse's lawyer.) In any event, they can tell you about their own experience with their lawyer and give you some help on what to look for and what to avoid. Listen to divorce stories from friends and colleagues. Ask the following questions, preferably from someone who is at least two years postdivorce:
  - What kind of settlement did your friend get?
  - What areas were settled fairly and quickly?
  - If your friend went through another divorce, would he or she hire this attorney again?
  - Overall, was your friend happy with how the case was handled?
  - Did the attorney's efforts interfere with or even jeopardize whatever relationship existed with your friend's spouse?
  - Did your friend feel that he or she was kept informed, or kept in the dark?
  - Did your friend feel comfortable with his or her attorney? (Some attorneys proposition their clients sexually—it's unethical, yet it still happens.)
  - In hindsight, did the fees paid and the overall results from the divorce seem fair?
- Check the referral services of your state and local bar associations, listed in the telephone yellow pages. Tell them it is a divorce case and ask for the names of a couple of people experienced in that area of practice. On a national level, if you want to find an exceptionally qualified and experienced divorce lawyer, call the headquarters for the American Academy of Matrimonial Lawyers in Chicago at 312-263-6477 for referrals in your area. Also ask for information on the criteria for membership in this organization.
- You can always call the local courts and ask for the name of the presiding judge for family law. Then, ask to speak to the judge's law clerk. More

than likely the judge will not talk to you, but the law clerk may be open with information about where to look for an attorney.

- Consult the *Martindale-Hubble Directory*, found in most large libraries. Remember, however, that the information found in this text is provided by the lawyers for a fee.
- Don't forget the Internet search engines if you use a computer and are on-line. If you don't have a computer, your local library does.

Put a great deal of effort into the task of finding a lawyer—it may be one of the most important decisions you make. The wrong choice can mean endless, painful, and expensive litigation; heartache; frustration; anger; and consequences you (and perhaps your children) will have to live with for the rest of your life.

If you have a referral source in whom you are totally confident, see the suggested person first. For example, if you have a great deal of trust in your business lawyer and he makes a very strong recommendation, see that person first. Then interview at least two more and compare them in terms of competence, personality, and price.

Since lawyers are now permitted to advertise, as a last resort you can now look to your local newspaper or yellow pages to find a lawyer who specializes or concentrates his or her practice in divorce law. Some states have a process of legal specialization in which lawyers can be certified as specialists in certain fields of law. This process is demanding and screens out those who have a passing interest in the field. If your state certifies specialists, concentrate on these specialists. Unfortunately, most states do not certify specialists, and there is no way to verify the truth of any particular advertisement without checking out that lawyer's reputation through the bar association or by asking other lawyers or friends who have dealt with that person. A lawyer's reputation among other lawyers is probably the most valid indication of his or her capabilities and weaknesses.

Be wary if your spouse suggests that you hire a particular lawyer. Ask yourself, "Is it likely my spouse wants me to have the best divorce lawyer in town—or even the tenth best?" But don't eliminate a particular lawyer who seems right for you just because of your spouse's recommendation—just make sure to check out that lawyer very carefully.

To Clinic, or Not to Clinic

One way to reduce costs is to use a legal clinic—a group of lawyers and paralegals who supply legal services at lower rates than the more typical firm. The bottom line is that the clinic's quality of service will depend on the lawyers and paralegals involved. The difference between law clinics and private offices is that clinic lawyers attempt to minimize the number of hours spent with the client. Clinics maximize the use of forms and the assistance of secretaries and paralegals who are paid at lower rates than those with law degrees. This approach is satisfactory if the case is simple and does not involve a lot of contact between the lawyer and client.

Even if the price seems right, of course you still must consider the lawyer's competence and personality. Ask yourself, "If this lawyer is really as good as he seems, why is he working for a clinic at one-fourth of the price of other, experienced lawyers?" But after your initial interview, if you are satisfied on the points discussed in this chapter, there is no reason not to hire the lawyer. Your pocketbook may benefit.

Always ask whether that lawyer will be the person representing you, or whether it will be an associate or other office personnel. Many people have been quite surprised to find out that the person they interviewed with ended up doing only a small amount of work on the divorce. If your case requires personal attention, then you want to know who will be giving you that attention.

Also know that just because a clinic may advertise a divorce for as low as $250 does not mean it won't be entitled to a larger fee if your case is more complicated and requires more time or court appearances. These matters should always be clarified at the outset of your relationship with the law clinic as with any other law office. Never assume anything.

Ask what the hourly charge for the clinic lawyer is. Compare that rate with what is commonly charged in your community and determine whether the clinic is really the bargain you expected.

Making the Right Choice (and Avoiding the Wrong One)

Your divorce (or any financial concern for that matter) is no place for on-the-job training. Doctors work as interns and residents under close supervision. There is no similar requirement for lawyers before they can hang out a shingle. If you are lying on a stretcher in the emergency room after a car accident, you want an experienced physician trained in emergency medical care, not a doctor who reads x-rays for a living.

The Personality Factor

Even if there are slight differences in other areas, the personality factor is very important. You will have to deal closely with this individual on potentially volatile and personal problems. While there does not need to be a perfect match, a clash of personalities may make this relationship uncomfortable or even contentious.

If your case is a simple one, avoid the lawyer who appears to be unnecessarily combative or more interested in preserving his or her ego than in obtaining a good result. This lawyer could turn a simple inexpensive case into a long expensive struggle. You can pay out big bucks. To some degree, you should rely on your instincts.

The following character descriptions should show you what you *do not* want in a lawyer. Think about them when you go see an attorney.

Trust me, leave it all to me. This "father (or mother) knows best" lawyer dismisses your questions and concerns. This lawyer may appear to offer you options as the case goes along but will probably try to manipulate you into approving his or her decisions.

On-the-one-hand, and on-the-other-hand. At the other extreme is this wishy-washy lawyer who will never express an opinion about anything. You will be lucky to get this lawyer to commit that the sun rises in the East. You will not get a straight answer no matter how hard you try. Over and over again, this lawyer will tell you that nothing is predictable and anything can happen. Favorite phrases are, "We'll check that out," or "Let's see about that," or "There's no way of telling."

Which way to the battlefield? Rambo lawyers will look at every issue as an opportunity to use everything from martial arts to nuclear bombs. Most of this enthusiasm probably will be directed at the other side, but you may need your own ninja if you disagree on some point of strategy or tactics. Unfortunately, this confrontational style may cause the other side to dig in its heels and turn your divorce into a bitter and expensive mother of all battles. Frequently these lawyers use the experience to build their egos at your expense.

Where do we sign, and which way to the back door? This marshmallow will avoid conflict at all costs, is always ready to settle every question, and readily sees the reasonableness of the other side's positions. This lawyer will try to avoid a trial at all costs. You will be lucky to leave the marriage with the clothes on your back. And if your case ever comes to trial, forget about having this person fight for your rights.

Hold that thought . . . Isn't call waiting wonderful? A visit to this center of the universe is a real treat. This lawyer is always talking on the phone while the intercom keeps buzzing. A stack of unanswered messages is always in a pile on the desk. During your interview, there will be calls and "urgent" interruptions parading through the office. If you are lucky, this lawyer may hear a word or two that you say and will manage to give you a word or two in response before sending you out the door.

I am your knight in shining armor. Sir Galahad takes the view that law is a secret world that only he or she can understand. Certainly, a layperson could never appreciate what this lawyer does and how he or she can orchestrate your case. Don't expect any information on the details or strategy of the case—only wait to be told where to sign and what to say. You will not be given options, just this lawyer's opinion.

Did you see me on the evening news? This celebrity lawyer is a master at self-promotion, and is more interested in looking good for the press and public than in obtaining a good result for you.

Oh, you poor dear. Nurse lawyer bleeds right along with you. But in the end you will have gotten more faulty therapy than competent legal advice. This lawyer will see to it that you use lots of Kleenex during your visits.

What to Look for in a Lawyer

Here are some things your lawyer should do for you:

- Listen attentively to you.
- Instill a sense of confidence based upon expertise and experience on the issues you face.
- Provide you with options and an explanation of the pros and cons of a particular course of action.
- Provide an outline of what you may realistically expect.
- Defend you vigorously to obtain every advantage you can get, including competent representation in a trial if that is necessary.
- Give you honest feedback when he or she thinks you are off track.
- When necessary, act as a peacemaker by explaining the benefits of negotiating terms that you and your spouse can accept.
- Have an active law practice from which you can benefit due to vast experience.
- Have a good reputation with the court and opposing counsel.
- Have an experienced and congenial support staff.

- Have the ability to be sensitive enough to the inevitable emotional struggles.
- Help you maintain perspective as to what is a fair settlement.
- Conduct aggressive discovery of all assets and income.
- To the degree possible, significantly control the case. (The lawyer should control you in order to avoid willful violations of court orders or agreements; and control the opposition by blocking attempts to take advantage of you.)
- File all pleadings and motions in a timely fashion—and not on the last day permitted.
- Respect you and your ideas and suggestions.

What to Avoid

Still not sure about your prospective lawyer? Here is some final advice: Run, do not walk, out the door if, during the interview with a prospective lawyer, you hear any of the following:

"I'll represent both you and your spouse. There is no reason for both of you to have a lawyer." One attorney cannot ethically represent both parties.

"Mediation does not work, so don't waste your time." Mediation can and does work, and should usually be attempted.

"Tell you what: I will charge you only a low, flat fee for your divorce." A lawyer who is not making a reasonable fee probably will not put his or her all into your case.

"I promise you . . ." Nothing is certain in a divorce. Ever.

"We will win this case." In the long run, a divorce is not about winning or losing, and a lawyer who believes that he or she has to win can be very expensive and often will push the other side into positions of unreasonableness.

"I'll win the kids for you." The children are not property to be won or lost, or to use as weapons.

Four Key Areas

We have consistently found that four types of questions pop up during the first few meetings with the attorney. It makes sense to determine whether any of these items are important to you. A word of caution here: Some lawyers are going to become incredibly defensive when you start probing into "their" territory. After all, they are the experts, right? Wrong. Too many make mistakes. And your objective is to avoid mistakes.

We suggest you lead your questions with something like this to your attorney (feel free to memorize and use verbatim):

Let's say that your child was to have brain surgery. I bet you would probe thoroughly into the surgeon's background and credentials before you would let him operate, wouldn't you? Me too. Well, I'm new at divorce and I feel like I'm going through a major and radical surgery. I need to know everything before we proceed. My intention is not to micromanage my case, but I'm going to be an involved client.

1. **The divorce process**
   - Who pays the legal fees?
   - If you must take your ex to court for nonsupport or for not complying with the divorce decree, who pays the legal fees and court costs? Will there be interest charges?
   - If you are the wife, do you want to take back your maiden name?
2. **Property**
   - Who gets which property?
   - Who gets which debt?
   - If the pension is to be divided, has the proper paperwork been prepared?
   - If there is a property settlement note, is it collateralized? Is there interest on it?
   - Does the spouse who gets the house get the whole basis in the house?
   - If the spouse who gets the house needs to sell it immediately, will that person be responsible for the entire capital gains tax?
3. **Alimony**
   - How much alimony for how long?
   - If alimony is not awarded now, can it be awarded later?
   - Will there be life insurance to cover alimony in the event of the payer's death?
4. **Child support**
   - How much child support will be paid, and for how long?
   - Will the child support change during college or when visitation times change?
   - Who has custody of the children?
   - What is the visitation schedule?

- Who pays related expenses for school (transportation, books, etc.) and unusual expenses (lessons, camp, braces, etc.)?
- Who will deduct the children on income tax forms?

The Overload Factor

Let's face it. Most of us today are overloaded. Your attorney is no different. A common postdivorce complaint is that clients feel that their attorneys didn't fully pay attention to critical issues and that at times, their cases were not managed well.

It may be that many attorneys take on more cases than they can really manage in the same way that airlines overbook. Some of their cases will eventually drop out, some will settle, some of the parties will change their minds and reconcile, and some will take longer than originally anticipated. To compensate for this, attorneys will fill their pipeline up with too many clients, primarily out of fear of not having enough work. In the end, it becomes a way of life for them. If this is a concern for you, get it out on the table now.

The Game Plan

This is the time to be proactive. You need to take the bull by the horns and force your attorney to respond when you ask a question along the line of:

- What happens when a court date is scheduled?
- What happens when the tax returns are delivered?
- What happens when we bring the appraiser in to evaluate the business?
- What happens when . . .?

Some attorneys will duck, waffle, equivocate, and otherwise refuse to answer the questions. Pin the attorney down, to narrow the field. If you ask, "When will my case go to trial?" and your attorney responds, "A long time from now," you, in turn can respond, assuming today is July 1, 1998, "By June 1999?" If the attorney responds, "Oh, before then," you know you have the furthest-out time or drop-dead date. You can then counter with, "December, 1998?" If the answer is, "No. Not that soon," you now have a six-month period where you have some idea when this will be going to trial, if it does. You can then respond, "Now I know approximately when it will go to trial. What has to happen prior to then and what will happen during? Let's work backward so I understand it." In other words, you need to say, "Give me the game plan."

Find out the order in which events will happen. If the attorney can't answer, you are better off leaving and finding a different attorney. If he or she responds, "I really can't tell you what will happen, but I can give you some guidelines," that's great—it becomes part of your game plan.

After the attorney gives you some guidelines, write them down and send a letter back saying the following:

This is my understanding of our discussion. These are the things that will happen: [fill in the blank]. I know you can't quote exactly how much time and effort you will put into them, but please do not spend any amount of time in excess of your original dollar estimate without my authorization.

Never give an attorney open access to your bank account. Avoid, with fear of your financial life, someone who says, "Don't worry. I'll take care of everything. Just pay my bill when it arrives." You really need to get fee and hour estimates and an overview of the game plan. If your attorney has to go on a fishing expedition looking for assets and documents, you are going to be spending a lot of money.

Your Initial Interview

Now that you have narrowed down your search, know the key areas of the divorce process, and have insight to the lawyer's turf, here are some questions to ask a lawyer during your initial interview:

- What percentage of your practice involves divorce? (You do not want an amateur. Look for someone who has specialized in family law for at least five years. This means that a minimum of 50 percent of his or her practice is dedicated to divorce.)
- Do you have trial experience in divorce cases, or do you usually settle out of court? What percent of your cases go to trial? (If you think this is where you are headed, you definitely want someone with experience in trial work.)
- Will you go to court to litigate the case if it cannot be settled?
- Do you consider yourself a litigator, negotiator, arbitrator, or mediator? (It depends on what you want. Do you want to negotiate a settlement or prepare for war?)
- Do you routinely represent clients in my county? (Never underestimate the old-boys-and-girls networks. Strangers are not always welcome.)

- Will you handle the case personally, or will an associate in your office handle it? (If another person is to be involved, you may wish to interview that person before retaining the lawyer. Also ask if there is a difference in rates.)
- Do you charge extra for work done by paralegals or secretaries? (If the answer is yes, ask what their rates are. They should be lower.)
- What is your procedure for calling you outside of normal business hours if it is necessary?
- In this jurisdiction, approximately how long does it take to resolve this case if an agreement is reached? How long will it take if it must go to trial?
- What do you expect of me?
- How do you charge for your services? Please show me your fee agreement and explain it to me.
- Do you think your fees are average, above average or below average for the area?
- Do you have a written contract or retainer agreement? Please show it to me and explain it. (The answer should be yes. It should state fee structures and his or her responsibility to you. If, at a later date, you decide to switch attorneys after signing an agreement, you can. An attorney cannot prevent you from taking your file elsewhere.)
- What do you estimate court costs will be?
- Which spouse will be liable for the fees and court costs? How will that be determined?
- Do you charge a retainer fee? How much will it be? Under what circumstances is it refundable in full or in part?
- Can you give a ballpark estimate on the total fee?
- Will there be monthly billings or will the fee be due at some particular time?
- Will there be charges for outside services by accountants or investigators? Will I be able to approve such services in advance?
- Based on the information I have given you, what results would you expect on any particular contested issue either by court decision or by negotiation? (Since predictions are risky and the information you have provided is probably incomplete, you should expect a guarded answer with no absolute assurances of a particular result.)
- If you have kids, ask what the attorney's attitude is about joint or legal custody. Make sure you probe and ask what has worked and what has not worked.
- How do local laws affect any issues that may be contested, such as child custody, support, alimony, or property division?

- Are you an active member of family law committees in your local state or national bar association? Are you a member of the American Academy of Matrimonial Lawyers? (Answers should be yes.)
- Ask any personal questions you have regarding your rights and responsibilities in connection with your spouse, e.g., whether you must continue to prepare meals if you both still reside in the same house, pay your spouse's charge accounts, file joint tax returns, etc.

You may think of other questions you'd like to ask. If an answer to a question is not satisfactory or you do not understand it, say so immediately. Don't be afraid to show your lack of understanding. A good attorney wants to know when you do not understand aspects of your case. You are paying to know the answers to your questions and to have them explained thoroughly, but you must ask the right questions.

Some of these points and questions may seem overwhelming. But if you don't ask questions up front, you will regret it as time progresses. None of your questions are unimportant to you—that's why you are asking. Ask each one, write down the answers, and review them. They will form a bible for you.

View this as a huge caution sign here: *People under stress are usually poor listeners—very poor listeners.* When you ask your lawyer a question, listen to the answers rather than thinking ahead to your next question. Don't be afraid to take notes. Again, if you brought a list of questions, you don't have to think ahead to your next one. Hint: Write down the answers you are given. If unsure what your attorney said, ask for clarification. Most people think they heard and understood what was said. Then they find out that they really didn't.

Paying the Piper

First let us put the billing process in perspective. Abraham Lincoln said, "A lawyer's time and advice are his stock and trade." That is, a lawyer has no goods on shelves to sell, only time and advice. Most people would never expect to walk into a store, take items to the cash register, and ask to be allowed to take the items out of the store without paying for them. But some people expect to be able to obtain legal advice without paying for it.

Attorneys have the reputation for charging for full hours of time when only a few minutes are spent. Don't be afraid to ask for exact documentation. We have been the recipients of and have reviewed with clients invoices that merely state services rendered, three hours, and a sum of money due. You have no idea what the services were and how much time was spent. It is your money. Ask, ask, ask.

Get in writing how charges are allocated—phone time, copies, faxes, mailings, filing fees, court costs, bonding requirements, paralegals, expert witnesses, mileage charges, attorney time, and the time of other members of the firm. Charges can mushroom overnight. Fees will range all over the map, depending on the area in which you live. New York and Beverly Hills will have a higher per-hour cost than Cedar Rapids, Iowa. The cost of living in your area is a factor, but so are experience and overall results. It's a good idea to keep a phone log of incoming and outgoing calls (the ones you make) to your attorney. Note the subject and amount of time for the calls.

If you have combined known assets and have limited funds, why pay $250 an hour when you can get adequate and reliable representation for much less? The key here is to ask around. Your local bar association can offer the average fee range in the area.

If you know your case is uncomplicated, consider using discount legal services found in your yellow pages or a clinic mentioned earlier in this chapter, or participate in one of the prepaid legal services available in your state. They have plenty of information they share for minimal costs. (Caution: Attorneys come and go at these establishments.) But if you are exploring or have minimal assets and hate paperwork, then this could be very worthwhile for you.

Again, *never, never, never* give an attorney carte blanche to run up enormous bills—many will. Sometimes attorneys can run up their bills to incredible proportions. They can do it in one of three ways:

1. They are often so busy coping with every deadline as each comes up, that they don't pay attention. Their meters don't get turned off because they are always scrambling and are not really organized.
2. Many don't understand the finances. When they look at an issue, they don't have the sense to say, "This is not my bailiwick. Let's talk to somebody who can tell you whether are looking at $5 or $50,000."
3. Some of them really and truly are deliberately goosing up their bills by being adversarial at every corner.

Most lawyers charge by the hour, and those who are in greater demand will usually charge more for their time. But price is not always a measure of skill. Find out the range of fees in your community for simple to more complex cases. Friends

> An important issue for hiring any professional is the cost—how much and how allocated (per flat hour, half hour, quarterly, fractions of time rounded up). You don't want surprises.

may discuss their experiences with you, but in shopping for a lawyer, inquire about fees and charges. If a lawyer you are considering charges substantially above or below the amount you have found, then find out why.

Another thing that you will find (not surprisingly) is that inexperienced lawyers charge less, unless they are really brazen. But it may take more time to finish the same work. Taking all things into consideration, if you can afford the more expensive lawyer who has a top-notch, well-earned reputation, you probably are better off using this lawyer. Many times his or her reputation may have a significant effect on the outcome of your case.

Retainers

In shopping, you will find that most lawyers require you to put up a sum of money up front before they will take the case. This is called a "retainer fee," and can run from a few hundred to several thousand dollars, depending on the expected problems with the case. State laws require that this money be deposited into a separate client trust account, not into the lawyer's regular bank account.

You need to understand clearly if the retainer is all or partially refundable. If the retainer is refundable, the lawyer likely will keep track of his or her time and charge against the deposit as the case progresses. If there is money left over, it will be refunded to the client. On the other hand, if the money is spent down, additional retainer funds will be required.

The retainer is normally not refundable if you drop your case or find a new lawyer unless the retainer was very large and little work was done. This is because divorce filings are frequently withdrawn, and much effort can go into the initial work.

We strongly recommend some type of fee agreement. This will be for the protection of the lawyer as well as the client. Go over the proposed fee agreement very carefully. If there is something in it that you do not like or understand, it is critical that you bring it into the open. For example, if there are payment requirements that you cannot make, ask if the provision can be changed.

In most cases, if you decide to fire your attorney, the retainer will not be refunded, and more money may be required if the time already spent on the case justifies it.

Do not be angry if the lawyer cannot tell you precisely how much your case will cost. It is impossible to accurately predict all of the variables that may arise. And be wary if the lawyer quotes a flat fee for a total package. If your case drags on, the lawyer will not be very motivated to put in the extra hours that will be required for taking the case to completion.

There is another element in the expense of divorcing—court costs, the miscellaneous charges made by the court in connection with the processing of the case. They include administrative filing costs of pleadings and the cost to transcribe the record if necessary.

Many other miscellaneous costs can be associated with a divorce: hiring an investigator; court-reporter charges for transcribing depositions; subpoena fees; process server fees; and costs for photocopying, postage, long-distance telephone calls, faxes, and the like.

> • • • • •
>
> Many good lawyers are not comfortable talking about fees. This does not necessarily mean they are not honest. You may have to bring up the subject.
>
> • • • • •

There are lots of excellent attorneys. We are adamant about good legal representation. Sometimes, you shouldn't rush full-bore into something. One client still lived with her husband but felt that her marriage was over. She came in to start divorce proceedings. When asked if she needed to be divorced right away, she said no. When asked if she needed financial support, she responded no.

> • • • • •
>
> Your attorney is *your employee*. Don't be afraid to take control. If you don't understand what is going on, ask. If you can't get a reasonable or clear explanation, shop for another attorney.
>
> • • • • •

She was advised to first deal with the emotional process of separation and getting on her own two feet before speeding unnecessarily into the legal hassles of a divorce proceeding. She should determine what she wanted to do with her life and what changes she needed to go through, and get herself gradually ensconced into a new lifestyle and pattern. There was plenty of time to work out the legalities later—when heads were clear.

Good attorneys often advise their clients to let the dust settle. It can give each of them a better handle on where they are going and how they feel, *really* feel about each other, whether the divorce is necessary or if the air just needs to be cleared and each party given some breathing room. It also eases settlement negotiations. When recently separated spouses are still hurting, their egos are not in great shape; emotions such as spite and anger can blind them as to what is in their long-run best interest.

> • • • • •
>
> No attorney can guarantee results.
>
> • • • • •

Working with Your Attorney Once You've Hired One

We have been advising clients for several decades. Whether we saw them as a couple or in a solo status, it didn't take any of us long to figure out that communications—missed, none, or wrong—was usually at the heart of their problems. The same holds true with communicating with your lawyer.

One of the corniest stories we've heard fits perfectly here. A distraught man made an appointment with an attorney. He said that his wife had decided to file for divorce. When the attorney asked, "Are there grounds?" he responded, "Yes, she owns 100 acres in the country."

The lawyer was a tad taken back, then said, "Well, that's not what I had in mind. If you have kids, does she want custody?" Again, the distressed man responded, "No, she rarely cusses."

"Well," the lawyer asked, "Does she need some support?" "No, she just lays down on the couch when she gets tired," came back the man's response.

This was getting to be too much. Maybe this guy didn't hear well. One more time, he asked, "One more question, did your wife tell you why she wanted a divorce?" This time he perked up and said, "Oh yes, but I don't get it. She says she wants to divorce me because we don't communicate."

That's an understatement! As your case progresses, communications with your attorney and other advisers are critical. Your relationship with your lawyer is central when it comes to orchestrating the various issues within your divorce. We hope this relationship is positive and continues to improve as your case progresses. Communications with your lawyer are important in creating a free flow of information between the two of you. If your lawyer does not want to listen to your ideas, watch out. There will be trouble ahead—we guarantee it.

One key ingredient in the relationship between a lawyer and the client is that the client should be open and candid with the lawyer. A relationship of trust and credibility is essential. The lawyer can't develop a strategy if he or she is not aware of the true facts, and predictions about the outcome of the case only will be inaccurate if he or she does not know the truth. One of the reasons some clients lie or withhold information is because they now realize that they have done something really dumb. But these are some of the most important details to tell the lawyer. Everybody makes mistakes, and it is unlikely that an experienced lawyer will be shocked by anything you say.

If you lie about facts such as assets or income, the truth usually will come out, and your attorney will have lost credibility with your spouse's attorney. This even can be disastrous if a judge finds out that you have lied. If your lawyer suggests that you should lie or keeps quiet while you continue deceiving the other side or the court, you have the wrong lawyer. A competent lawyer does not have to rely on such tactics.

Aside from violating ethical and legal standards, it is stupid to lie because your spouse usually will know what the truth is. And lies can pour gasoline onto the fires of litigation. The old adage is true, "If you tell the truth, you will not have to worry that you forgot what you said."

When you have an appointment, organize your thoughts, questions (write them down), and the information you are providing the lawyer. Have some specific goals in mind. This practice is better for you and your lawyer, and especially your pocketbook. This is one of the times to remember your lawyer is not your therapist or rent-a-friend.

> • • • • •
> Tell your lawyer all the facts, and then let him or her worry about protecting you.
> • • • • •

Frequently you may need to call your lawyer rather than making an appointment for an office visit. During your initial interview you should find out his or her preferences about telephone calls. Many lawyers who have a hectic day will return calls in the evening, so be sure and make it clear if the lawyer should not call you at home or leave messages.

Busy lawyers will not block out time every day to receive calls, so it is likely that you will have to leave a message and have your call returned. Before you call, think of a way to condense your question or information in the event you need to leave a message. This can minimize the need for telephone tag. In addition, it may be that the secretary or paralegal can answer your question or obtain the information you need. This may save you money because the lawyer will bill for calls and the secretary probably will not. If the secretary does, it should be at a substantially lower rate.

Don't call a lawyer's home unless it is a true emergency that must be dealt with immediately. Remember, if the problem is domestic violence, call 911, not your lawyer. Your lawyer is not going to come to your house and get in the middle of a confrontation. Most matters will have to wait until the next morning before they can be acted upon anyway.

The telephone can turn into a source of irritation and conflict between a lawyer

> • • • • •
> Do not make a pest of yourself on the phone. If the lawyer knows that you will want to spend a long time on the phone every time he or she calls, you will be less likely to have your calls returned promptly.
> • • • • •

and the client. This can result from a client who calls too much about unimportant matters and the lawyer who seldom or never returns calls. If a problem develops, honestly consider whether you are the problem. Look at your log of calls. (You *are* keeping a phone log, aren't you?) Find out from the lawyer's secretary if this is a normal practice, and if so, find out if there is something that can be done about it, be-

> • • • • •
>
> If you use the telephone prudently, the lawyer may put you at the top of his or her callback list because he or she can get quickly on and off the call.
>
> • • • • •

cause you need to know if this is just the lawyer's style, or if he is avoiding you. You may need to schedule an appointment to discuss this with the lawyer or write a letter with your concerns.

Sometimes a lawyer may not be aware of what is going on. A good lawyer will want to know if there is a problem in the relationship.

Getting Along with the Really Important People

Not only is it critical to have a good relationship with your attorney, it is equally critical to have a good relationship with his or her receptionist or parale-gal. A paralegal has formal training and experience in legal matters, and many lawyers place great responsibility on these people. It is customary for the administrative support staff to know more about some aspects of your case than your lawyer does.

Have you ever thought about who keeps track of stuff? Don't count on the attorney—it's the staff! They will usually keep track of information about dates, court times, depositions, and office appointments. Save your contacts with your lawyer for more important issues.

> • • • • •
>
> Get ahead of the pack by being nice to the administrative support staff. A thank-you note, flowers, or candy works wonders for these overworked and underappreci-ated cogs in the wheel of a good law office.
>
> • • • • •

Remember to treat the administrative staff with respect—not just because it is the civil thing to do, but because it is in your own best interest to do so. If they conclude that you are easy to get along with, your case can get priority—maybe in scheduling appointments and in having your calls returned. They are usually the gatekeepers of the lawyer and have significant indirect power.

13 Questions to Ask a Lawyer

• • • • •

1. What percentage of your practice involves divorce?

2. Do you have trial experience in divorce cases, or do you usually settle out of court? What percentage of your cases go to trial?

3. Would you consider yourself a litigator, negotiator, arbitrator, or mediator?

4. Will you handle the case personally, or will an associate in your office handle it?

5. How do you charge for your services? Do you charge a retainer fee? How much will it be, and is it refundable in full or in part under any circumstances?

6. Do you have a written contract or retainer agreement?

7. Can you give a ballpark estimate of the total fee?

8. Will there be monthly billings or will the fee be due at some particular time?

9. Will there be charges for outside services by accountants or investigators? Will I have to approve such services in advance?

10. Do you charge extra for work by paralegals or secretaries? If the answer is yes, ask what their rates are. (They should be lower.)

11. If you have kids, ask what the attorney's attitude is about joint or legal custody.

12. How do local laws affect any issues that may be contested, such as child custody, support, alimony, or property division?

13. Are you an active member of family law committees in your local state or national bar association? Are you a member of the American Academy of Matrimonial Lawyers?

• • • • •

13 Most Common Mistakes Lawyers Make

• • • • •

1. They overcommit, don't manage their time well, and make promises they can't deliver on.

2. They aren't fully prepared in the courtroom and don't use expert witnesses appropriately.

3. They can misrepresent your position by not knowing certain tax areas that impact you.

4. They don't refer their clients to divorce therapists.

5. They take on cases in which they don't have full expertise and shoot from the hip.

6. They turn a professional, adversarial relationship with their client into a personal battle or a fairly simple procedure into a war zone.

(continued)

7. They don't keep up with technology.

8. They bill clients for educating themselves in matters they should know.

9. They are horrible communicators, failing to keep their clients informed about the status of their case.

10. They wait until the last minute to accomplish routine tasks and miss important filing deadlines.

11. They poorly manage their support staffs.

12. They fail to design an overall case strategy.

13. They don't listen to or respect their clients.

• • • • •

What If You Don't Need (or Want) an Attorney?

Mediation and Arbitration

Going to battle is definitely not the only way to resolve the issues that are guaranteed to arise during your divorce. If an attorney tells you that the only place your divorce can be settled is in the courtroom, tell him or her adios. You are dealing with someone who is not tuned in to the possibility of mediation, arbitration, negotiation, or even a friendly parting.

Mediation or Arbitration

Before entering into mediation or arbitration, you need to know the difference between them. In arbitration and mediation, a neutral third party is used. But this is where the similarities end. In arbitration, both husband and wife agree to give the arbitrator the power to decide the dispute as a judge would. In binding arbitration, you agree beforehand to abide by the decision as if it were law. In straight arbitration, if you don't like it, you can go elsewhere.

The purpose of mediation is for both husband and wife to come to a mutually acceptable settlement. The mediator does no individual counseling, and is limited to gathering data, setting the ground rules, and keeping both parties on track. Throughout mediation, alternative solutions are offered, issues are clarified, and a settlement is arrived at. If you and your spouse are communicating, then mediation should be explored.

Elizabeth chose to go into mediation, but only after she went attorney shopping. She interviewed eight different attorneys over a variety of issues. When she told one of them about her husband's temper, he advised her to get an injunction immediately. That way, if Harold became threatening or harassing, she could throw him out. By law, he would have three days to respond. The thought of it made her extremely upset. There had never been any physical abuse, more along the lines of yelling, shouting, and stomping around the house. She didn't like the idea of throwing him on the street.

To her dismay, she discovered that the $3,000 retainer fee that this attorney requested would merely cover the cost of filing for the injunction. Her divorce would cost much, much more. The total marital assets she was looking at amounted to $200,000, mostly from the family residence. She called a friend of hers, a divorce attorney in another state, for advice and a reality check.

He countered what the first attorney had said, adding, "An injunction is merely a piece of paper that says you aren't to do anything that is harmful. Most times, it is plain B.S. If someone has his socks knocked off with such an order, it will incite him to actually be violent, even if he ordinarily wouldn't be violent. Throwing someone out of the house will create a negative mode and will make mediating the dissolution even tougher. If you do not feel that you are physically threatened, do not get an injunction."

Mediation as a Choice

Mediation doesn't eliminate your need for a competent attorney. It does require voluntary participation of both husband and wife.

Mediators can be retired or active family law commissioners or judges, a lawyer who is skilled in family law, or a lawyer who is skilled in family law and has some counseling background. Mediators can also be psychologists or other professionals who have been trained in mediation.

Gary Friedman is an attorney and director of the Center for Mediation in Law, located in Mill Valley, California. His book, *A Guide to Divorce Mediation* (Workman Publishing, 1993) is one of the best on the market today. Since the early 1980s, he has trained thousands of attorneys nationwide in the skills of mediation. When we first spoke with him, we asked if one of the objectives of mediation was to attempt to get couples through the divorce process with the least amount of pain. His response was, "In many ways, mediation is more painful than divorce because you face each other directly. You experience conflict in a very intense way, so that in terms of what you go through, many times mediation is harder. Mediation is a face-to-face situation—both parties often hear things they don't want to hear."

He stated that plenty of lawyers support the mediation process but added that many only pay lip service to it. "Most lawyers are quite attached to law as the standard to be used in determining how people should decide their disputes and don't believe that such a thing as fairness exists," he said. "When mediation is brought up, many lawyers are very cynical about it."

Why? Money is one good reason. Mediation costs a fraction of what it would for standard lawyers to work out the settlement. It is charged on an hourly basis and it usually takes from four to ten sessions for couples to go through the whole process. Friedman said that the best lawyers and the most competent divorce lawyers have no problems when their clients participate in mediation. In fact, they actually encourage them to do it, know how to support them as they go through the process, and encourage them to come back and consult. "This way, the husband and wife have the protection of their lawyers and, at the same time, the ability to control the decisions that are made in meetings face-to-face with spouse," he said.

This is not to say that attorneys have no place in mediation; the contrary is true. A good lawyer will help you guard against one of the dangers of mediation—that this more informal approach could miss or inappropriately value properties that are divided in the marital settlement. Before you sign any agreements that come out of mediation, have them reviewed to determine whether they represent your best interests.

The bottom line is that no single person has all the answers and any answers he or she offers will often be muddy. Some

> • • • • •
> If a couple keeps communications open, the divorce is less costly.
> • • • • •

type of compromise may well be the only solution. In reviewing our files of men and women who achieved successful divorces—from which they came away with their self-esteem intact and a reasonable or acceptable property settlement—we noticed two key similarities: They had a nonadversarial attorney representing each side and they kept channels of communication open.

How to Make Mediation Work

Obviously the selection of the mediator is critical if this process is to be given a chance to work. An experienced divorce lawyer (another time when experience counts) in a metropolitan area will know a variety of mediators with varying backgrounds and strengths. Get recommendations from your lawyer before you turn to other sources.

You may be thinking, "I bet my lawyer does not want the mediation to work because he will make a lot more money if we cannot settle." Again, the better lawyers would be pleased to see their clients avoid the trauma of a contested divorce. These top-notch lawyers want what is best for their clients.

Mediators come from different professions: mental health, financial planning, law, or social work. Most important, however, the person must have training in mediation, and be knowledgeable about issues confronted in a divorce.

You'll also want to focus on the mediator's style, and decide which will work best for your situation. Some will simply be a third party to facilitate communications as you and your spouse sort through issues. Others will provide advice about particular issues such as child custody or property division. And still others will assist the parties in working through some of the emotional issues of divorce.

In shopping for a mediator, ask the following questions:

1. Do you specialize in family law?
2. How many mediation cases have you handled in the past 12 months?
3. How long have you been a mediator?
4. What kind of training do you have?
5. Do you have any certifications?
6. What is your professional background?
7. How much do you charge and how do you bill?
8. Do you see the parties individually or only as a couple?
9. What is your schedule like for the next two weeks?
10. What guidelines or checklists do you use to make sure you address all issues?
11. Are you aware of how courts in this county resolve certain issues such as child custody and spousal support, and does that influence you?

A goal of the mediation process is to draft the outline of a settlement. The parties will then have an attorney take the outline and prepare a formal separation agreement based on the terms of the mediation. If you are using only your spouse's lawyer in your case, seek a second opinion from your own lawyer. Have this lawyer explain the pros and cons and significance of each provision. Remember, you will have to live with this the rest of your life.

Arbitration

Arbitration is another tool for avoiding lengthy and expensive litigation. An arbitrator acts as your own private judge who conducts a "mini-trial" of sorts, in which the parties and their attorneys present their cases. Arbitration is used more in some areas than in others, and can be particularly attractive if you live in an area with a huge backlog of cases. If you agree in advance to what is called binding arbitration, the arbitrator's decisions are final and become a court order just as if you had gone before a judge. On the other hand, you can agree that the decision of the arbitrator is only "advisory," in which case you would not be required to follow his or her decision.

An arbitrator can be used for the entire process or only to resolve certain issues. The arbitrator may even offer a combination approach, mediating initially, but making a decision for you if you cannot agree.

> • • • • •
> Be sure you understand whether the arbitrator's decision will be binding or only advisory.
> • • • • •

Shop for an arbitrator in the same way as you would for a mediator, but you will find that it is rare that an arbitrator is not a lawyer. Retired judges frequently open arbitration practices. If this is something you want to consider, ask your lawyer to recommend some good arbitrators.

In some jurisdictions the court, upon request, will approve a lawyer to act as what is called a "special master" to get past a problem area. This appointed lawyer usually will have a particular area of expertise, such as the division of pensions. Again, your attorney should play a significant role in deciding whether to use a special master and who that person should be.

> • • • • •
> There is no attorney-client privilege with a mediator, arbitrator, or special master, so anything you say could come out in court.
> • • • • •

We are not thrilled when we hear that divorcing couples are gearing up for a courtroom encounter. It's rare for both sides to come out of the courtroom content with the aftermath of a divorce. It you feel that you may be caught up in someone else's agenda—yes, attorneys sometimes *do not* act in your best interest—consider strongly getting a second opinion and input from one of the experts identified in this chapter.

13 Requirements for Mediation or Arbitration to Work

· · · · ·

1. Since only you and your spouse (not your lawyers) will be with the mediator, you both need to be communicating reasonably well.

2. Both of you should want the divorce.

3. Both of you should want to use the mediator or arbitrator.

4. You should both be able to be assertive and stand up for yourselves.

5. You both should be able to compromise when necessary.

6. You should know what your assets and debts are, because a mediator or arbitrator does not have the power to order that documents be provided.

7. You should believe that the mediator is trying to be fair to each of you.

8. You should not have a lot of anger or resentment toward your spouse.

9. You should be able to control your emotions when the chips are down.

10. You must be careful in your selection of a mediator or arbitrator.

11. You should have the excess emotional energy to make it work.

12. You should be organized.

13. You should have some understanding of financial affairs.

· · · · ·

9

Ready, Set, Go!
Your Case Begins

You've got an attorney and have set up a few rules so that you both communicate effectively. During this second phase of your divorce, you will have an unbelievable number of questions. Some, you have already asked; some surface during the process; and some come after the final decree. Most of it will sound like legal gobbledygook. Our job is to tell you what it all really means.

Fault or No-fault?

For the purposes of this book, we aren't taking any positions on who is at fault for your divorce. Let's just talk about what "fault" is, in a legal sense.

In the majority of states, a resident can get a divorce without proving that the other party was at fault. In these "no-fault" states, all the person has to do is to claim—and prove grounds that exist in that state. The most common "no-fault" grounds are *incompatibility* and *irreconcilable differences leading to the irretrievable breakdown of the marriage.* The proof may be as simple as answering a few questions such as, "Do you consider the marriage to be irretrievably broken?" If you answer "Yes," then you have grounds.

Some states still maintain a type of fault system in which proof is required of such misconduct as mental and physical cruelty, adultery, desertion, or imprisonment. The existence of "fault" and "no-fault" states sometimes causes a person to move to a "no-fault" state in order to obtain the divorce. Check the Appendix for a state-by-state listing.

You will see an increasing number of magazine and newspaper articles about whether the move to a "no-fault" system has caused an increase in the divorce rate. And you will see, there is a growing movement toward restoring a "fault" type of system. As evidence of this trend, one state, Louisiana, recently implemented a system of two types of marriages—one that can be dissolved without establishing fault, and another, which will require a finding of fault before a divorce can be granted.

When Fault May Be an Issue in a No-Fault State

Even in some "no-fault" states, misconduct, such as adultery or abandonment, can still be an issue when considering such matters as spousal support and child custody. If there has been misconduct by you or your spouse, discuss the possible uses of this with your attorney.

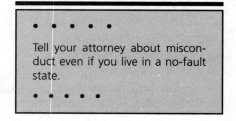

Tell your attorney about misconduct even if you live in a no-fault state.

Where to File

A sturdy building must be built on a sturdy foundation. And deciding when and where to file for a divorce is the foundation of the divorce process. Before you file for a divorce, a decision has to be made on where to file. This decision will be made jointly by you and your attorney. You will first consider all the places you can file, and then the places you should file. The county in which you file will be determined by convenience, where you live, even the experience and reputation of the judge in that particular county. Each state has its own requirements for filing. As an example, our home state of Colorado permits a person to file on the 91st day after arrival in the state.

It is important to understand that the term *residence* means more than just physical presence in a state. A more accurate legal term is *domicile*. That means that the person is not only residing (living) in the state, but he or she also intends to make it his or her primary residence. Registering to vote in that area, or getting a new driver's license, are two simple ways to show your intent.

If you are domiciled in the state where you want to have your divorce, but intend to leave the state, then discuss this with your attorney. You should file before you leave.

There are also choices of locations within a state. It is common to require filing in the location of one of the spouse's homes or where the marital home is or was. In short, knowing where you can or must file is very important.

Where It All Begins—Serving Divorce Papers

The divorce process begins when you or your spouse files a document asking for the divorce. This is usually called a *complaint for divorce* or *petition for dissolution of marriage.* This document must then be served on the other party by one of several methods, depending on how cooperative the other party is and where the party lives. The court where the case is filed will not have jurisdiction if the proper method of service is not followed. Ask your attorney to explain how this works so that you can understand what lies ahead for you.

For example, you may believe that your spouse will avoid being served and you should understand the process that can be followed if this happens. In this case, ask your attorney about how your spouse will be served, and how the process can continue if service is never obtained.

If your spouse lives out of state and does not want to cooperate or participate in the divorce process, the court where the case is filed will have limited power to dispose of issues. For example, the local court could dissolve the marriage, assuming the residency requirement has been met, and can also dispose of property in the state and establish custody of children who live in the state. Frequently, out-of-state defendants believe that they can just ignore a summons and there will be no adverse consequences. This is a mistake.

Whether in or out of state, seek counsel immediately after being served divorce papers. It may be that the ultimate decision will be to cooperate in the action, but that decision should be made only after talking about it with a competent lawyer. Just as the person filing gets the process started with the filing, the person being sued for divorce continues the process by filing a response to the petition. The response may be short and to the

> • • • • •
>
> The advice of a lawyer should always be obtained before making a decision to ignore the petition for divorce.
>
> • • • • •

point, or it may be elaborate and detailed, depending on the facts of the situation and the strategy laid down.

You may hear the term *contested divorce*. This simply means that some of the issues have not been resolved, such as child custody or support. In essence, every case starts out as contested, so proceed as

> • • • • •
>
> Property awards, support, and such issues are not determined by who fires the first shot.
>
> • • • • •

if the case may go to trial until you find out otherwise. The general process of pleadings, discovery, negotiation, and motions are the same in all cases, but the amount of cooperation affects the speed and expense of the process.

Who's Pleading Now?

In the world of the law, certain formal rules and procedures must be followed for both sides to notify each other and the court of their demands. These are called *pleadings*. These rules and procedures not only specify the format of each pleading, but also tell when each must be filed.

The pleading that is filed in response to the initial complaint or petition for divorce is usually called an *answer* or *response,* and contains provisions that either admit to or deny the allegations contained in the original complaint. If the answer raises new issues, a *reply* may be filed by the person who filed the complaint.

There are other pleadings that have a specific purpose, such as to force the other side to produce documents or to dismiss a motion or to set a trial date. A *petition to show cause* is filed when one of the parties claims that the other party has violated a court order. If the party really has violated the order, the other party may then ask that this person be held in contempt and suffer certain penalties.

Other examples of pleadings are petitions asking for temporary support, custody, visitation, or a court order limiting the rights of you or your spouse to do something, such as come to the marital home.

Some states require that pleadings containing allegations of fact be sworn to or supported by your sworn affidavit. In that case, the response to the pleading must also be under oath.

> • • • • •
>
> A lawyer who knows the ins and outs of the rules of procedure in the jurisdiction where your case will be tried will have a great advantage over a lawyer who is ignorant.
>
> • • • • •

And you may see, as your case progresses, the form of a filing or its timing sometimes overshadows the substance of the allegation.

Temporary Orders

You may hear the term *temporary order* throughout your divorce process. A temporary order requires a *temporary motion,* a short-lived document that serves until final orders are created.

In this action, one party asks the judge to make an order before the final judgment for divorce or legal separation. If the other side opposes the motion, a hearing will be necessary. Sometimes it is necessary to have witnesses testify at one of these hearings. In any event, whoever asks the court to act must prove that the action is necessary and within the power of the court to grant. If the judge agrees that the action must be taken, then an order is issued on that subject.

A common temporary order is one that orders one spouse to pay support to the other until the divorce trial takes place. Before the judge can grant the motion, it must be shown that the support is needed and that the spouse is capable of paying the amount requested. Much of the information you gathered for your first meeting with your lawyer will be used in this process.

To show the need and the ability to pay, some states require that a sworn statement be prepared, detailing your and your spouse's living expenses and incomes. This hearing is to be taken very seriously, because it will set the tone for the final support order that is contained in the final decree.

Here is another opportunity to work out an agreement without the necessity of a hearing. Some states and judges require both spouses to try to work out an agreement before a case will be heard. At this stage, each side will be required to exchange information. In essence, the temporary motion becomes a form of *discovery* (discussed further in the next section) and provides a basis for you to reach a compromise temporary order.

This may be your first opportunity to find out if your spouse is open to compromise and negotiation, and it may set the tone for future efforts to bring the case to a swift close.

There is usually an advantage to making an agreement you both can live with. Judges, overloaded with cases, usually don't have time to devote to the stack of temporary motions on their desks. This can lead to some unfair and arbitrary results that may be next to impossible to overcome for some time, even years or decades.

One point to understand is the term *without prejudice*. A temporary order issued without prejudice means that either party can seek a hearing to modify the order at a future time. If this term is not used, you will have to prove a change in circumstances before the temporary order can be modified or terminated. But understand that a temporary order issued without prejudice is completely valid until it is overturned in court.

A final word about enforcing a temporary order. If either of you fails to comply with a temporary order, then the "wronged" spouse can ask that his or her spouse be held in contempt, requiring a hearing. The alleged violator will have an opportunity to show why he or she should not be held in contempt. If the violator is found to be in contempt, fines can be levied, assets could be seized, or the violator can be sentenced to serve time in jail. A good lawyer will explain exactly what is needed to comply with an order even if the client does not like the terms of the order.

> • • • • •
>
> Caution: An unfair temporary order places you or your spouse at a tremendous disadvantage in future negotiations. For example, if you are the recipient of a low level of temporary spousal support, you may have to settle in order to shorten the process and to prevent financial ruin.
>
> • • • • •

What You See Is What You Get: Discovery

As you may know by now, *discovery* is the process of gathering information about the cards your spouse will be playing. Many cases are won or lost at the discovery stage, well before a trial ever begins.

The theory now in civil cases is that the ends of justice are best served if both sides have access to the same facts and evidence. Nice "theory." With a spouse knowledgeable about financial affairs and willing and able to manipulate records, discovery can turn into a life-or-death struggle.

Consider a skilled cook who has these ingredients for a stew of deception: tax shelters, trusts, limited partnerships, deferred compensation packages, unregistered stocks, annuities, retirement plans, and custodial accounts. You will begin to see why the discovery process is often the most difficult, expensive, and time-consuming aspect of a divorce.

Thankfully, most cases go smoothly, but in case you become embroiled in a knock-down, drag-out case, you need to be forewarned. Obviously before your lawyer can begin to negotiate a financial agreement or go to trial to obtain a judgment, every effort has to be made to discover the full extent of the property to be divided.

What if your case looks like it will be World War III? If your spouse works for someone else, be thankful, because tracking down accounts and investments will be easy compared to the situation if your spouse is a self-employed professional or runs his or her own business. Watch out if your contentious spouse is a doctor, dentist, lawyer, accountant, financial consultant, stockbroker, real estate agent, store or factory owner, or independent contractor. Hiding assets is relatively easy for this group. You will need a skillful, savvy attorney and maybe a private investigator and accountant to dig out the truth. Of course, you'll need to consider your potential gain before you go to the expense of hiring these professionals.

This is where discovery rules come into play and must be used for all they're worth. The law gives your lawyer wide discretion to review tax returns, business and personal records, contracts, canceled checks, credit card receipts, and other documents; and to question your spouse, his or her friends, relatives, and business associates about your spouse's financial dealings. And it gives your expert witnesses liberal access to inspect and evaluate the books of any enterprise your spouse owns, controls, or profits from.

A really great attorney will have more information about discovery than we can give in a book like this.

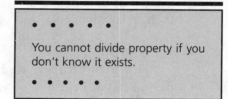

You cannot divide property if you don't know it exists.

Depositions and Interrogatories

In addition to the gathering of documentary evidence, there are two other important discovery tools—depositions and interrogatories.

Depositions. A deposition is the testimony of a witness taken outside a court in the presence of lawyers for each side, and put in writing for use as evidence in court. The contents of the deposition are usually transcribed by a court reporter. Because of the logistics and expenses involved, depositions are rarely used in divorce cases.

A deposition is like a dress rehearsal for the face-to-face questioning and testimony that will take place if the case goes to trial. Because it is a sworn statement, it becomes part of the record of the case. When the witness is on the stand, his or her testimony will be challenged if it is not the same as was given in the deposition. Depositions are used for many purposes—for example, to gather information that the witness may have that would be difficult to obtain in a written exchange of questions (interrogatories) or to test the competence and reliability of an expert witness.

Expert witnesses aren't cheap. Here's why you would want to use one: Sometimes after a deposition is taken, an issue or an entire case will settle when it becomes apparent that the witness is credible, competent, and articulate, and it would therefore be a waste of time to go to trial on that issue.

As another example of the use of a deposition, lawyers may question your spouse. This is particularly useful if your spouse has been evasive in interrogatories and pleadings. Your lawyer's objective is to pin your spouse down before the trial or prepare to catch any lies on the witness stand. A question as simple as this can be a blockbuster: "Is anyone holding any money or property for you?" If your spouse is uncooperative or argumentative, a deposition can help show the judge that your spouse has something to hide.

If you will be testifying at a deposition, your attorney should spend a fair amount of time preparing you for your testimony. If he or she does not schedule such an appointment, insist on it. For some general hints and tips, see our discussion on preparing for testimony at a trial later in this chapter.

Interrogatories. An interrogatory is a series of written questions used in the judicial examination of a party or of a witness. Because interrogatories are in writing, they are used more frequently than depositions. A common use of an interrogatory is to obtain more information about a particular item that has been provided by the other side. For example, once the parties exchange financial statements, they could be followed by interrogatories requiring the other side to provide more details about a particular item.

Suppose the husband gives a bare statement about his salary. The wife's lawyer could use interrogatories as a powerful tool for obtaining more detail. How could that be helpful? Here are some smart questions to ask:

- Does he have an employment contract?
- Does the contract provide for a severance package?
- Does he have any pensions? Describe them.
- What benefits does he have? A company car; free membership at the country club; free medical, life, and disability insurance? Were they included in his stated annual income?

- What kind of expense account is he on when he travels? For example, does he draw cash advances for expenses that are not later accounted for?

Any answers to interrogatories may lead to the demand to produce certain documents, such as his employment contract and pension plan account information.

> • • • • •
>
> In a divorce, it is difficult to imagine a situation where you can have too much information about the financial affairs of your spouse. Be thorough, be tough, and be tenacious. In the right case it will pay big dividends.
>
> • • • • •

Alternatives and Settlements

Do not conclude that a knock-down, drag-out fight is inevitable. A good lawyer will explore several possibilities to settling the case. The most common are negotiation, mediation, and arbitration. People who have never been through the ordeal of a divorce or even a lawsuit rarely appreciate the advantages of a settlement. See Chapter 8 for details on mediation and arbitration.

Negotiation

Men and women often view negotiating differently. For men, it's part of the game. For women, the fear of losing something becomes a factor. Negotiation requires give and take. It also demands that you do your homework and know what is really important to you and what you can give up, if needed. Following are several advantages to a negotiated settlement.

You'll be more likely to get what you need and want. During the negotiation process, each lawyer will keep in mind his or her client's needs and wants. These will be taken into consideration as the deal is hammered out, and sometimes both parties will get what they want because their priorities are different.

Let's say that you want to keep the house. Your spouse obviously needs a place to live and is open to either keeping the house or moving out. Both your desires can be accommodated. If you really want the house, you should be willing to give up or trade something else that your spouse wants. If there is conflict, good negotiators will give up one item in exchange for another. That's why you really want to spend some time thinking about what is important to you and what is not. The "nots" are what you're willing to give up.

By contrast, if the case goes to trial, it is unlikely that the judge will devote much effort to trying to strike a balance between what each party wants. In most trials, each side is trying to get all it can, in hopes of getting something.

An example here could involve a piece of property that has special significance for your spouse, not you. It is unlikely that this will come out in a trial and the judge could award it to you thinking that he or she is doing the best thing for you. Through successful negotiations, you can steer the process toward the assignment of a certain piece of property to the one who really wants it.

Lawyers can be more creative in structuring the agreement to the mutual benefit of everyone. An example is when tax benefits can be reduced by allocating income to the party with the lower tax rate. A judge would rarely spend the time necessary to structure the order in this way, and may not even have all the facts needed to make such a decision.

A court-ordered judgment may not be as comprehensive as a well-drafted agreement. The negotiated agreement will be more deliberately prepared over a period of time, and if something is left out, there will be time to address it. By contrast, some court orders are made by the judge from the bench at the end of the trial, and some details may be omitted.

There usually will be greater cooperation in carrying out the terms of the agreement because both parties are more likely to feel that they got something in return for their sacrifice. By contrast, both sides may feel as though everything has been forced upon them by the court, and they had little opportunity for input.

Most lawyers are good negotiators. But an experienced divorce lawyer is more likely to be a good negotiator than is someone who is unaccustomed to the ins and outs of the issues that must be resolved. In addition, a lawyer with an excellent reputation will be perceived as being more persuasive. There will always be posturing between the lawyers—it's part of the game.

If you are going to use negotiation, you will need to have a rather lengthy session with your lawyer as you decide what issues are really important and which may be "throw-aways" to the other side. During this session, ask your lawyer for the checklist of items that he or she will be using to help minimize the possibility that something is left out.

If It Goes to Trial—A Visit to Purgatory

If you feel that you have been wronged, the courtroom is usually not the place to settle matters. Often, judges' opinions are very black and white. The last thing they want to hear is bickering and blame-casting. They do not care who did what to whom.

In your attorney selection process we hope that you found an attorney who is comfortable in the courtroom. Because few divorce cases go to trial, relatively few divorce attorneys are really polished trial attorneys. Even if your attorney is not Perry Mason, careful preparation can make up for courtroom weaknesses. If you feel you have tried absolutely everything to bring your differences forward and nothing has worked to resolve them, then you may have no option but to go forward with a court trial.

If your lawyer suggests that you find another attorney for the trial, do it. The attorney may have come to dislike the case, or may be genuinely concerned about his or her ability to represent you in a litigated trial. (To a large degree this decision will be affected by the lawyer your spouse will have at the trial. For example, if that attorney has a lot of trial experience, you will want one with equal or greater experience.) In any event, ask for some recommendations and find another lawyer immediately. Understand, however, that unless you discharge the first one, you will now be paying for two lawyers. How deep are your pockets?

Your Day in Court

When it is time to actually appear in court, a number of do's and don'ts can help make you more believable to the judge, as well as to yourself. These are listed in the Baker's Dozen at the end of this chapter.

Be prepared. If any of your testimony concerns specific events or places, make sure you review your notes prior to going in (but don't memorize them). Visualize where you were.

Dress neatly and conservatively. This is not the time for you to look as if you are either poverty-stricken or dripping in gold.

Show respect to other members of the court as well as the judge. Don't smoke, laugh loudly, or demonstrate what could be perceived as threatening behavior.

Don't talk about your case outside of the courtroom. Remember that the people who participate in the courtroom—the judge, the bailiff, the recorder—all wear regular street clothes during their off hours. You may not recognize them in the halls or elevators, but they are sure to recognize you. Loose talk can hurt your case.

> • • • • •
>
> Your conduct in the courtroom can have a profound impact on the judge, for better or worse.
>
> • • • • •

Try not to fidget, and when you take the oath, do so in a strong and clear voice. Remember to breathe. If you are likely to feel nervous or tense, we suggest that you yawn several times before going into the courtroom and before you are called to the stand. It lets a lot of air in and brings you on bright-eyed. In addition, avoid any dairy products, even coffee with milk, before testifying. Sip warm or hot water instead. It helps keep your throat from tightening up.

Make sure you understand any questions you are asked. If you can answer with a yes or no, by all means, answer only yes or no. Your attorney will guide you.

Learn how to edit your responses. Too often, we talk too much. You may end up giving out too much information or the wrong information in trying to explain an event. Make sure your answers include the vital information and, without question, the truth. If you don't remember a situation or fact, say so—don't try to fill in the blanks. If the judge, your attorney or your spouse's attorney interrupts you during testimony, stop talking immediately.

Your attorney may want to develop some body language signals with you. Pay attention. Your attorney is your guide through this whole procedure. The opposing attorney may be trying to push your buttons. Do whatever you can to remain composed.

Sometimes information gets jumbled. If recounting another event triggers something that you already testified about, correct yourself immediately on the stand.

If you feel nervous, and more than likely you will, and have been on the stand for a period of time, don't hesitate to ask

> • • • • •
>
> Listen to the objection. The judge or your own attorney may be trying to clarify the question, even protect you from what may be spilling out.
>
> • • • • •

the judge if you can have a short recess. Better yet, if your attorney has set up a few signals that you can give to make it known that you need a break, use them.

Finally, when you go to court, it doesn't hurt to have a few friends in your corner. Everyone needs moral support now and then. You are no exception. If your pending court date looks and feels intimidating, a friend in tow can make the difference.

Why Go to Court?

You may be wondering why a trial would be needed if you live in a no-fault state. While the grounds for divorce may not have to be litigated, all other issues that cannot be resolved must be tried. The most common areas litigated are child custody and visitation, property division, and child and spousal support.

When approaching the trial date, be aware that most cases are settled close to the trial date. There are many reasons for this. A primary concern is the looming expense as well as a realization that there may be more to lose than there is to gain. Be sure to discuss this with your lawyer. The proverbial settlement "on the courthouse steps" really does happen.

Another important issue to discuss with your lawyer is the probability that your case may not be heard the first time it is scheduled, or even the second or third. This phenomenon is more prevalent in some jurisdictions than in others. Ask your lawyer how many other cases are scheduled on the same day as yours. In some jurisdictions, more than 20 cases are docketed on the same day at the same time! This overbooking is the result of overloaded trial systems and the fact that many scheduled cases are either canceled or settle at the last minute.

The Anatomy of a Trial

Court cases follow a specific, predetermined sequence of events. That's a strong reason for you to visit the courthouse so you can see firsthand what all the players do, what "events" happen, and in which order they come. Following is the most typical format:

1. *Pretrial conference.* Some judges use this step in which the lawyers and judge meet to narrow down the issues that must be litigated and identify those that can be agreed upon in advance. A well-run pretrial conference can save you thousands of dollars. The judge also may explain the procedures that will be used and sometimes his or her preferences.

2. *Opening statements.* The lawyers give an overview of their positions and what they intend to prove. Keep your cool when the other side gives the opening argument, because what is said is not evidence and cannot be used in the judge's deliberation. Some weak attorneys will use this to posture and impress their clients. Frequently the opportunity to give statements is waived.

3. *The petitioner (or plaintiff) presents its case.* Whoever filed suit presents evidence in support of the complaint.

4. *The respondent (or defendant) presents its case.* The respondent presents evidence to deny or counter the petitioner's case.

5. *Rebuttal by petitioner.* Evidence is offered to deny or counter new matters raised by the respondent. (This step is frequently skipped.)

6. *Surrebuttal by defendant.* Evidence is offered to deny or counter new matters raised in the rebuttal. (This step is skipped if there is no rebuttal.)

7. *Closing arguments.* The lawyers summarize their evidence. As with opening arguments, closing arguments impress clients more than they do the judge, who has probably made up his or her mind by this time. For that reason, these arguments are often waived.

8. *The judge gives the ruling.* This can be done at the close of the trial, or it can be done at a later date, with the attorneys being notified by mail with the judgment.

Ask your lawyer to go over each step in your case and explain in general terms what evidence will be presented.

An attorney can—and should—go over your and other witnesses' testimony before the trial. The same set of facts can be presented effectively and poorly. Most witnesses have never testified before and need help organizing their testimony and putting it into perspective. In other words, the preparation will cover what is said and how it is said. In discussing what is said, it is normal for the lawyer to have a list of questions that will be asked. In preparation for the trial, the witness can study this list.

Caution: The preparation just described is not illegal or unethical. Nevertheless, time and again, when asked on cross-examination whether he or she has discussed this case with anyone, the witness, with the trial questions burning a hole in his pocket, will answer no. The witness presumes from the question that there must be something shady in discussing the testimony beforehand. There is not. The cross-examination can be—and often is—used to intimidate a witness.

When preparing for a trial, be sure to follow the Baker's Dozen at the end of this chapter, as well as any guidelines your lawyer may have. Forget the Perry Mason courtroom scenario—very few lawyers have Della Street or Paul Drake sitting in the courtroom to run errands for them. It's just too expensive. Because of this simple fact, ask your lawyer if there are any ways that you can help administratively before or during the trial. It can range from keeping track of types of questions asked to managing the box with the exhibits and handing them to the lawyer as needed.

Using an Expert Witness

Sometimes it will be necessary or helpful to present testimony from people who have a special expertise. These witnesses will usually be called for one specific purpose. An example would be to testify as to the value of a business or pension. The people you will most likely use are identified in Chapter 6. We have worked on countless cases where the expert has made a substantial difference in the final settlement. Your lawyer should coordinate the use of these experts.

The Final Decree

The final decree is the document that will rule the rest of your life. Have we got your attention? This is not much of an exaggeration. The contents of the decree may be issued as the result of an agreement; a knock-down, drag-out battle; or a mixture of the two. Regardless of how the contents are determined, a great deal of thought should go into the preparation.

Don't Let Your Guard down Now

This document can be called such things as *judgment of divorce, decree of dissolution,* or *permanent orders,* and the judge usually assigns the job of preparing the document to one of the lawyers. In rare cases, the judge will prepare it. This order may contain the details of all the issues such as child custody and division of the property, or it may refer in a simple statement to your detailed agreement.

Ask your attorney to tell you as soon as possible what procedure will be used in your case. Sometimes, drafts of the final order may be exchanged between the lawyers before being sent to the judge. In other cases, the lawyer who drafts the order will send it to the court directly, with a copy to the other attorney. If this procedure is followed, the attorney who did not draft the order must let the judge know within a certain period (spelled out in state law) if there are any objections to the form and content of the order.

If the judge writes the decree, you may have little input until it is filed as the final order. But if it is to be drafted by one of the attorneys, stress to your attorney that you want to have him or her do it. Yes, it will mean more expense to you, but this can pay big dividends in the long run. You also want to see the draft before it is submitted to your ex's attorney or to the court.

Why would you want your attorney to write the draft? Sometimes the lawyer who is assigned the task will put it off, especially if that party will benefit from a delay. Also, it is rare that the judge is so precise in what is ordered that a little freedom is not allowed in the wording of at least some of the provisions. In some cases, the judge may not have been clear as to what was intended. In other cases, the lawyer who prepares the order might misunderstand the judge. If your lawyer does not prepare the order, he or she should carefully review the order and discuss it with you.

> • • • • •
> Ask your lawyer to urge the court to have him or her prepare the final decree.
> • • • • •

An experienced domestic relations attorney will have a checklist that is followed in the preparation of a final order so that nothing is left out. In addition, and this is where experience is invaluable, an experienced attorney knows and understands where the land mines are in a typical case, and will do everything possible to help you work around them.

The Final Orders or Ruling

At the end of some trials, the judge will say that he or she is taking the matter *under advisement*. This means that he or she wants to review the evidence and reflect on the issues before making a final decision. In some instances there may be a matter of law that the judge will want to research. A good example of a case where the judge will make a ruling later is if many items of property of substantial value, especially pensions and businesses, must be divided.

But don't worry if the judge rules immediately at the end of the trial. This does not necessarily mean that he or she has not considered the evidence. For experienced trial judges there is rarely anything unique for them to consider.

Don't expect the judge to rule solely for one of you; instead, the ruling will be favorable to you on some issues, and to your spouse on others. As strange as it may seem, compromise can be a large part of the ruling. That is why trial judges are given wide discretion in their rulings and successful appeals are rare.

In some cases it will be necessary to have a written transcript prepared so that the attorneys can see exactly what the judge ruled. (Since judges hear hundreds of cases, it is unlikely they will remember much of what was ordered. And sometimes the transcript will reveal confusing or contradictory rulings.)

Because of their expense—sometimes upwards of $1,000—transcripts are not prepared in every case. However, in every case in which an appeal is taken, a transcript must be prepared.

The Problems with Do-It-Yourself Divorces

After getting this far in this book, you may be thinking, "This is just too complicated and scary. I think my spouse and I should do our own divorce." We suggest you think again. We have seen cases where one party concealed from the other that he was secretly seeing a lawyer and was getting advice on how to take advantage of his unrepresented spouse.

Here are some examples of mistakes made by couples who are trying to be honest and open in a do-it-yourself divorce. Imagine the mistakes that could be made if one spouse (or both) were shrewd and dishonest!

Income taxes. If you do not understand the tax consequences of the transfer of certain property, such as a house, you may be stuck with a huge tax bill.

Forgotten and missed assets. If you don't understand what constitutes marital property, some property may be mistakenly transferred, such as inherited property that has been kept in your own name.

Pensions. In many cases, the retirement accounts are the most valuable marital asset, so mistakes in this area can be very costly. Spouses who do not fully understand their own retirement plans could grossly undervalue what is to be divided. Some also fail to understand the consequences of the death of the nonemployee. In these cases, the nonemployee died, and the company ended up with that person's share of the retirement, not the employee. This means that your heirs would get none of your earned pension.

The settlement agreement. Drafting a comprehensive agreement can be a real challenge. For example, a couple with children may leave out some of the major points of their understanding about visitation rights. They could forget to state who will be responsible for some major credit card debt and underestimate the amount of child support that the noncustodial parent owes.

Selection of the state in which to get divorced. Consider this example: The parties had separated because of the husband's abuse, and the wife left the state. Several years later, the husband called the wife to see if they could agree on a divorce. One of the topics discussed was whether to file the action in the state where the wife lived or in the state where the husband lived. They agreed to a divorce in the state where the husband lived. In that state, the property rights of the spouses end when they separate, but in the state where the wife now lived, the property rights continue right up to the time of the divorce. Although a victim of serious abuse, the wife lost the opportunity to have a larger portion of the husband's pension plan.

Postdecree matters. The details of completing the final paperwork are often put aside for another day. Some couples don't understand how to transfer some real estate in another state, taking months to get things straightened out. One couple we knew never prepared the final orders. They did not find out for many months that they were still married.

Do You Appeal?

Maybe. This is a critical phase of the case. The period within which you may file an appeal varies from state and state and from case to case, depending on the procedure followed to wrap up the case. The clock could start running when the judgment is signed by the court, or when the clerk sends a copy of the judgment to the lawyers. If you are unhappy with the results and strongly believe that they are challengeable, you need to know what your appeal window is.

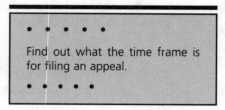

Find out what the time frame is for filing an appeal.

Summing Up

Legal matters can be overwhelming and confusing. Shakespeare is credited with writing, "The first thing we do, let's kill all the lawyers." We know that there will be times when you would gladly eliminate your attorney. It's not a fun thing you are going through, and they often become the brunt for all that ails you.

The reality is that unless your situation is so uncomplicated that you don't have kids and little or no assets, you need a good attorney on your team. The information we have given you should ease your way through this legal maze.

13 Dos for the Courtroom

• • • • •

1. Be careful about what you wear. Dress as you would for an important event, and discuss your specific plans with your attorney.

2. Be on time.

3. Tell the truth and be straightforward. If telling the truth means that you will lose, then consider settlement.

4. Keep your emotions under control, no matter what is said.

5. Try to act natural.

6. Listen to the entire question before answering.

7. Speak up so that you can be heard.

8. Ask to have a question repeated if you do not understand it.

9. Answer "yes" if asked if you and your lawyer went over your testimony to prepare for the trial.

10. Write notes to your lawyer if you must communicate with him or her before a recess.

11. Respond to the judge when he or she asks you any questions.

12. Be pleasant to opposing counsel, even if you want to attack them.

13. Come in with a positive attitude.

• • • • •

13 Don'ts for the Courtroom

1. Don't chew gum.

2. Don't make faces at your spouse, the judge, the lawyers, or witnesses.

3. Don't tell lies—even small ones.

4. Don't try to be cute, a wise guy, or flippant.

5. Don't try to memorize your answers.

6. Don't act hostile.

7. Don't worry if you forget something.

8. Don't try to get sympathy from the judge.

9. Don't act defensive or suspicious on cross-examination.

10. Don't interrupt the person who is asking you questions.

11. Don't use the threat of custody or withholding visitation of your kids.

12. Don't wear seductive or flashy clothing.

13. Don't keep the court waiting.

10

Keeping Your Head above Water

How to Make It through Your Divorce without Going Broke

One of the great myths of separating and divorcing couples is that it is cheaper to live as a single than as a couple. Here's the fallacy in that thinking: Presently you both contribute to your lifestyle. And if you're like most couples, you struggle each month to make the paychecks stretch to pay the bills.

If you could barely live on your combined incomes before the divorce, how do you think you can continue to live at the same standard after divorcing and setting up two households—one for you and one for your ex?

After the divorce, expenses that you didn't think about begin to surface. Let's look at some of these additional expenses—both small and big:

- Two house payments (or rent payments)
- Two utility bills (one for each house)
- Two telephone bills (one for each house)
- New furniture for the second home
- Kitchen staples (flour, sugar, cleaning supplies) and utensils (pots, pans, dishes)
- Automotive maintenance and repairs
- Convenience foods (New singles spend more money on take-out, eating out, and fast foods.)
- Kid's expenses (You may want to double up on many things so that your kids have belongings at Mom's *and* Dad's.)

113

Most women and men feel they have been taken to the cleaners when the divorce is finally over. They did not consider these "extra expenses" when negotiating a settlement. The first thing that most do is to liquidate some of the assets received in the divorce settlement to pay for the extra expenses. No wonder everyone feels they got cheated.

The Credit-Card Dilemma

So how do you pay for this? An increasing amount of divorcing couples are showing up with large amounts of debt, mostly credit card debt. The good news is that you are not alone.

Credit Wisdom

It's tempting to overcharge. If you're like most people, your mailbox is packed with credit card applications offering a very low percentage rate, even 0 percent interest for a six-month period on outstanding balances. Who can resist? It looks like free money.

The problem is that this low interest charge prompts even more spending and six months later, with an even larger credit balance, the interest rate jumps up to somewhere between 14 percent and 20 percent. Now you are in trouble! You have to stretch just to make the minimum payments. Suddenly you realize that you are living beyond your means. You'll be paying for that sweater or new CD unit you couldn't afford yesterday—but charged anyway—for many tomorrows to come.

It's tempting to start living off your credit cards when the spouse who moves out stops sending money. If there is absolutely no money, it may be necessary to use credit cards, but do so sparingly. It is more important to pare down your living expenses to the bare bone. This means no vacation, new clothes, even car repairs—unless you have the cash to pay for it.

As in most cases, there seems to be another side. Some attorneys advise their clients to buy whatever they need and run up the credit card balance. Why? Because it's considered marital debt and your about-to-be-ex will have to pay for half of it. This is bad advice. Too many times spouses max out the credit cards before the divorce. After the divorce, each spouse has difficulty paying off his or her share or getting any other type of credit. Once you run into trouble making credit card payments, you have put your credit standing into jeopardy. It just isn't worth it.

Evaluating Your Expenses

So, where does this leave you? Remember the sleuthing you were doing digging up papers and information for your attorney to fill out the various forms you file during the divorce? Your hard work will come in handy here.

You'll also need to take a hard look at what you consider necessary expenses. If you are used to taking a nifty vacation each year, you probably feel that it should be part of your regular life style postdivorce. That's not necessarily so. Spending the day golfing or lounging by the country club pool may not be in the cards, either. Also, if your normal expenses include $350 per month for clothes and you have two closets full of clothes, you may need to make them last longer than before.

Typically, divorce changes everybody's life. Yours, your ex's, your kids', your pets', even your friends'! To determine your minimum financial needs, ask yourself the following:

- Will I have enough to support my current lifestyle?
- Will I be able to keep the assets from our division of marital assets without having to deplete them to pay living expenses?
- Will I be able to contribute to savings and retirement funds?

If any of the answers are "no," you will have to look seriously at your budget and adjust your standard of living. It has been proven that most of us can easily live on at least 10 percent less than we currently do.

Two Friends

At one of our workshops, we met Sally and Jean. They had been best friends since growing up in a small midwestern town. Both their fathers worked at a local factory and there never seemed to be enough money to go around in either family. In college, Sally met and married Don, whose career skyrocketed. She became active within her community, chairing fund-raisers for charitable events and participating in several clubs. They moved to a mansion complete with two maids, and later, two children. Ah, the ideal life!

Jean, on the other hand, married Stan, who also worked at the factory where her father worked. Like Sally, Jean had two children. She became skilled at sewing their clothes and making good, budget-conscious meals.

As time went by, both couples decided to divorce. Sally was used to living on an allowance of $138,000 per year, while Jean could do well on $21,000 per year. Sally's husband Don argued that her best friend, Jean, could live on $21,000 per year—why couldn't she?

Sally didn't see how she could possibly cut her budget to less than $92,000 per year. When Sally's divorce was final, Don agreed to pay her alimony of $60,000 per year for six years, the $850,000 house, and $262,000, half of his retirement account.

After the divorce was final, Sally continued to spend $92,000 per year. She retained her membership in the country club and continued as the chair of their annual fund drive. She felt it was important to keep up her image of a successful, dynamic woman doing volunteer work within the community. She knew that there was a shortfall between the alimony she received and the actual amount she spent each year. She also knew that she could tap into the retirement account to cover any shortages, and she did.

No one initially told her that the money she withdrew from the retirement account would be both taxed and penalized for early withdrawal. Although once she was aware of it, it didn't stop her. After all, she had her image to keep up. Within six years, the retirement account was depleted. On top of that, her alimony payments of $60,000 came to a screeching halt. Her only asset was her $850,000 house, which certainly was not a measly amount of money! But, with Sally's track record, whatever equity she had accumulated would be gone within a few years at her spending pace.

She had no paying job, no income from alimony, and no retirement fund. Just the house. She cried to her friend Jean, "If I had only known how fast my money would disappear, I would have spent more carefully or gotten a job or something!"

And how did Jean fare during this same time? Stan paid her half his salary, $19,000, for five years, and half his retirement account. She earned another $7,500 per year from a part-time job. With her sewing skills and ability to get along well with few resources, she was able to add $5,000 per year to her mutual fund and retirement accounts that totaled $22,000 when her divorce was final. In the same six years while Sally was going broke on $60,000 per year, Jean's mutual funds and retirement accounts had grown to $81,135.

What Should Sally Have Done?

Choice is an important word for most people today. Sally had plenty of them.

She chose not to work for pay. With her country club connections, she could have tapped into a well-paying job from someone who knew of her organizational and fund-raising skills. Or, if her pride wouldn't let her ask her friends for job leads, she certainly could have gotten some training and some coaching from a career counselor to secure a position.

She chose to keep the $850,000 home, which was free and clear of a mortgage. She felt she had an image to keep up and couldn't make do with a more modest house. She chose to sit on an illiquid asset that did not produce any income for her. If she had decided to buy a smaller home at half the cost of her current home and invest the difference, she could have realized an extra $40,000 per year in interest income at 8 percent.

She chose not to reduce her expenses. Large homes cost money. Hers required the use of caretakers, which included a maid, housekeeper, and gardener.

She chose to continue to buy clothes at the rate of $1,000 per month. It didn't matter that she had four closets full already. But she didn't want to be seen in the same thing over and over.

She chose to continue to have lavish parties and entertain on a large scale. Her image was more important today than how she would look tomorrow. "What will people think if I don't stay visible in the community?" She asked.

She chose to continue to travel for relaxation and leisure. "I have to get away once in a while to recuperate," she said.

She chose to have her hair, nails, and facials done weekly. "After all," she said, "I must look my best."

Eliminating Financial Misery

This whole chapter is about evaluating your expenses. It is important to make reasonable decisions when facing divorce.

Are you willing to change your spending patterns and live at a reduced lifestyle in return for not having to live with your spouse anymore? This is a critical question. It doesn't make sense to trade one kind of misery for another kind. You don't have to live in financial misery after divorce if you:

- can negotiate a reasonable settlement;
- can adjust your spending patterns so you don't tap into your assets, however minuscule they look; and
- can take responsibility for some of the financial issues (this may mean getting a better job, or even just a job).

What about the Kids?

Let the kids help, and tell them the truth. Parents often hate to deprive their children of the designer jeans and shoes they have been getting. Instead, they go without other necessities to avoid letting the kids know the extent of the financial situation. This is insanity.

Our experiences are that when the kids are part of the financial decision-making and are privy to the income and expenses of the household, wondrous things can happen. The "gimmes" that are so prevalent, especially when parents attempt to soften the emotional blow of divorce by buying things, almost vanish. Your kids can be incredible troupers at wanting to help cut costs and make things work. It becomes a game for them. That's what brought Carol and her teenaged daughter Marie together.

After the divorce, Marie lived with her mom during the summers and with her dad the rest of the year in another state. Carol was ashamed of how little money her job was paying. In desperation, she had no choice but to share her financial situation with her daughter. She just couldn't afford all the teenage things Marie wanted. But what Carol thought was an embarrassment turned into an adventure. Carol would come home from work and find that Marie had found a bargain at the grocery store and had whipped up dinner for just a few dollars. Marie was so proud the day she found a bookcase at a garage sale that she knew her mother needed. All summer long, they found bargains and were able to laugh at their creativity.

Contrast that with the situation with Stella and her son, Josh. Stella was too proud to share her financial situation with Josh. When she grew up, her family didn't talk about money—it was not the proper thing to do. The end result was that she and Josh would argue over every purchase he wanted to make, creating a real strain in their relationship. He was convinced that his mother was a real miser and didn't care about his wants and needs. Or Stella would give in and buy the designer clothes for him instead of paying her credit card bill. Her money woes only deepened, and her relationship with Josh worsened.

Whose shoes would you rather be in: Stella's or Carol's? The choice is yours.

If You Don't Own It Now, Don't Buy It

Darrell and Laurie argued all the time about money. When they decided to get divorced, they made an effort to stay out of the war zones and make sensible decisions to make it as easy as possible through a trying time. One day when Laurie got home from work, Darrell was unpacking a new computer. Laurie blasted at him about his irresponsible spending habits—he had just spent the money they were going to pay to the attorney. Darrell tried to defend himself by explaining that he was expecting to learn new computer skills that would help him earn enough to ease their financial situation and besides, he felt he deserved the computer to help him through this emotionally difficult time.

Needless to say, with this additional financial burden, Laurie became so angry that their efforts to have a friendly divorce were sabotaged.

This is not the time to buy the new house or a new car. This is also not the time to invest in any product or to shift investment assets. Investments that you make during this time could have enormous financial strings attached, including Uncle Sam's. Your property may be divided in a different way than you thought it could be. There will be costs to split it up, even penalties in shifting assets from one spouse to the other.

Unless the property division has already been decided before purchase, how do you know who is going to get which asset? Shifting assets could create difficulty in tracking the location and ownership of the asset, and a suspicion that someone is hiding assets.

Guerrilla Warfare—Do You or Don't You Raid the Accounts?

This is a tricky one. There is a balance between having enough to live on and taking money just to be vindictive. Then there is the situation where you may just want to make sure you get what is rightfully yours before it disappears as Sarah did in Chapter 5.

Take Molly. Her husband, Daniel, walked out after years of bitter fighting. He was the breadwinner and she stayed home and raised their four kids. Before he left, he gave her money each month for bills and groceries. After he left, she didn't hear from him, nor did he leave any money for her. She did hear from the bank. Nothing had been paid on the car or mortgage. She borrowed from friends to feed the kids until she could borrow no more.

Molly knew it was time to hire an attorney. The first three attorneys she called wouldn't take her case because she had no money to pay a retainer. The moral here is that it would have been prudent for her to have taken money from a bank account immediately when Daniel left home to allow for such emergencies.

Then there's the opposite. Consider the case of Patricia and Ken. When Ken left, Patricia was so angry that she went to their bank and raided their accounts. She depleted them and moved the money to a different bank in a different city. Now, Ken had a hard time making ends meet when he needed cash. That point was brought out strongly in their court trial, which prejudiced the judge against Patricia.

> • • • • •
> If you decide to withdraw money, be reasonable. You should not take more than half from any account!
> • • • • •

Summing Up

Know what you spend money on and where you spend it. Determine which areas can and should be trimmed back if necessary. Don't make any financial commitments that you don't understand or are not absolutely clear about. Don't take out loans or add additional credit obligations on to your balance sheet. And, if you have kids, don't keep them in the dark. They have ESP and know all is not well. Game-playing doesn't deal a fair hand.

13 Emotional Facts of Divorce

• • • • •

1. The wife may not be able to keep the house.

2. The husband may need to share his pension.

3. In divvying up household items, you may not be able to keep your favorite painting or casserole dish.

4. After a difficult divorce, you may find it difficult to ever trust the opposite sex again!

5. You may never be able to trust your ex-spouse, who used to be your best friend.

6. The custody arrangements may be the pits.

7. You may not have as much money as you want, need, or used to have.

8. You may have to set up a visitation schedule for your family pet.

9. The kids will go to your ex for permission when you say "no."

10. Your old friends may not be your friends anymore.

11. You may not get invited to couples parties anymore.

12. You may dread running into your ex with your "replacement."

13. It's a lonely time—but possibly a time of positive transformation, if you play your cards right.

• • • • •

11

When Love
Takes a Backseat
Controlling Your Anger

Have you said or thought any of the following?

- "When my ex says those things to me I could just explode!"
- "If only I could think of a great retort to my ex's smart-aleck remarks, or go one better!"
- "My ex makes me so angry!"

If so, it may not come as news to you that you're feeling some anger. Anger, as you may have guessed, is a natural byproduct of divorce. But you may be surprised to learn that you are on the wrong track in dealing with your anger.

In this chapter, we will give you some tips on managing your anger. Volumes of books are dedicated to the topic of anger—we can only scratch the surface. But because of the emotional charges that bounce around during a divorce, it is essential that we discuss it here.

Is your ex really the one *making* you angry? Think about it—who is the one *being controlled* and who is the one *in control*?

Remember that you have choices—life does not just happen to you. You have the choice to deal with your own emotions, including anger—you can choose to be reasonable, rational, or irrational.

> No one can make you have a certain emotion. You choose to have it. People can choose their attitudes and beliefs as well as their actions and behaviors.

Can Anger Really Be Reasonable?

Common sense requires you to meet your physical needs—food, clothing, shelter, and possibly the care of any children. Dealing with anger, grief, fear, shock, and even shame in a rational way is usually the last thing anyone thinks of and consciously tries to deal with.

What is considered reasonable anger during a divorce? That depends on how you interpret the situation.

Unreasonable actions may include:

- Purposely concealing assets.
- Telling friends, family, children, coworkers, and bosses things whose primary purpose is to belittle and undercut your spouse.
- Destroying personal property.
- Making slanderous statements about your spouse.
- Draining bank, savings, and investment accounts.
- Running up excessive credit card debt.
- Harming or destroying cherished items or pets.
- Misdirecting personal mail and phone calls.
- Falsifying documents.
- Destroying documents.
- Canceling insurance policies.
- Canceling credit card accounts.
- Soliciting someone to lie as a witness.
- Firing your lawyer at the last minute in order to get a delay.
- Using your kids.
- Faking illnesses to get a delay.
- Selling assets without your spouse's consent.

Anger is a warning signal—like smelling or seeing smoke before the fire erupts—that something is not right. It may be that needs, wants, or expectations are not being met or that you are being hurt or abused. When you start to feel anger, it is a signal. Pay attention to it and try to figure out what must be done.

Your body is designed with an automatic emergency response system. Once apparent danger, crisis, or distress is detected, the body produces energy by releasing adrenaline. It provides power for the fight, flight, or freeze response.

How you respond may depend on whether the divorce was expected or served out of the blue. The more unexpected, the more anger, grief, and fear are generated. Even when anticipated, those emotions surface about the future.

Your response also may depend on your social or family background. Our society is quite fickle. Anger is usually considered an acceptable emotion. The flip side of anger, hurt or helplessness, is considered unacceptable. Your upbringing also comes into play here. How your family responded and acted around anger will impact how you respond to that emotion today. Many people have never learned what to do with their anger and have no idea that they can control it or choose a response rather than *react* to it.

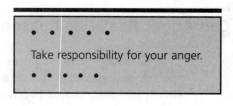

Take responsibility for your anger.

The meaning you attach to a negative event determines your emotional response. It's that simple. By taking responsibility for your anger, you have the advantage of being able to choose what you want to do instead of feeling helpless about controlling your emotions. When you feel helpless about your emotions, any external event—such as a divorce—can send you into turmoil.

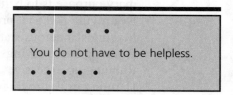

You do not have to be helpless.

Ways to Cope with Anger

There are a variety of ways to deal with the anger and emotional turmoil that takes place when you face divorce. First, consider these rather basic tools.

Walk before You Run

Use community resources and support systems. Seminars or support groups may be sponsored by a government agency, a business, or a place of worship. Many religious institutions provide excellent, low-cost divorce recovery workshops and child care programs. And don't forget to check your local library for books as well as audiotapes and videotapes. Tip: Check to see if the book or tape has a workbook and, if so, use it. There's no need to spend lots of money on these things when you can check them out when you need them. But you may need to visit a bookstore as well to see what is available.

Talk it out with family and friends. They frequently are willing to listen and be there for you. They may offer helpful suggestions or ideas.

Write an "anger letter." Write a letter to the person with whom you are angry. *Do not mail this letter!* Write down every rotten thing that you think, even suspect, your ex has done. You will be amazed at how much this can release you from your anger.

Exercise. Physical exercise, even a walk around the block, can dissipate some of the energy generated by the anger.

Relaxation therapy. Deep breathing or other relaxation techniques such as listening to calming music can help.

Seek professional help. Trained therapists can assist even when you feel your case is hopeless.

Picking up Speed

As you begin to learn more about your anger, you will want to move to the next level. You've walked, now let's run. Here are more complex ways to deal with your anger:

Develop an "anger plan." Do what? Plan to be angry? No, plan what to do when you are angry. Having a plan to follow when you become angry can assist you in using your energy to make decisions and accomplish tasks that must be completed when a divorce occurs.

Your anger does not help you on most occasions, it just immobilizes you and mires you in a situation rather than allowing you to move forward in your life. If you have a plan for using the anger energy to seek positive solutions, you may have a chance to change your situation. Having such a plan in place can help eliminate that helpless, out-of-control feeling and replace it with a sense of assertiveness. It makes you a winner.

Remember, you have a choice about how you will feel and what you will do about any situation. When you become aware of the event, consciously decide how you want to respond. You have the advantage of being in control so that you can act rather than react.

Here are a few suggestions to help you put together your anger plan:

- *Begin to understand your thought processes.* Deal with the thought processes that either keep the "fire" of your anger burning or allow you to stop adding fuel to the flames.

- *Practice thought-stopping.* When you have a thought, stop and think about what you are thinking and how you feel when you have that thought. Thoughts are not the same as feelings or emotions. First you think, then you feel, and then you act. Your thoughts fuel your angry feelings. So, stop the thoughts first, then move to the next stage of the plan.
- *Replace negative thoughts with positive thoughts.* When you stop the thought and identify whether it is negative or positive, you then have a choice. If the thought is negative, choose a positive one to put in its place. Let's say your ex is having dinner at the same restaurant you are. Just seeing him with a new "friend" makes you want to explode. Your reaction re-fuels the anger you felt when you found out he was cheating on you. Instead of focusing on how ticked off you are (and hurt), think about the fact that he can no longer cheat on you, and that he is now her future problem. Or, rather than "I'm so stupid," say "This is a difficult situation, but I can get through it."
- *Use assertiveness rather than aggressiveness.* Being aggressive and looking for a fight is not a healthy way to deal with anger. Being assertive means acknowledging that you are angry, choosing to say so in more appropriate ways than fighting. Use *I* messages. Avoid using *you* messages that use blame rather than assertiveness. For example, "When *I* hear you speak in that tone of voice, *I* know it is not a good time for a discussion. *I* will talk with you later."
- *Try role-playing different ways of acting when you are angry.* Just as if you were learning lines in a play, practice what you want to say in front of a mirror, with a friend, or to an empty chair. If you have trouble, write out a script and practice it until you can be calm and sure of your words.
- *Don't think of revenge.* Almost everyone going through a divorce thinks about retaliation and revenge. These thoughts will not help you achieve any positive goals in your dealings with your ex, the lawyers, or the judge. Acting out revenge will make matters worse. Anything you think you have gained will be short-lived.

The key question to ask is, "Will my anger benefit me and work to my advantage, or will it deplete my energy and distract me from what is really important?" If your heart and soul are filled with revenge, you will rarely be able to focus on more positive, productive goals.

> Attempting to control someone other than yourself rarely works.

Recognize—and correct—your misconceptions. People who are angry tend to misinterpret and personalize events. By identifying and replacing misconceptions with the facts and the facts alone, you can reduce your anger significantly.

Let's say you think that the judge hates your guts because of the way he looks or acts. Get a reality check from your attorney. Perhaps this judge seems irritable and impatient to *everyone*. While this may not be what you want to hear, at least you now understand why the atmosphere in the courtroom is so tense, and can take it less personally. (This is why we recommend that if your case is going to trial, you should sit in on a few cases tried by your judge to get a feel for how he or she acts.)

Misconceptions are normal in divorce, can be the at the heart of much anger, and can have a powerful effect on how you act and react. Following are the ten most common ways you can misread an emotional situation. Do you see yourself (or your soon-to-be-ex) in any of these?

1. *Having an all-or-nothing attitude.* You measure yourself and those around you against perfection. Everything is black or white; no gray areas. There is no in-between. Everything is yes or no.
2. *Having a negative outlook.* You know that everything will turn out badly; if anything good happens, it's an accident or even a mistake.
3. *Leaping to conclusions.* You take small "hints" and expand them into a muddled reality. You constantly see the dark side of any incident, even when there is no evidence to support it. You practice a "self-fulfilling" approach to events—if you believe it will be negative, you actually support the negative to happen. You assume that others are negative toward you without verifying whether they are or not.
4. *Over-generalizing.* If one event turns out negative or badly, you interpret it as the pattern for the rest of your life.
5. *Over-personalizing.* You assume that you are the cause of negative situations for which you are not responsible.
6. *Not letting go.* You focus and refocus on negative events, trying to figure out how and why they occurred.
7. *Emotional rationalizing.* You assume that your bad feelings must be the "truth." Do a reality check with a friend.
8. *Tunnel vision.* You stretch and expand on the negativity of items—yours or someone else's—or you reduce and minimalize major issues and events until they become a minor hiccup. If something appears to be wrong, you may view it as the pending outbreak of World War III. Or, you dismiss, ignore, or deny an issue that could radically affect you.

9. *Marking and Mismarking.* This is an extreme form of overgeneralization. You have no flexibility in your judgments of youself or others. Everything is grounded in cement.

10. *"Should," "Ought to," "Must," and "Have to" Statements.* Using any of these within a statement can set you up for failure. Using them on others sets their defensive verbiage in play. The result is often anger, frustration, and resentment.

Make a List

If you are feeling angry, make a list of the pros and cons of being angry, both for the near and long-term effects. Next, determine which is the bigger plus—the cost or advantage of your anger. You must decide whether it is worth the effort to be angry and resentful, or if it is better to forgo such strong feelings and focus your attention elsewhere.

Irrational Anger

A final word of caution. As you have seen by now, some anger can be reasonable. Sadly, there also can be irrational, sometimes violent, out-of-control anger.

During a divorce, most people feel that they have been treated unfairly and some react accordingly rather than choosing to act after checking out the facts. It's like putting your mouth into gear before your brain has started its engine. If you allow your angry thoughts to grow, irrational or extreme behavior can result.

If you think your anger *might* reach this level, get professional help *immediately.* During a divorce there is usually enough legal maneuvering for a lifetime, so why add more difficulties on your plate?

In the past, you probably put your mouth in gear before your brain kickstarted. You know you said things you wished you hadn't. The following statements are used when anger, hurt, and the feeling of wanting to get even are experienced. When used, they only negatively compound your situation.

13 Things Never to Say to Your Soon-to-Be-Ex

• • • • •

1. Any sentence that starts with "You will (I will . . .) *never*" or "You will (I will) *always*."

2. "Over my dead body . . ."

3. "I'll work until I die before you get a dime of _____" or something that sounds like this.

4. "If I have to pay alimony, I'll quit working."

5. "If you get custody, I'll take the kids and you will never see them again."

6. "I'll destroy/break/smash _____ before you get it."

7. "I'll tell the kids (parents/friends/coworkers/boss/new girlfriend or boyfriend) the *truth* about you."

8. "I'll cancel all the insurance policies and credit cards."

9. "I'll destroy/break/ruin you."

10. "You'll never get a dime of *my* money."

11. "I'll declare bankruptcy so you won't get anything."

12. "I'll take the kids and move to _____."

13. "I'll ruin your career."

• • • • •

12

Property
A House Divided

What do you think about when you think of property? Your joint savings account? The house you jointly own or that may be in your spouse's name, yet you have paid for half of it? You may think you already know all about property. But do your views meet the legal tests of what property is?

Although each couple is different, there are some averages when it comes to property. Most divorcing couples have household furnishings (89 percent), cars (71 percent), and some savings in the form of money in bank accounts, stocks, or bonds (61 percent). Almost half (46 percent) of the couples own or are buying a family home, which is likely to be a couple's most valuable asset. Only a small proportion of divorcing couples have a pension (24 percent), a business (11 percent), or other real estate (11 percent).

It has been said that most divorcing couples have a net worth of less than $20,000. If this is so, it may be that couples are investing in their careers and earning capabilities instead of their savings accounts. The majority of today's couples both work. Many are professionals who have earned one or more degrees or have undertaken special training. They may see their careers as being more valuable than tangible assets. Because future income is typically of greater value than property, the main financial issues at divorce, particularly for women and children, are those of spousal and child support.

When looking at the property issues in divorce, couples usually ask these four questions:

1. What constitutes property?
2. What is it worth?

3. At what date will it be valued?
4. How will it be divided?

Our objective is to cover these questions, and show how to protect what belongs to you.

What Constitutes Property?

Property includes such assets as the family home, rental property, cars, and art or antique collections. It can also include bank accounts, mutual funds, stocks and bonds, cash value life insurance, IRAs, and retirement plans. And yes, career assets and PHTs or PWTs (putting husband/wife through school). As you can see, there is virtually no limit to what can be considered property.

Laws vary from state to state on how to divide it. Property issues account for a large number of appeals! Although there are exceptions to just about everything, when it comes to property, it is usually divided into two categories: separate and marital.

In general, separate property, property that will not be divided, includes what a person brings into the marriage, inherits during the marriage, or receives as a gift during the marriage.

On the other hand, marital property, which can be divided, is everything acquired during the marriage no matter whose name it's in. In some states, marital property also includes the increase in value of separate property.

Do you know what kind of state you live in and what rules of property division your state follows? There are three different types of states: *community property, equitable distribution,* and *equal distribution.* The differences are subtle. Once you know how your state handles property division, you can decide which property is yours or your spouse's, and which is owned jointly. The great majority of states have detailed statutes that categorize property. (For more information, see the Property Division table in Appendix A.)

In community property states (Arizona, California, Idaho, Louisiana, Nevada, New Mexico, Texas, Washington, and Wisconsin), property that is not subject to division of the court—your and your spouse's separate property—is the first to be identified. The court then may decide on how your marital, or community, property is divided. Again, separate property is owned before the marriage, or obtained by gift or inheritance during it. Everything else is community property and is subject to equal division. Some community property states require that all property acquired during the marriage be split equally, while others divvy up assets in the same way as equitable distribution states do.

The equitable distribution states usually agree that your marital property be divided equitably, or fairly, between you and your spouse. In equal distribution states, the property is divided—you guessed it—equally.

What Is It Worth?

Let's look at an example. Beth and her husband are getting a divorce. When Beth got married, she had $1,000 in a savings account. During the marriage, her $1,000 earned $100 in interest. Her account is now worth $1,100. She did not add her husband's name to the account when they married.

Her property is $1,000, because she kept it in her name only. In some states, the $100 in interest goes into the pot of marital assets to be divided because that is the increase in value of her separate property. If Beth had put her husband's name on the account, she would have turned the entire account into a marital asset. She would have made a gift to the marriage.

In second or third marriages, both people may bring a house into the marriage. Suppose that Beth had a house when she got married, which she kept in her name only. At that time, the house was worth $100,000 and had a mortgage on it of $70,000, so the equity was $30,000. Now Beth is getting divorced. Today the house is worth $150,000. The mortgage is down to about $50,000. Equity has increased to $100,000.

At Marriage		At Divorce	
$100,000	Value	$150,000	Value
−70,000	Mortgage	−50,000	Mortgage
$ 30,000	Equity	$100,000	Equity

These numbers lead to only one conclusion in the valuation of property. The increase in value is the increase in the total equity, or $70,000.

Let's reverse the situation. Assume Beth put her husband's name on the deed to the house when they got married. After all, they were going to be together for the rest of their lives.

As soon as Beth put her husband's name on the deed, the house was turned into a marital asset. She gave what is called a *presumptive gift* to the marriage.

What if Beth owned stock worth $10,000 when she got married? On the day of the divorce, it is worth $9,000. Is that a $1,000 marital loss? Yes. If there is a marital increase on one asset, it can be offset with a marital loss. If Beth had owned a house and it had decreased in value, the same would apply.

Assume that when Beth got married, her husband gave her an eight-carat diamond ring. Let's assume that they are in court and she is testifying that the ring was a gift from her husband so it is her personal property. He says, "Are you kidding? I would not *give* you an eight-carat diamond. That was an investment, so therefore it is marital property."

The judge decides. Typically, however, women get to keep their jewelry, their furs, and similar types of gifts. Men get to keep their tools, their guns, and their golf clubs.

What if Beth's husband had given her an $80,000 painting for her birthday? She claimed it was a gift and he claimed it was an investment and therefore should be treated as marital property.

In this case, the judge called it an investment. Because it was not the type of thing that most people would freely give as a gift, it was seen as an investment for the family so it was considered marital property. But remember, you can never predict what the judge will decide!

What happens when both parties want the same item? Let's say Beth and her husband had divided all their property except for one item. They couldn't agree who was going to get the set of antique crystal that had come from England.

Reason and logic is needed here. Negotiation skills come into play, along with a need to prioritize what is wanted, along with the value of the item. We know that emotional value is a factor and can't be measured. When both spouses want the same item, obtaining an item can become an out-of-control quest. We have seen cases where the item may have originally cost a few thousand dollars, and the couple spends megathousands trying to "win" it in the courtroom. Instead of spending the money for attorneys, Beth and her husband could take the savings and return to England to buy a new set!

When it comes to home furnishings, most values are fairly low. Home furnishings aren't usually included on the list of assets, because couples just divide them up. If they are to be valued, the typical value is what you can get from a garage sale.

At What Date Will It Be Valued?

States vary as to the cutoff date for ending the accrual of marital property. For example, some would value the property on the date of physical separation of the parties, while others would continue until the final decree is granted. Therefore, you must ask your attorney how your state decides.

How Will It Be Divided?

Dividing property almost always takes some finesse. It's not as simple as taking the total value of marital assets and just divvying them up. Emotions, perceived value, even not wanting a spouse to have something because, well—just because—it all plays a part.

Let's look at an example of how a case can play out. Marilyn and Tom Baxter have been married for 35 years. She's a homemaker caring for their four kids and has not worked outside of their home for pay. Tom earns $150,000 per year and has started a business in the basement of their home. He expects the new business to create revenues after he retires. Their home is worth $135,000 and mortgage-free. His pension is valued at $90,000. Their joint savings is $28,000. Tom estimates his basement business is worth $75,000. Their combined assets total $328,000. If you assume a 50-50 property split, each would receive $164,000.

Here are the Baxters' assets at the time of their divorce:

House	$135,000
Pension	90,000
Savings	28,000
Business	75,000
Total	$328,000

Splitting the property and assets down the middle is often not the most equitable division. In this scenario, Marilyn wants the house. The value of the house will remain in her column on a typical property settlement worksheet. Tom wants what most men want in the distribution of assets, the pension. We'll put the pension in his column.

Tom also has some other thoughts. With the demands of his growing basement business, he needs cash. He wants the $28,000 savings account. Add the savings account to his column. Since Tom feels the business in the basement is his, he wants it all as his property. Put the business in his column.

The division now looks like this:

		Marilyn	Tom
House	$135,000	$135,000	
Pension	90,000		$90,000
Savings	28,000		28,000
Business	75,000		75,000
Total	$328,000	$135,000	$193,000

Her assets total $135,000 and his assets total $193,000. If we were to look at a 50-50 property split, he would owe her $29,000. Although Tom has a large income of $150,000 a year, he does not want to give up any of the business or pension or savings.

Property Settlement Note

We could even out this division with a property settlement note. Tom could pay Marilyn $29,000 over time, like a note at the bank. He can make monthly payments with current market interest. Or, he can borrow funds directly from the bank, since he has assets, including a savings account comparable to what he would owe. A *property settlement note* is an agreement to pay a specified amount for an agreed-upon length of time with reasonable interest. It is still considered division of property, so the payer does not deduct it from taxable income. The payee does not pay taxes on the principal—only on the interest. It is important to collateralize this note, meaning that the payer should pledge something of value to guarantee it, in case the payer doesn't pay on the note.

If no other asset is available, it is possible to collateralize this note with a qualified pension by using a qualified domestic relations order (QDRO), a legal document that directs the administrator of a pension plan as to what amount (either percentage or dollar amount) is to be given to a nonemployee spouse. If the payer defaults on the payments of a property settlement note, then the payee can collect pursuant to the terms of the QDRO agreement from the pension. A QDRO can be used to collaterialize a property settlement note.

Suppose Marilyn does not like the settlement suggested. She believes she is owed the house and wants half of her husband's pension because, in their 35 years of marriage, she helped him earn his pension by caring for their children and managing their household. She also wants half of the savings, because she doesn't want to be left without any cash. But she agrees that the basement business is Tom's.

Adjust the columns, keeping the house in Marilyn's column; splitting the pension, putting $45,000 in each column; dividing the savings, placing $14,000 in both columns; and crediting Tom with the business.

The property split now looks like this:

		Marilyn	*Tom*
House	$135,000	$135,000	0
Pension	90,000	45,000	$45,000
Savings	28,000	14,000	14,000
Business	75,000	0	75,000
Total	$328,000	$194,000	$134,000

Marilyn's assets are now valued at $194,000, and Tom's at $134,000. Marilyn now owes Tom $30,000 to make a 50-50 property settlement. It's not that simple. She does not have a job and has limited skills. It is unlikely she would be able to get a job that pays her a high income.

Her largest asset is the house, an illiquid asset. It is paid for, but it does not create revenues to help her buy groceries. She could rent out rooms for additional income, but that rarely works and it creates a different lifestyle that she may not want. How is she going to pay this $30,000 to Tom? The prospects are bleak. Given that Marilyn is in her mid-50s, has never worked outside the home, and her largest asset is illiquid, this unequal division may be considered the most equitable.

Awarding alimony comes after the property is divided. The reason for this is that alimony can be based on the amount of property received, so it is important to look first at the property division.

Equal versus Equitable

In property division, you trade assets back and forth until the couple agrees on the division. In an equitable property division state, you split the property equitably. It does not mean *equal*—it means *fair*.

On the other hand, the word *equality* suggests fairness and equity for all parties involved. Unfortunately, the required equal division of property in most states has forced more sales of family assets, especially the family home, so that the proceeds can be divided between the two spouses. The net result is increased dislocation and disruption, especially in the lives of minor children. This is not fair, in that the needs and interests of the children are not considered in many cases.

A second problem of equality is that a 50-50 division of property may not produce equal results—or equal standards of living after the divorce—if the two spouses are unequally situated at the time of divorce. This is most evident in the situation of the older homemaker. After a marital life devoted to homemaking, she is typically without substantial skills and experience in the workplace. Most likely, she will require a greater share of the property to cushion the income loss she suffers at divorce. Rarely is she in an equal economic position at divorce. Our example of Marilyn Baxter fits this description.

Generally, a 50-50 division is started when property is divided in an equitable division state. A major consideration can be how much separate property the client has. Let's say your spouse has $2 million in separate property. Your marital estate totals $200,000. A judge who knows your spouse has $2 million worth of separate property may not give your spouse 50 percent of the marital property. Instead, the judge's attitude may be, "Well, you have $2 million in separate property, so you get none of the marital property."

What's a Career Worth?

With many couples, one spouse has significant assets tied to his or her career. These career assets include insurance (life, health, disability); vacation and sick pay; Social Security and unemployment benefits; stock options; and pension and retirement plans. Future promotions, job experience, seniority, professional contacts, and education are also considered career assets. In many cases, career assets should be considered in arriving at an equitable settlement.

In 1998, a highly publicized battle over career assets made the cover of *Fortune* magazine. Lorna and Gary Wendt were married for 32 years. He was the CEO of GE Capital; she was a "corporate wife." At the time of the divorce, he declared the marital estate to be worth $21 million and offered her $8 million as her share. She balked, saying that the estate was worth $100 million. Her counter to him was that she wanted $50 million—half.

Lorna Wendt's position was that her husband's future pension benefits and stock options had been earned during their marriage. She argued that her contribution as the homemaker and later, wife of the CEO, enabled him to rise through the ranks to the top of an international organization. Her husband didn't agree.

In the early years of their marriage, she worked to support them while he attended Harvard Business School. They moved often while she handled the details of the household and took care of him and their two children. When he became CEO, she was expected to entertain often and extravagantly as his position required. She felt she was a 50-50 partner in the marriage and the accumulation of all assets.

The Wendt case broke through the long-held belief that "enough is enough"— that a spouse deserved enough to maintain her lifestyle—nothing more. In a landmark decision, the judge awarded her $20 million—far less than the $50 million she had requested, but far more than the $8 million her husband initially offered.

Putting Husband/Wife through College

Consider the example of a family of simpler means, in which the husband is the dominant wage earner. It is not unusual for the wife to put the husband through school or help him become established while abandoning or postponing her own education. She may have quit her job to move from job to job with him.

Together, they made the decision to spend the time and energy to build his career with the expectation that she would share in the fruits of her investment through her husband's enhanced earning power. Over time, he has built up career assets, which are part of what he earns, even though they may not be paid out directly to him.

Even in two-income families, one spouse's career often takes priority over the other's. Both spouses expect to share the rewards of that decision—at least, in the beginning of their marriage.

Some states even place a value on degrees such as the medical degree, the dental degree, or the law degree. In a 1980 case a couple, both medical students, agreed that the husband would finish his education first while the wife supported him. When he finished, she would complete her education.

After his first year of residency, the couple separated. The court held that the husband's medical school degree and license to practice medicine were obtained during the marriage, and therefore were "property" and to be considered assets to be divided. It established the value of the husband's medical education as the difference in earning capacity between a man with a four-year college degree and a specialist in internal medicine. With the help of a financial analyst, the court valued the education at $306,000. The wife was awarded, in addition to alimony, 20 percent of this amount over a five-year period.

Myths and Realities in Family Business

Whenever one of the marital assets in a divorce is a business, there are challenges in dividing this asset. A business can be a dental, medical, law, or accounting practice; a real estate firm; or a home-based business. It can be a sole proprietorship, a partnership, or a corporation.

Valuing the business. Any time there is a small, family, or closely held business, it makes sense to do a little probing. In fact, you may have to do a lot. For more on this subject, see Chapter 6. We do throw out a caution here. If you know that the business creates cash flow, it's definitely worth looking into. If you know that it's barely making it, or showing a true financial loss, strongly consider where you want to spend your investigative monies.

Dividing the business. Dividing up a business is another issue. There are four options when deciding how to go about doing it:

1. One spouse keeps the business.
2. One buys the other out.

3. Both spouses keep the business.
4. Both spouses sell the business outright and split the proceeds.

If one spouse is the primary driver in keeping and running it, it usually surfaces early that the person will continue with it by buying or giving assets of equal value. If there are no assets large enough to give, a property settlement note could be created or a loan obtained. If the spouse owns shares of the company, the company could buy back her shares over time.

Care needs to be taken when buying out shares of stock. If there has been an increase in the value of the stock, the selling spouse could be liable for capital gains tax. If one spouse buys the shares directly from the other, it would be considered a transfer of property incident to divorce, which is not a taxable issue.

It is much more difficult to divide a family-owned business where the husband and wife have worked next to each other every day for years. They both have emotional ties with the business. In addition, if they try to divide the business, it may kill the business. Some couples are better business partners than marriage partners, and are able to continue to work together in a business after the divorce is final. This doesn't work for everyone, but should be considered as an option.

Some couples opt to sell the business and divide the profits; this way, both are free to look elsewhere for another business or even to retire. The problem here may be in finding a buyer. Sometimes it takes years to sell a business. In the meantime, decisions need to be made as to whose business it is and who runs it.

Revisiting the scavenger hunt. Remember when we talked about hidden assets in Chapter 4? Discovering and determining what property should be identified as marital assets takes a little work. We know that at times, it seems as though you've been sent on a scavenger hunt to find assets. Here's a quick review to tweak your memory of places to look:

- *Tax returns.* They show interest and dividend income and name the source. Look at Schedule B. If you see $5,000 interest from a mutual fund or bond, you know someplace there is an asset worth about $62,500 (if it is earning 8 percent). If instead that $5,000 is from a bank or credit union, it is probably earning more like 4 percent and the asset may be worth about $125,000.
- *Financial statements.* When used to secure a loan, these usually have values assigned to assets to pump up the net worth. If your spouse was trying to impress the bank with your combined net worth, there may be some assets there worth tracking down.
- *Canceled checks.* A large sum made out to a brokerage firm, mutual fund, or insurance company would indicate that an investment was made. And

that money is sitting someplace even though you may not have known about it. Make sure when looking through the checks that you have all of them and there are no missing numbers.

- *Copies of investment statements.* This will show values. If you have several months of statements and you see that the value declined within the past few months due to a withdrawal, find out where that money went. It may be sitting in a different account someplace else.
- *Deferred compensation.* Did your spouse talk about an expected bonus that somehow never got paid? Perhaps the bonus is still owed but the employer is helping out by holding that bonus until after the divorce is over. Check it out!
- *Cash business.* Does your spouse own a business that takes in a lot of cash? It is important to know how much cash flow there really is.
- *Retirement plans.* These are biggies. Remember that in most states, retirements plans are marital property even if held in only one name. It is important to have the paperwork on each one.
- *Payroll stubs.* Is your spouse having money withheld that goes into a special account nobody else knows about?
- *Contracts or agreements that pay out in the future on work done in the past.* Because the work was done during the marriage, the future payout is marital property. This category includes royalties, patents, and commissions.

Dividing the House

Most assets are in houses and pensions. How one spouse gets his or her share out of either creates some anxiety, and tension is in the air. There are three basic options to approaching the issue of who gets the house. You can sell the house, buy out your spouse's half, or continue to own the property jointly after the divorce.

1. Sell the house. Selling the house and dividing the profits that remain after sales costs and the mortgage is paid off is the easiest and "cleanest" way of dividing equity. Concerns that will need to be addressed include: the basis and possible capital gains (addressed later in this chapter), buying another house versus renting, and being able to qualify for a new loan.

2. Buy out the other spouse. Buying out the other spouse's half works if one person wants to remain in the house or wants to own the house. There are difficulties with this option that need to be considered.

First of all, you need to agree on a value of the property (for purposes of the divorce, value is the equity in the house). Next, decide on the dollar amount of the buyout. Will the dollar amount have subtracted from it selling costs and capital gains taxes?

Next, a method of payment needs to be selected. If payments will be made over a specified period, the terms need to be comfortable for both parties. The payment could be as simple as giving up another marital asset in trade for the equity in the house. The house could be refinanced to withdraw cash to pay the other spouse, or a note payable can be drawn up with terms of payment that are agreeable to both parties. Reasonable interest should be attached to the note, and it should be collateralized with a deed of trust on the property. One problem with this arrangement is that it keeps you in a debtor-creditor relationship with your ex.

There is another problem with buying out your spouse's half. Let's say you get the house and both names are on the deed. The ex can quit-claim the deed to you so that only your name is on the deed. Now, you can sell it whenever you want. Although your ex's name comes off the deed, it remains on the mortgage. What happens if you don't pay the mortgage? The mortgage company will come to your ex for payment. It doesn't care that you are divorced. The only way to remove your ex's name from the mortgage is to assume the loan in your name, refinance it, or pay it off.

When your ex's name is kept on the mortgage, it also may impact credit by making you appear overextended unless there is proof that you have been making the mortgage payments. This could create, continue, even enhance an adversarial relationship between the two of you.

3. Own the house jointly. The other option—continuing to own the property jointly—is used when you and your ex want the kids to stay in the house until the children finish school or reach a certain age, or until the resident ex-spouse remarries or cohabits. You agree to sell the house after the kids have graduated from school and split the proceeds evenly. Whoever stays in the house in the meantime can pay the mortgage payment, while all other costs of maintaining the house plus taxes and repairs are split evenly. Again, this continues a tie between the two of you that may create stress.

Here are some examples to help put all these options into perspective. Mark and Susan had very good jobs when they decided to divorce in 1986. Susan wanted to stay in the house with the three children and buy out Mark's half of the house with a property settlement note. Interest rates were high. The note was drawn with her agreeing to pay Mark his half of the equity at 14 percent interest. Then property values began to decline. Susan's half of the equity was losing value, while Mark's was earning 14 percent, even after the interest rates plummeted.

At the time they drew up this agreement, no one presumed that interest rates or property values would go down. It is always a risk when you make agreements that extend out into the future. These risks run both ways.

Lila and Keith had divided all their property, with her owing him $5,000. She kept the house and was going to sell it in three years when their daughter was out of high school. The house had $20,000 of equity in it at the time of divorce. They both agreed that when she sold the house in three years, she would give him his $5,000. Lila's attorney knew Susan's lawyer and had heard about the case where Susan was paying 14 percent interest. Lila's attorney suggested, "Since $5,000 represents 25 percent of the equity, why don't you agree on a percentage? That way, when you sell the house you give him 25 percent of the profits. If the house declines in value and you only get $10,000 profit, you are not paying him half. Or if it goes up, you both win because you both get more."

If you are considering dividing assets beyond one year of your divorce, we suggest you discuss negotiating a percentage versus an exact dollar amount. If dividing assets prior to a year, specifying hard dollars usually works better.

When the wife should not get the house. We have mentioned several times in this book that women are usually more attached to the home. Should a woman always negotiate to keep it? Not necessarily. There are cases when the wife should not keep the house.

Consider Bob and Cindy. Cindy is 32 years old and Bob is 33. They have been married 12 years. They have two kids, nine and five years old. Cindy is the custodial parent.

Cindy needs three more years to finish college and get her degree and another year to earn her teaching credential. She estimates that she will earn $33,000 a year as a new teacher. Between going to school and caring for the kids, she will not be able to earn income. Bob is offering to help Cindy through school by paying maintenance of $2,400 per month for one year, then $1,500 per month for two additional years.

Cindy's expenses with the two kids are $3,000 per month. This includes her expenses for school, which average $350 per month. Bob earns $75,000 per year and brings home $57,570 per year after taxes. His expenses are $2,000 per month. Cindy and Bob had trouble staying within their budget while they were married. Cindy loved to shop and tended to overspend, maxing their credit cards to their limits.

The family home has a fair market value of $220,000 with a mortgage of $125,000. Monthly payments are $1,500 per month, including real estate taxes. Cindy wants to remain in the house with the kids.

It doesn't make economic sense for Cindy to keep a house with a $1,500 monthly payment when she has no income of her own and is relying on maintenance to make that payment for her. She could rent a smaller house close to where she currently lives for $750 to $800 per month.

Some type of alimony will be received for a few years, as well as child support for the kids. Selling the house will release cash that in turn can create income to supplement the alimony and child support she will receive until she gets her teaching credential.

Maintenance cannot be counted on. What if Bob loses his job? Both need counseling on cash flow and budgeting. Both must understand that whatever scenario is followed, it will have a major impact on their financial, emotional, parenting, and relationship lives.

Tax Considerations

The Taxpayer Relief Act of 1997 has created a big tax boon to the majority of taxpayers, and is a disaster to others when it comes to capital gains. It has also created some complications. The details of the new tax law are anything but simple. Let's take a look.

The previous law taxed net capital gains at 28 percent. This was great for those in the 31 percent, 36 percent, and 39.6 percent tax brackets. But it gave no benefit to those who were taxed at 28 percent or lower.

The new maximum tax rate on net capital gain is generally lowered to 20 percent for all taxpayers (except those in the 15 percent tax bracket, for whom it is now 10 percent).

For years, taxes on capital gains from the sale of the home were subject to deferral or a one-time exclusion. First, homeowners have been able to defer the capital gain by buying another home within two years before or after the sale of their home. Second, homeowners age 55 or older had the one-time opportunity to exclude $125,000 from their capital gain when figuring their taxes.

The new tax law eliminates these two options for sales made after May 6, 1997, and replaces them with a new exclusion that should help most—but by no means all—homeowners. The new tax law provides an exclusion of up to $250,000 for single people and $500,000 for married couples. This is a big plus.

What do the terms *capital gains* and *basis* mean? Basis is the original investment in your first home increased by selling costs and any improvements. Another common term used is *adjusted basis*. Capital gains are the amount of profit you made when comparing the adjusted basis with the selling price of your last home.

The rollover is no longer available. And the home must have been used as the principal residence by the seller for at least two out of the five years before the sale. The new tax law also provides fulfillment of the residency requirement by the nonresident spouse. In other words, if you get the house in the divorce, sell it four years later, and split the profits with your ex, you both get to take a $250,000 exclusion because one of you fulfilled the residency requirement.

Let's look at some examples:

John and Mary are getting divorced. John is awarded the jointly owned family home for four years. At the end of four years, John sells the home and 50 percent of the proceeds are sent to Mary.

Scenario A: John sells the house for $400,000. Mary will receive $200,000 and will be entitled to use her $250,000 exclusion, even though she has not lived in the house for the previous four years.

Scenario B: John sells the house for $750,000. Mary will receive $375,000. If the basis in the property was $100,000, Mary's portion of the basis is $50,000, leaving her with a $325,000 gain. Even though she uses her $250,000 exclusion, she will be taxed on $75,000 of gain.

Sales Price	$750,000	Sales Price	$750,000
Basis	−100,000	John's Half	375,000
Capital Gain	$650,000	Mary's Half	375,000

Mary's Half of Sales Price	$375,000
Mary's Half of Basis	−50,000
Mary's Half of Capital Gain	$325,000

Mary's Exclusion	−250,000
Amount on Which Mary Will Be Taxed	$75,000

The 1997 tax law would be disastrous in some situations. Here's how:

Vicki and Stan are getting divorced and Vicki is taking the house, worth $750,000. The basis in the house is $200,000. Vicki decides to move to another city and buy another house for $750,000. She wants to maintain her current lifestyle and, as often happens, does not check into tax law or get financial advice before making a decision that may haunt her at a later time.

Her gain on the sale is $550,000. She will be able to use her $250,000 exclusion but will still have to pay taxes on the gain of $300,000, even though she bought another house of equal value! Remember, the capability of rolling over personal residential gains is a thing of the past.

Sales Price	$750,000
Basis	−200,000
Capital Gain	$550,000
Exclusion	−250,000
Amount on Which Vicki Will Be Taxed	$300,000

One good thing that the new tax law created was a recurring exclusion. You can use it over again every two years. If you buy a house and sell it after two years, you can use the exclusion again.

Bank Account Blues—Debt, Credit, and Bankruptcy

We have referred to property as either marital or separate. The same classifications apply to debt. In general, both you and your spouse are responsible for any debts incurred during the marriage—it does not matter who really spent the money. When the property is divided up during the divorce, the person who gets the asset usually also gets the responsibility for any loans against it.

It's in both of your best interests to pay off as many debts as possible before or at the time of the final decree. To do so, use whatever liquid assets you have—bank accounts, money market funds, stocks, bonds, or cash values from life insurance. It may make sense to sell assets to accumulate some extra cash. The most easily sold assets include extra cars, vacation homes, and excess furniture. (Don't expect to get much for used furniture unless it has value as an antique or collector's piece.)

If you can't pay off the debts, then the decree must state who will pay which debt and within what period of time. There are generally four types of debt to consider: secured debt, unsecured debt, tax debt, and divorce expense debt.

Secured Debt

Secured debt includes the mortgage on the home or other real estate, and loans on cars, trucks, and other vehicles. It should be made very clear in the separation agreement who will pay which debt. If one spouse fails to make a payment on a debt that is secured by an asset, the creditor can pursue the other spouse.

Unsecured Debt

Unsecured debt includes credit cards, personal bank loans, lines of credit, and loans from parents and friends. These debts may be divided equitably. The court also considers who is better able to pay the debt.

For unsecured debt, any separation agreement needs to include a *hold-harmless* clause. This will indemnify the nonpaying spouse, which means that the paying spouse gives the nonpaying spouse the right to collect not only all missed payments, but also damages, interest, and attorney's fees if payments are not made. Without a hold-harmless clause, the nonpaying spouse has the right to collect only the missed payments.

Often, the legal decision and the financial outcome are very different things. This is a lesson Paul learned the hard way. Tracy and Paul were married eight years, during which time Tracy ran her credit cards to the limit with her compulsive spending. The court held Tracy solely responsible for paying the $12,000 in credit card debt. After the divorce, however, Tracy didn't change her ways and was unable to pay off her debt. The credit card companies came after Paul, who ended up paying them off.

> • • • • •
> This is very important—even though something was agreed upon, it doesn't necessarily happen as planned.
> • • • • •

In a case like this, one solution would have been to pay off the credit cards with assets at the time of divorce or for Paul to have received more property to offset this possibility.

Tax Debt

Just because the divorce settlement is final doesn't mean you are exempt from possible future tax debt. For three years after the divorce, the IRS can perform a random audit of your last joint tax return. In addition, the IRS can question a joint return—if it has good cause to do so—for seven years. It can also audit a return whenever it believes fraud is involved.

To avoid surprises, the divorce agreement should spell out what happens if any additional interest, penalties, or taxes are found, as well as where the money comes from to pay for defending an audit. We know of countless horror stories where the unsuspecting spouse (usually the ex-wife) is all of a sudden obligated for a huge tax bill and doesn't have a clue how it happened.

Divorce Expense Debt

Although it isn't always clear who is liable for debts incurred during the separation, typically these debts are the responsibility of the person who incurred them. An exception would be if one spouse runs up debts he or she is unable to pay to buy food, clothing, shelter, or medical care for the kids. The other spouse is probably obliged to pay those expenses.

You will accrue other costs during the divorce process, including court filing fees, appraisals, mediation, and attorneys. Other less obvious expenses are accounting, financial planning, and counseling. The separation agreement needs language that states who is responsible for these expenses.

Divorce expenses may accrue after the decree, such as attorney fees for doing QDROs, title transfers, tax preparation for the final joint tax return, mediation fees, and long-term divorce counseling for the parents or the kids. Who pays? You do, unless it is spelled out clearly so there are no disputes at a later date.

> • • • • •
>
> At times, you may have paid some divorce expenses before the divorce process was officially started. In the final agreement, you may want to get a credit offset for these expenses.
>
> • • • • •

Dividing Marital Property and Debts

Many people try to divide each asset as they discuss it—your half of the house is $4,000, my half of the house is $4,000. Since you will rarely divide the house like this, this may not be the most useful way to go about it. It may be more practical to list each asset as a whole item under the name of the person who will keep it.

For example, in the wife's column, list the marital equity in the house if she is thinking of continuing to live there. List the entire value of the husband's retirement in his column, if that is your initial inclination. An advantage to this method is that it allows you to see the balance, or lack of it, of your initial plan as you develop it. If you want to know dollar values, you may need a third party, such as an appraiser, to help you determine them.

This is the time to have a real heart-to-heart discussion with your about-to-be-ex about the range of his or her sense of fairness. Ask:

- Is the only possibility for a 50-50 division of things by value? By number?
- Are you more interested in cash than in things?
- Will you take less than 50 percent if your share is all cash?
- Are you more interested in future security than in present assets?
- Are you willing to wait for a buyout of your share, such as house selling or retirement, and are you looking for more than 50 percent to compensate you for waiting?
- Are you interested in a "lopsided" agreement (more to one of us than the other) to compensate for the larger earnings made by you or your spouse?
- Do you want to be "made whole"—meaning ending up where you were at the beginning of the relationship?

- Do you need to be compensated "off the top" for some contribution you made to the acquisition of property?
- Is there a possibility that any assets or investments are hidden?

If you both can agree on a generic plan that meets each of your ideas of fairness, you will find you have an agreement that practically writes itself. The bonus is that you save on lawyer's fees.

As you allocate the debts, decide first whether they are marital, separate, or a mix. Then agree who will pay off the balance of each. Remember that the problem of unsecured debts may be handled more easily as if it were a monthly credit card payment than a division of your property.

Think about the long-term effect of the division of assets and debts you are considering. For example, suppose you get all assets that appreciate slowly or depreciate, and which take money to maintain (home, car, furniture). Then suppose your spouse takes all assets that increase in value or produce income (stock, retirement accounts, rental home). Guaranteed, in a few years after the divorce, what in the short term appeared to be "fair" or "equal" will look quite different. Your spouse's net worth will far exceed yours—and the gap will just continue to widen.

Bankruptcy

The word *bankruptcy* strikes fear in the hearts of many people—especially those going through divorce. You may be trying to decide whether it is better to ask for alimony or a property settlement note and are caught in indecision. Perhaps your spouse has threatened either to leave the country if alimony is required or to file bankruptcy if money is owed or a property settlement note is due. Let's look at some of the rules of bankruptcy as they apply in divorce situations.

Two types of bankruptcy are available: Chapter 13 and Chapter 7. Chapter 13 allows you to develop a payoff plan over a three-year period, and Chapter 7 allows you to liquidate all of your assets and use the proceeds to pay off debts, erasing debts that cannot be paid in full.

Chapter 7 bankruptcy forgives all unsecured debts and requires the forfeiture of all assets over certain minimum protected amounts. Creditors have the right to repossess their fair share of the assets. The net proceeds from the sale of assets are divided *pro rata* among the creditors.

Chapter 13 bankruptcy may preserve the assets and allow the debtor to pay off all the secured debt, as well as a portion of the unsecured debt, and discharge the rest of the unsecured debt. The debtor needs to make payments under a plan that is approved by the bankruptcy court.

Here are some things to remember:

- If a spouse files bankruptcy before, during, or after divorce, the creditors will seek out the other spouse for payment—no matter what was agreed to in the separation agreement.
- While you are still married, you can file for bankruptcy jointly. This will eliminate all separate debts of the husband, separate debts of the wife, and all jointly incurred marital debts.

Caution—promissory notes or property settlement notes, especially unsecured notes, are almost always wiped out in bankruptcy. Some secured notes, depending on the property that secures them, can also be discharged. Here's what happened to Cheryl: Sam and Cheryl divided all their assets. To achieve a 50-50 division, Sam still owed Cheryl $82,000. He signed a property settlement note to pay Cheryl the $82,000 over a ten-year period at 7 percent interest. After the divorce, Sam filed for bankruptcy and listed the property settlement note as one of his debts. Cheryl never received a penny of the money that was due her.

> • • • • •
>
> Certain debts cannot be discharged in bankruptcy. These include child support, maintenance, some student loans, and recent taxes.
>
> • • • • •

13 Property Nuggets

• • • • •

1. All earned income acquired during the marriage, no matter whose name it's in, is considered to be marital property, unless there is a prenuptial agreement stating otherwise.

2. A property settlement note can be used to even up a property division and should be collateralized.

(continued)

3. Be careful when dividing assets if one spouse gets all the cash while the other spouse gets illiquid assets (such as real estate) or all retirement funds, which, when taxes are deducted, are not worth as much.

4. The expert who appraises the family business should not work for that business.

5. If the house has a large capital gain, that should be taken into account when dividing assets.

6. Even though your desire to keep the house is emotional, get some advice on the financial ramifications of keeping it.

7. If your spouse declares bankruptcy, any alimony and child support awarded will not be affected.

8. Most household furniture is valued at garage-sale value.

9. Any cash-value life insurance purchased with marital assets is considered property to be divided.

10. A gift or inheritance received during the marriage and kept in your name only should be considered your separate property.

11. If you or your spouse supported the other while he or she earned a degree or built a career, it may have value as property.

12. Before alimony is awarded, all property is divided.

13. The 1997 tax law created a $250,000-per-person ($500,000 per couple) exclusion when selling the home. It can be reused every two years.

• • • • •

13

Pensions and Retirement Plans
His, Hers, and Theirs

Pensions (also referred to as retirement plans) are recognized as part of the joint property acquired during the marriage and as part of the assets to be divided upon divorce. Pension and retirement benefits earned during the marriage are potentially of great value. In a longer marriage, they may be the most valuable asset that the couple owns.

Divvying up Pensions

There are two main schools of thought when it comes to dividing pension benefits:

1. The *buy-out* or *cash-out* method, which awards the nonemployee spouse a lump-sum settlement—or a marital asset of equal value—at the time of divorce in return for the employee's keeping the pension.
2. The *deferred division* or *future share* method, where no present value is determined—each spouse is awarded a share of the benefits if and when they are paid.

In a defined-contribution plan, there is very little problem identifying the value of the account. Monthly or quarterly statements show the dollar amount available to be divided in either the buy-out method or the future share method.

Basic Plans

There are two main types of retirement or pension plans: defined-contribution and defined-benefit. Following are some ways to split up the treasure chest:

Defined-Contribution Plans

One type of defined-contribution retirement plan is the 401(k). But even in the overall group of 401(k)s, there are different types with different rules. Each company can set its own rules for its retirement plans—as long as the plan is approved by the IRS.

Let's look at the defined contribution plans of employees A, B, and C. Each participates in a defined-contribution plan, yet has different results.

1. Employee A is married and works for a company that has a 401(k). He puts all of his retirement money into the 401(k) and the company does not match any of his funds. He has worked there for three years and he has accumulated $1,500 in his plan.

    Any money that employee A puts into his 401(k) is his—he is 100 percent vested. If he quits or is fired, he can take all of this money with him. He can use it as income, declaring such to the IRS (and most likely, receiving a penalty of 10 percent of the withdrawn amount) or he can roll it over to an IRA.

    After a three-year marriage, employee A and his wife begin the divorce process.

	Employee A
Length of Employment	3 years
401(k) Value at Time of Divorce	$1,500
Percent Vested	100%
Marital Portion	$1,500

2. Employee B works for a company where only the employer contributes money to the 401(k); the employee does not put anything in. He has worked there for three years and his 401(k) is worth $1,500. The company uses a vesting schedule, which regulates how much money he can take with him if he quits or is fired.

    The amount depends on how long he has worked for the company. Employee B is 30 percent vested. Therefore, his 401(k) today is worth 30 percent of $1,500, or $450. The lower amount, $450, is assigned to the marital pot of assets.

	Employee A	Employee B
Length of Employment	3 years	3 years
Value at Time of Divorce	$1,500	$1,500
Percent Vested	100%	30%
Marital Portion	$1,500	$450

3. Employee C works for a company that matches every dollar he puts into the 401(k) with 50 cents. He has worked there for three years and he has $1,500 in his 401(k). Out of $1,500, he has put in $1,000 and the company has put in $500 with its matching program. He is 30 percent vested. However, the $1,000 that he put in was his money, so he is 100 percent vested in that amount and he can take that whole $1,000. He can take 30 percent of the $500—or $150. Employee C's marital portion of this 401(k) is worth $1,150.

	Employee A	Employee B	Employee C
Employee/Employer Contribution		$1,500	$1/50 cents
Length of Employment	3 years	3 years	3 years
Value at Time of Divorce	$1,500	$1,500	$1,500
Percent Vested	100%	30%	30%
Marital Portion	$1,500	$450	$1,000/$150
			$1,150

Defined-Benefit Plans

A defined-benefit retirement plan promises to pay the employee a certain amount per month at retirement time. In many pensions, there are choices as to how it is to be paid out, such as life, years certain, life of employee and spouse, etc. The value of a defined-benefit plan comes from the company's guarantee to pay based on a predetermined plan formula—not from an account balance.

For instance, the amount of the monthly pension payment could be determined by a complex calculation that, in addition to the employee's final average salary, could include an annuity factor based on the employee's age at retirement, the employee's annual average Social Security tax base, the employee's total number of years of employment and age at retirement, the method chosen by the employee to receive payment of voluntary and required contributions, and whether a pension will be paid to a survivor upon the employee's death. As you might guess, the valuation of such a plan poses a challenge and has fostered much creativity!

To see how a defined-benefit plan works, let's look at the example of Henry and Ginny. Assume that, based on today's earnings and his length of time with the company, Henry will receive $1,200 a month at age 65 from his pension. He is now age 56, and has to wait nine more years before he can start receiving the $1,200 per month. Because of the wait, it is called a *future benefit*. The value of a future benefit is determined by mathematical assumptions and calculations.

You could, for example, divide the defined-benefit plan according to a qualified domestic relations order (QDRO) by saying that Ginny will receive $600 a month when Henry retires. When he retires, his benefit will probably be worth more than $1,200 per month because he will have worked there longer, and most likely will be earning more than what he is presently. When Henry retires, he may get $1,800 a month. If the QDRO stated that Ginny would receive $600 per month, she won't get any more even though the value of the fund has increased.

It is important to find out whether the $1,200 per month is what he will get at age 65 based on today's earnings and time with the company, or if the $1,200 per month assumes it is what he will get if he stays with the company until age 65 with projected earnings built in. If it is not clear on the pension statements, these questions must be asked of the plan administrator.

If the couple has fewer than eight years to wait until retirement, Ginny may choose to wait to get the $600 per month so she can have guaranteed income. However, if they are nine or more years away from retirement, she may wish to trade out another asset up front. This way, she'll be assured of getting some funding, which she would not get if the retirement plan disappears due to mismanagement or the company going out of business.

Assume that Ginny decides to wait nine years until Henry retires to receive her benefit. They have been married 32 years. Instead of stating in the QDRO that she will receive $600 per month, it may be more prudent to use a formula that states she will receive a percentage or half of the following:

$$\frac{\text{Number of years married while working}}{\text{Total number of years worked until retirement}} = \frac{32}{41}$$

If Henry's final benefit would pay him $1,800 per month:

$$\frac{32}{41} \times \$1,800 \div 2 = \$702$$

This may be a more equitable division of the pension based on the premise that Ginny was married to Henry during the early building-up years of the plan.

It is also important to ascertain if the plan will pay Ginny at retirement time (when Henry is 65) in the case that Henry doesn't retire. He may decide not to retire just so Ginny can't get her portion of his retirement plan! Some companies do allow the ex-spouse to start receiving benefits at retirement time even if the employee's ex-spouse has not retired. This depends on the QDRO's dividing method and the plan—another reason to have a pension expert involved in your case.

To QDRO or Not to QDRO

The qualified domestic relations order directs the administrator of a pension plan as to the amount to be paid to the nonemployee spouse after the divorce is final.

You need to know that many plans don't allow for this order. The parameters and language of a pension plan take precedence over court rulings. Plans that are divisible by a QDRO include defined-contributions and defined-benefit plans, 401(k)s, thrift savings plans, some profit-sharing and money-purchase plans, Keogh plans, tax-sheltered annuities, and employee stock ownership plans (ESOPs).

> The rules that apply to dividing a corporate pension do not apply to governmental pensions.

Plans that are not divisible include some of the plans of small employers who are not covered by the Employee Retirement Income Security Act (ERISA), and many public employee group funds including police and fire groups; and city, state and federal government employees.

If you or your spouse are participants in any type of pension plan, you need to read the plan documents to ascertain how that company handles any division of retirement assets. Do it before your divorce is final.

> A QDRO should only be prepared by an expert who specializes in pensions.

Common Pension-Related Mistakes

We don't mean to pick on lawyers. But when it comes to snafus in the distribution and division of assets, especially in the area of pensions, they win the prize. To help you avoid the pension trap, we have listed the most common mistakes lawyers make in this area:

Mistake 1: Not Identifying All Retirement Plans

In the discovery process, some lawyers fail to identify all the retirement plans of the other party. This may be due to ignorance, sloppiness, or both.

Mistake 2: Not Understanding the Characteristics of the Retirement Plans

Usually through ignorance, lawyers are confused about the different types of retirement plans, and therefore mishandle the division of the retirement. On top of that, few judges are well versed in pensions. They depend on the lawyers in the case to keep the issues straight. You end up with the blind leading the blind.

> • • • • •
>
> Do not rely on the judge to keep the pension issues straight. Most of them are just as ignorant as the lawyers and sign whatever order is prepared for them.
>
> • • • • •

Mistake 3: Waiting Until after the Divorce to Obtain an Approved Order

If the employee dies after the divorce, and no order is in place, the nonemployee will lose every bit of the interest in the retirement. And, if the employee had remarried, the new spouse will receive all the survivor benefits.

If your case involves a pension, discuss this early on and demand that the lawyer give priority to the preparation of a pension division order. If the lawyer does not know how to prepare one, have the lawyer contact a pension order consultant *immediately*. You are forewarned; don't get caught in this abyss.

> • • • • •
>
> If no pension division order is in place after a divorce, the nonemployee has no more rights to the pension than would a total stranger.
>
> • • • • •

Mistake 4: Not Taking Responsibility for the Preparation of the Order

Even though your lawyer does not know how to prepare the order, you must be the one to find the person to prepare the order, especially if the agreement or decree of dissolution is vague. It makes sense to obtain the advantage for your side when you can.

Mistake 5: Not Anticipating What Will Happen if the Parties Die

The order should specify what will happen if death occurs before or during retirement.

Mistake 6: Not Properly Handling Medical Care for the Nonemployee Spouse after the Divorce

This is especially true in governmental plans, where it is frequently possible for the nonemployee to continue coverage indefinitely after the divorce. In each plan, there is a particular process that must be followed, and there are strict deadlines for completing the applications.

> • • • • •
>
> Make a priority of getting the pension division order signed at the time of the divorce.
>
> • • • • •

Transferring Assets from a Defined Contribution Plan

What happens when the ex-spouse receives the 401(k) asset? There are some specific rules to be aware of.

Consider the example of Esther, who was married to an airline pilot nearing retirement. They were both age 55 at the time of the divorce. There was $640,000 in his 401(k) and the retirement plan was prepared to transfer $320,000 to her IRA.

She could transfer the money to an IRA and pay no taxes on this amount until she withdrew funds from the IRA. But Esther's attorney's fees were $60,000 and she needed another $20,000 to fix her roof. She said, "I need $80,000." She held back $80,000 of the monies before transferring the remaining $240,000 into her IRA. She was able to spend the $80,000. Esther does have to pay taxes on the $80,000 because she had to declare it as income, but she does not have to pay the 10 percent early-withdrawal penalty.

Normally, distributions made before the participant attains age 59½ are called early distributions, and are subject to a 10 percent penalty tax in addition to any income tax. The penalty tax does not apply to early distributions upon death, disability, annuity payments for the life expectancy of the individual, or distributions made to an ex-spouse by a QDRO.

> • • • • •
> The IRS says that any money received from a qualified plan in a divorce situation can be spent without penalty, even if the recipient is under age 59½.
> • • • •

After the money from a pension plan goes into an IRA, which is not considered a qualified plan, Esther is held to the early withdrawal rule. If she says, "Oh I forgot, I need another $5,000 to buy a car," it's too late. She will have to pay the 10 percent penalty and the taxes on the monies that were not rolled into the IRA.

It is important to understand the difference between *rolling over* money from a qualified plan and *transferring* money from a qualified plan. The Unemployment Compensation Amendment Act (UCA), which took effect in January 1993, stated that any monies taken out of a qualified plan or tax-sheltered annuity would be subject to 20 percent withholding. This rule does not apply to IRAs or simplified employee pensions (SEPs).

Here's how this would work:

The Rollover

Gordon was to receive his ex-wife Yvonne's 401(k) of $100,000, which was invested in the ABC Mutual Fund. He told the 401(k) to send him the money so he could roll over the proceeds into a different mutual fund of his choice. The 401(k) sent Gordon $80,000, which was the amount remaining after they withheld the 20 percent withholding tax.

Gordon deposited the $80,000 in his new IRA mutual fund. He could have added the $20,000, which was withheld for taxes, but he didn't have $20,000 to spare even though the IRS would have refunded that amount to him after filing his taxes.

Since he could not come up with the $20,000, the next April when he filed his tax return, he paid an extra $6,600 in state and federal taxes for the "distribution" that

> • • • • •
> To avoid tax, 401(k) transfers must be made directly between trustees and not by a rollover.
> • • • • •

was withheld for taxes. Of course, when he eventually takes his IRA money, $20,000 in taxes already will have been paid.

The Direct Transfer

If Gordon had instead *transferred* the $100,000 from the 401(k) to his new fund, he would have $100,000 in his new fund (instead of $80,000) and would have saved $6,600 in taxes and penalties. It is important to remember the effect of having an extra $20,000 growing tax deferred.

To transfer funds, all Gordon had to do was instruct the 401(k) to send his $100,000 directly to the new IRA account he had just set up with his new mutual fund.

Summing Up

We do a lot of interviews with the media on the topics of divorce, pension distributions, and money. We continue to be amazed when a caller or an interviewer expresses naïveté about property and distribution. We shouldn't be; we know it can be complicated. What surprises us is that most people believe that property is fairly easy to identify and distribute.

13 Important Things to Know about Dividing Pensions in Divorce

• • • • •

1. In most states, most pensions are treated as marital property to be divided in divorce.

2. In order to make an intelligent decision on how to divide a pension, it is necessary to understand the nature of the pension, how it is funded, and how it pays out.

(continued)

3. In most states, a pension can be divided three ways: value it and trade off assets; divide it now using a formula approach; or reserve jurisdiction and divide it when payout to the retiree starts.

4. Different laws and rules apply to dividing corporate pensions and government pensions.

5. You'd be smart to gather information about the pensions as early in the divorce process as possible.

6. Unless your attorney is very knowledgeable about dividing pensions in divorce, use an expert who specializes in that area.

7. Do not merely follow the pension division order form provided by the plan. It rarely offers all of the choices that you might want to consider in dividing the pension.

8. If a pension division order is not in place when the parties divorce, the nonemployee former spouse has no more rights to the pension than would a total stranger.

9. Have the pension division order in place at the time of the divorce.

10. Plan ahead. Many plan administrators take months to review an order and give feedback on whether it can be implemented.

11. The pension division order should provide for what happens if the employee or nonemployee dies before or after the retirement.

12. Have your attorney take responsibility to prepare the pension division order, even if it means hiring an expert.

13. If you are the nonemployee, make sure you understand the plan's rules about continued coverage under the health care plan.

• • • • •

14

When Money Talks, Listen
Alimony, Child Support, and Taxes

Money is one of the primary factors and causes of divorce. It also can be a huge problem after divorce. You can almost feel Naomi's frustration and fear as she tells her story of her postdivorce finances:

> I am bitter. Sometimes I am so bitter, I can't stand myself. It galls me to know that I won't have the vacations we have had in the past, that he continues in his lifestyle, going everywhere, treating friends to dinners out and entertainment, while I, on the other hand, have to count every penny. I am scared about what will happen to me as I really get old. The holidays are a disaster. My whole family is not together and I can't even afford to buy presents.
>
> I had absolutely no idea or concept of the financial and legal aspects [of divorce]. I didn't know what to pay anybody. I didn't know it was going to cost so much money. I had no idea how we were really paying the taxes John reported that we paid. I am always behind paying my bills, literally turning into a penny-pincher. I have cut down on everything. I shop for bargains and at discount stores. I used to think having a wallet full of credit cards was my right. Now I have none. I feel like I am in a marathon race with John for the kids' attention, for their affection. He can buy them everything. I sometimes think I will lose my sanity.

Marcia is 35. Before her divorce, she never thought about how much money was spent on housing, food, or entertainment. Now she is extremely careful and makes an effort not to spend more than the money she earns at her job. She reports that money is her biggest problem.

> I don't entertain in my home unless it is potluck, or go out with my friends anymore. I have fewer clothes, I have given up my weekly house cleaner and I have actually found myself cutting coupons. Somehow I just didn't think that this was the way it would be when I filed for divorce.

What's happening here? No money? The misuse of money? Unreasonable expectations? Not enough money? Possibly, a little bit of everything. We couldn't complete this book without mentioning money—in this instance, alimony, also known as spousal support or maintenance. For the payer, it can be a burden. For the receiver, a lifeline—and sometimes a sinker.

The Big *A*—Alimony

For practical purposes, alimony, maintenance, and spousal support mean the same thing. Simply put, alimony is a series of payments from one spouse to the other, or to a third party on behalf of the receiving spouse. In most cases, the wife is the recipient. Alimony is taxable income to the person who receives it and, with few exceptions, it's tax-deductible by the person who pays it.

In a long-term marriage (more than ten years) that would be defined as "traditional" (meaning the wife has not worked outside the home and has stayed home with kids until they are older or left home), the wife's ability to build a career is somewhat limited.

In most cases, if the wife did hold a job, her income was less than her husband's, sometimes substantially lower. If a transfer or move was indicated, the decision would be based on his job and career. If they moved, she usually would have to quit her job and start over somewhere else. This situation is more typical of couples who are over 50. In most marriages of those under 50, both spouses work, and earn comparable salaries; the wife may very well make more than the husband.

Career decisions and divorce can negatively affect the husband, as well. If the wife makes more money, the husband may have refused a job transfer so that his wife could pursue her career. He can't leave his dead-end job without jeopardizing his pension.

Criteria for Alimony

Deciding whether a spouse should receive alimony (and if so, how much) is based on certain criteria. Most state statutes give detailed criteria (see the Appendix). It used to be that fault was the primary factor in determining alimony. Today, in addition to fault, alimony is awarded based on other criteria, including:

Need. To determine need, you basically have to assess whether the recipient will have enough money to live on after the divorce. To make this determination, you need to consider the spouse's earning ability, earnings from property received in the property division, and earnings from separate property. Alimony may be necessary to prevent the wife (and sometimes the husband) from becoming dependent upon welfare.

Minor children are also considered when evaluating need. Although child support is a separate issue, the custodial parent must be able to care adequately for the children. That means keeping a roof over the kids' heads—utilities to heat, light, and provide water in their home, and food on the table.

Even though a spouse may think an alimony award is needed, the court sometimes finds otherwise. Take the example of Sofia. She wanted maintenance from her husband. However, she had a trust of more than $1 million set aside that was separate property. The court believed that she did not need maintenance because she had property that would provide income to her.

Ability to pay. Can the payer afford to pay what is needed and still have enough to live on? The payer's ability to pay also may be based on having enough money left to meet expenses to support a lifestyle roughly equivalent to the marital lifestyle.

Length of marriage. The longer the marriage, the more likely alimony will be awarded. A two-year marriage may not qualify for alimony but a 25-year marriage probably would. In addition, the longer the marriage, the longer alimony will be paid.

Previous lifestyle. In a 23-year marriage where the husband earns more than $500,000 per year, he probably won't be able to justify a claim that his wife only needs $50,000 per year in alimony. In contrast, a young couple who didn't earn much money should not expect to become wealthy as a result of the divorce.

Age and health of both parties. The following questions are considered when determining whether age or health affect the disposition of alimony:

- Is either spouse disabled?
- Is either retired? Is there a guaranteed permanent income?
- If a wife is 60 years old, does she have a work history? If she has never worked, it will be very difficult for her to find employment, and permanent alimony is a strong option.
- If a spouse is in poor mental or physical health, adequate employment may be difficult to find, and permanent alimony is likely to be granted.

> • • • • •
> Alimony stops upon the death of the payer. If the recipient remarries, it usually stops.
> • • • • •

Rehabilitative Alimony

In the 70s, courts began to recognize the need for a transition period following marriage. It was unrealistic to expect or assume that the wife (or husband, when the wife was the breadwinner) could instantly earn what her husband did, if ever. With that awakening, rehabilitative alimony was born.

If the wife, for example, needs three years of school to finish her degree or time to update old skills, she may get rehabilitative maintenance. This will give her financial help until she becomes able to earn enough to support herself. If you are considering this, stretch your coverage by a few years. If you have kids, you may take longer to complete a degree or obtain new skills than someone who has no child-care responsibilities.

Modifiable versus Nonmodifiable Alimony

Given that the one constant in life is change, it doesn't make much sense to assume that the final settlement decided in court will apply to all future scenarios. One spouse may become unemployed; the other may become ill. Change can be positive, too: You may land a job that includes lucrative stock options and incentives; you could inherit a substantial sum of money; or win a lawsuit or even the lottery.

To accommodate these potential changes, the court where the divorce is granted often maintains jurisdiction over the case. This allows any order of support to be modified when a change of circumstances makes it reasonable to do so.

These changes in circumstances include increases or decreases in the income or expenses of either or both spouses, especially when such changes are beyond the individual's control.

What if you get a roommate or co-habit with someone who pays all the expenses? Your ex's attorney could use this as a fact to reduce current alimony payments. Many states presume that when a spouse who receives alimony moves in with another person, less monetary support is needed.

Be aware that judges do deny requests for modification. Not only that, but

> • • • • •
> After the divorce is final and an order of support is given, either spouse can go back into court and ask for a modification, either up or down.
> • • • • •

they could even rule in the opposite direction! So, before you go back to court to ask for a modification, be sure to examine the position and soundness of your reasons and that you have backup evidence to support your requests. (For information about documentation, see Chapter 13.)

Advantages and Disadvantages of Nonmodifiable Alimony

There are certain advantages to nonmodifiable alimony. Let's say that the divorce decree says that you are going to receive six years of alimony that is nonmodifiable. This means that even if you get married in two years, you still receive four more years of alimony payments. This also could work against you. What if you become disabled or otherwise need more income? Under the nonmodifiable alimony agreement, you can't. When six years are up, all payments stop. Legally, you have no way to continue the alimony income.

What happens if the alimony payer retires early and wants to reduce the amount of alimony being paid? To change the original orders, a new court order is needed. That means you go back to court and a judge will make the final decision. You both will have to hire attorneys to represent you. Even if they both agree to modify the original court order, a new agreement must be drawn up.

It's a Taxing Time

To be considered alimony under the tax code, the payments must meet *all* of the following requirements:

- All payments must be made in cash, check, or money order.
- There must be a written court order or separation agreement.
- The couple can't agree that the payments are *not* to receive alimony tax treatment.
- The couple may not be residing in the same household.
- The payments must terminate upon the payer's death.
- The couple may not file a joint tax return.
- No portion of alimony may be considered child support.

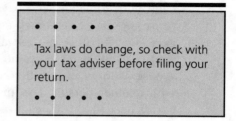

Tax laws do change, so check with your tax adviser before filing your return.

Let's look at each requirement in more detail:

Form of payment. To qualify as alimony, payments made from one spouse to the other must be made in cash or the equivalent of cash. Transfers of services or property do not qualify as alimony.

Payments made to a third party on behalf of his or her spouse may, however, qualify as alimony. Consider the case of Stanley and Marilyn. Under the terms of their divorce decree, Stanley is required to pay his ex-wife, Marilyn, $5,000 per year for the next five years. Six months after the decree is entered, Marilyn decides to return to school to qualify for a better-paying job. She calls Stanley and asks him to pay her $5,000 tuition instead of sending her the monthly alimony checks. Stanley agrees, and on September 4, 1997, pays $2,500 for Marilyn's first semester tuition. For Stanley to deduct this payment as alimony, he must obtain a written statement from Marilyn indicating that they agreed that his payment of the tuition was alimony.

This written statement must be received *before* Stanley files his original (not an amended) income tax return for 1997. Here's why. Let's say that as tax return time approaches, Stanley is eager to get his tax refund. On February 14, he files his 1997 return without waiting for the written statement from Marilyn. On March 1, he receives the statement from Marilyn. He may not deduct the payments as alimony because he failed to get the required written statement before the return was filed.

Here's another example of third-party payment. Under the terms of their separation agreement, Robert must pay the mortgage, real estate taxes, and insurance premiums on a home owned solely by his ex-wife, Julia. Robert may deduct these payments as alimony. Julia must include the payments in her income, but she is entitled to claim deductions for the amount of the real estate taxes and mortgage interest if she itemizes her deductions.

One important exception is that payments made to maintain property owned by the payer-spouse may not qualify as alimony.

Written court order or separation agreement. There must be a written agreement or court order in order for the payments to qualify as alimony. As an example, Craig and Sally are separated. Craig sends Sally a letter offering to pay her $400-a-month alimony for three years. Sally feels this is a slap in the face, since she raised his kids and kept his house clean for 18 years. She does not respond. Craig starts sending the $400 per month. Sally cashes the checks. Since there is no written agreement, he may not deduct the payments as alimony.

Here's another example. According to their divorce decree, Allen is to send Marian $750 per month in alimony for ten years. Two years after their divorce, Marian loses her job and prevails on Allen's good nature to increase her alimony for six months until she gets started in a new job. He starts sending her an extra $200 per month. This was an oral agreement, not a written one. Because no post-decree modification was made, he may not deduct the additional amounts.

Taxes. The divorcing couple must not opt out of alimony treatment for federal income tax purposes. Maintenance is taxable to the person who receives it and tax-deductible by the person who pays it.

Cohabitation. After the final decree, the divorcing couple may not be members of the same household at the time payment is made. Sometimes a couple gets divorced but neither can afford to move. They reach an agreement: She lives upstairs and he lives downstairs. He pays her alimony as specified in the decree, but he cannot deduct it on his tax return. Since they live in the same house, it is not considered alimony.

Death of a spouse. The obligation to make payments must terminate upon either spouse's death.

Joint tax returns. Many couples file a joint return for the year they got divorced. This is an error. The filing status is the status they have on December 31st of the year they are filing. If they are divorced during 1998, they may not file a joint return for that year.

Child support. If any portion of the maintenance payment is considered to be child support, then that portion cannot be treated as alimony. *Family support* is a common term today. Use it carefully. When alimony is combined with child support, the IRS considers the entire payment to be child support. That's great news for the receiver, because the payment does not have to be declared as income. It's bad news for the payer, since none of it is deductible from gross income at tax time.

If the separation agreement specifies a certain amount for family support instead of clearly stating a specific amount for child support and a specific amount for alimony, there could be adverse tax consequences.

If the family support is reduced within six months before or after the child reaches the age of majority and is reduced by the amount that the parents had allocated for child support, the entire amount of the reduction could be deemed child support and nondeductible as alimony. This will be retroactive to the date of the first payment, and any deductions for these payments as alimony will be retroactively disallowed.

A Sure Thing? Protecting Support

Even though the divorce decree stipulates one spouse is to pay the other a certain amount of maintenance for a certain period of time, that doesn't mean it will happen. Several things can happen to the payer that can cause payments to stop or decrease. Fortunately, there are ways to guard against this and ensure that payments will be made. These include life insurance, disability insurance, and annuities.

Life Insurance

Alimony payments stop upon the death of the payer. A simple way to cover future payments is to have your divorce decree stipulate that life insurance will be carried on the life of the payer to replace alimony in the event of the payer's death.

If you are to receive alimony or any other payments, we recommend that you own the life insurance policy and make the premium payments. This prevents any changes in the policy without your knowledge. Consider what happened to Joan. She was receiving $400 per month in alimony from her ex-husband Jerry. The court had ordered Jerry to carry life insurance on his life, payable to Joan as long as alimony was being paid. After three years,

> The recipient spouse should either own the life insurance or be an irrevocable beneficiary for three reasons: to make sure the premiums are paid, to receive tax-favored treatment, and to make sure the beneficiary is not changed.

Jerry was tired of making the insurance payments so he stopped and the insurance was canceled. Nobody knew about it until one year later. Jerry was in a car accident and died two weeks later of complications from his injuries. Alimony came to an abrupt halt and there was no life insurance! Yes, Jerry was in contempt of court, but it didn't make any difference.

The type of insurance you purchase may depend on your cash flow. You could select a whole life policy that accumulates cash value over time, or a term policy that will initially be less in cost for the life of the alimony owed. If you select a term policy, discipline yourself to invest the difference in costs between the two into a mutual fund.

If the court orders a spouse to purchase insurance to cover alimony, child support, or both, and that spouse owns the policy, the premium payments are treated like alimony for tax purposes and can be deducted from taxable income. Likewise, the beneficiary of the policy will need to declare the paid premiums as taxable income.

> • • • • •
>
> If new insurance is needed, it should be applied for before the divorce is final. If the spouse paying the alimony cannot pass the physical and purchase new insurance, there is still time to modify the final settlement to make up for this possibility.
>
> • • • • •

Disability Insurance

A second way to protect the stream of alimony income is to have disability insurance on the payer's ability to earn income. Assume, for example, that you pay your ex $1,200 per month based on your salary of $6,000 per month. Then, you become disabled. If you had disability insurance, you might then be able to receive $4,000 per month tax-free and could continue making maintenance payments. If you had no insurance and no income, you would probably go back to court and ask to have alimony reduced.

You must own your own disability policy. Your ex may make the payments on it so that there is a guarantee that it stays in force (at least, as long as the premiums are paid).

Annuity

A third way to protect alimony is to have the payer buy an annuity that pays a certain amount per month that equals the alimony payment. To do this, the payer of the alimony needs to make a large lump-sum deposit to an annuity with an insurance company and instruct it to make the specific payment. The annuity in turn will send a monthly check. Once the alimony obligation has been met, payment will revert to the payer. Here's the drawback—once an annuity is annuitized (meaning regular payments are being made), you are stuck. You cannot cancel it or get back the original lump sum. You will receive income for the remainder of the annuity.

Child Support

Every parent is obligated to support his or her children, regardless of divorce. In a divorce situation, the noncustodial parent usually is ordered to pay some child support to the custodial parent. The remainder of the child's expenses are paid by the custodial parent.

All states now have child support guidelines that help the courts decide the amount of child support to be paid. The support obligation of each parent is often based on the ratio of each parent's income, the percentage of time the child spends with each parent, and the amount of alimony paid to the custodial parent. (For more information on child support, see Chapter 16.)

Health Insurance

One of the concerns that comes out of a divorce involves health insurance— Who pays for it and how does the nonworking spouse continue with coverage? Usually, the greatest impact is for the woman who has had a long-term marriage and is not covered by an employer's health care plan. It is not uncommon for women over 40 years of age to develop severe health problems. Some become almost uninsurable, at least at a reasonable cost. This is a real concern where, all of a sudden, they are on their own and responsible for acquiring health insurance.

The Older Women's League (OWL) worked hard to get the COBRA law passed in 1986. COBRA stands for the Consolidated Omnibus Budget Reconciliation Act—quite a mouthful. The normal COBRA provision states that, if an employee is fired or leaves a job, he or she can get health insurance from that company for 18 months. However, in a divorce, the nonemployee former spouse coverage is extended to three years or 36 months. It allows a nonemployee former spouse (it doesn't matter which spouse) to continue to get health insurance from the employee spouse's company, which must have at least 20 employees, for three years after the divorce.

The health insurance company is not obligated to offer someone who is covered by COBRA the discounted group rate but will charge the full rate. If any premiums are missed, the insurance company does not have to reinstate you. It is important to shop for health insurance. Even though the COBRA provision may supply a quick solution to health care coverage, it may not be the best. It may be purchased at a lesser cost somewhere else under a totally different plan.

If you are over 40, explore other options. If you can match the rate from your spouse's company or get a lower premium with another company, buy your own. Then if something happens, you are covered as long as you pay your premiums. Otherwise, at the end of three years, COBRA drops you, and then you have to start shopping again. By that time, you might be uninsurable and not able to find insurance. Special rules apply to governmental plans because they are not covered by COBRA.

Most states have insurance for those who are uninsurable and cannot get health insurance any other way. As may be expected, this insurance is very costly. It is better to look ahead and get individual health insurance for a lower premium while you are healthy than to gamble that you will still be healthy three years later.

Is health insurance a marital asset? Maybe. Some companies provide health benefits for employees after they retire. Some lawyers are starting to consider this an asset since the Financial Accounting Standards Board in 1993 began requiring employers to calculate the present value of the future benefits and show a liability for that value in their financial reports.

13 Things to Know about Money and Divorce

1. In general, the longer the marriage, the longer alimony will be paid.

2. It is possible for a husband to get alimony.

3. The amount and length of alimony depends on factors such as the length of the marriage, the needs of the spouse, the ability to pay, the previous lifestyle, and the age and health of the parties.

(continued)

4. Sometimes alimony is paid so that a spouse can obtain a degree or update job skills.

5. Most alimony is not paid on a permanent basis.

6. If properly structured, alimony will be taxable to the recipient and deductible by the payer. Child support is never taxable to the recipient or deductible for the payer.

7. Since alimony payments will stop if the payer dies, consider purchasing life insurance on the payer to protect the income stream.

8. Alimony should not change or end within six months of any child's eighteenth, or twenty-first birthday, or age of emancipation in his or her state.

9. If you are to be the beneficiary of life insurance, you should own the policy and pay the premiums.

10. The amount of child support depends on a number of factors, most importantly the incomes of each parent.

11. Child support is not deductible by the party who pays it and is not income to the parent who has custody of the child.

12. In some states a parent is not legally obligated to pay for a child's college education. Ask your attorney.

13. Depending on who the employer is, health care insurance coverage may be continued for the nonemployee after divorce.

● ● ● ● ● ●

15

Don't Turn Your Kids into Casualties of War

Many couples have kids—a byproduct of when the marriage enjoyed happier times. Kids often soak up the pain created through a divorce. As a caring parent, you should strive to lessen whatever fears and trauma your kids go through now.

In 1960, the number of marriages in the United States outnumbered divorces by nearly four to one. By 1970, it was three to one; and since 1980, two to one. This so-called divorce boom has allowed behavioral scientists to complete volumes of research on its effects on children. They have found that the effects can range from mild to disabling and last much longer than psychologists once thought.

Children can survive divorce with healthier psyches if parents keep their hostilities under control, pay attention to the kids, and understand that more is at stake than the parents' feelings.

What Do Kids Want?

If you ask most kids whether their parents should get divorced, the almost-universal response will be, "No." Most kids would rather see their parents slug it out—physically or mentally—before breaking up the family. They view their parents' differences as minor when they compare (at least in their eyes) the significant changes that they are forced through because of the divorce.

If kids had their druthers, their security is more important than their parents' happiness. In their landmark book, *Surviving the Breakup: How Parents and Children Cope with Divorce* (New York: Basic Books, 1980), authors Judith Wallerstein and Joan Berlin Kelly found that few of the kids in their follow-up survey agreed with their parents' original decision to divorce, even several years after it was completed. Throughout the 1990s the Wallerstein-Kelly team continued with their follow-up studies. The results? Kids don't want their parents to split.

Staying Married for the Kids' Sake

Some couples stay together because of the kids. Most don't. We would like to think that when there are kids involved, you looked at all angles of your situation before you decided to divorce.

> • • • • •
> If getting a divorce is the best solution, then do it. Procrastinating will compound the stress and agony for you and your kids.
> • • • • •

How Do I Tell the Kids?

You and your spouse should decide on the best time to tell your kids that a separation or divorce is in the works. The longer you wait, the more you risk an aura of painful confusion for everyone. Not to mention the fact that people talk—friends, neighbors, and family members. Wouldn't you rather your kids hear this kind of news from you and your spouse, the two most important people in the world to them? If they don't hear from you, and get the news through others, you have created a schism between you and your kids and have set the stage for future distrust.

Start with a Family Meeting

You are still a family—one that is undergoing structural changes. There are several important things to get across at this first meeting. Ideally, you and your spouse should be together at this first meeting. We know that this is not always possible—you and your spouse may find it impossible to be within 50 feet of each other; or your spouse may have vacated the family residence suddenly. If either has occurred, you get the honors of setting the stage alone. How you do it will impact your kids, and yourself, for years to come.

Your job is to get across two key points: that each of you still loves your kids, and that your children are in no way responsible for the divorce. There will be lots of questions, usually starting with "why?" Your kids will wonder where they will live, with whom, whether they will be able to see their friends, even if they can keep their toys. This first meeting can go something like this:

You: Your dad [or mom] and I have spent a lot of time talking about this. We have decided not to live together anymore. That doesn't mean that we don't love you. We do love you—very much. It doesn't mean that we don't want to be with you. We do and we will. We will always be your mom and dad. No one else can take that from you. And there will always be a room (space) for each of you in each of the homes we live in.

Your Spouse: Your mom [or I] will be staying in this house until we decide what to do—either stay here [kids will vote for this] or sell it and both of us will get a different place to live. Whatever we decide, we will include you so that you will always know what is going on. There will be room for whatever things you want to keep at each place and you can decorate or put up posters in your rooms. Each of us wants to participate in school activities. We will be checking with the school. Please let us know what is going on so that we can both keep time free for any activities you want us to attend. If you need help on homework, we both want to help. I'll [or your mom] will call each night to check in. You can always call me [or Mom] for help or with questions.

You: We know that this may surprise and hurt you!! We aren't doing this to be mean. It just isn't working with us now. We tried to work out our differences. We are sorry. We will work out how time will be spent, when stayovers occur, and the details of where you will spend most of your time when you're not in school.

[Note—If your kids are very young, input from them is probably not going to be solicited. If your kids are ten or older, they are often cemented in their neighborhoods; if teens, their activities focus around school—the last thing they will want is to be uprooted and moved to a different school.]

Your Spouse: Mom [or Dad] and I are figuring out which special days and holidays we split, and which ones we will share. There will be times when we will all be at the same event, like at school nights. We want you to still have your friends and to know that your grandparents and other relatives will always be there for you.

You: We know you have lots of questions. You can ask us together, or you can talk to either of us later. Please remember that we love you and will do whatever we need to do to help you through this.

Okay, you've taken the first step, and what a big one it is. Your kids will not hear everything you say. In many cases, they will be numb, not believing what is being spelled out. Make sure you get across the following points:

- *Blame*—It's not their fault that you are separating.
- *Living*—Tell them where they, and you, will be living.
- *Offsite parenting*—Tell them who is leaving, where he or she will be, and when the children will be able to see him or her.
- *Timing*—Tell them when all this will happen.
- *Communicating*—Make sure they understand how, when, and where they can communicate with the offsite parent.
- *Changes*—Keep them informed of what will happen.

Your kids will have questions—some for you, some for themselves. Don't be surprised if your kids hold their own version of the family meeting. This is when their fears really surface and they'll ask, what will *really* happen to us? No matter how much attention, detail, and caring went into the first meeting, they won't care. Their world is being shattered. And you, dear Mom and Dad, caused it.

Besides all the other stuff on your plate, you must now roll up your sleeves and deal with these fears and budding anger. Your therapist may be a great help here; sometimes family members who are good listeners make a great addition to a support team; and don't forget a minister or rabbi. Your kids need to know that you are available to them, no matter how small the issue seems.

We think it makes sense to hold family meetings every month or so, just to check in. It's easy to get so caught up into all the details of your divorce that the kids' needs and concerns get sidestepped. Or, the opposite occurs. Parents become so guilt-ridden that they give their kids everything from Disney World to carte blanche to their wallets. Don't. If you have to cut back on expenses, tell them. If you are on an emotional roller-coaster, tell them. If you are happy, share the good news. But, never, never leave your kids in the dark.

> • • • • •
> *Never* bad-mouth your spouse. We know it's tempting, but it *never* pays off. Bite your tongue, take a bath, or go for a long walk.
> • • • • •

Required Reading When Kids Are Involved

If you have kids, do yourself a favor and get involved with your kids' welfare during this extraordinary time in everyone's lives, especially theirs. Read Isolina Ricci's book *Mom's House, Dad's House: Making Shared Custody Work* (New York: Collier Books, 1981).

This book offers a guide for parents, showing how two homes can be built for children after a divorce—even when parents are on unfriendly terms but have a *genuine desire* to do what's best for their kids. One of the goals for kids, the book stresses, is that they understand there are two different homes and that rules that apply in one house may not apply in the other house. No set of rules is better than the other, the book says, it's just that one goes with Mom and the other goes with Dad. This book has guidelines for putting together a questionnaire to deal with the principal issues in dealing with your child's welfare, as well as sample agreements.

We highly recommend two other books that will be helpful to you: *Separate Houses: A Handbook for Divorced Parents,* by Robert Shapiro (Lakewood, CO: Bookmakers Guild, 1989) and *The Divorced Parent: Success Strategies for Raising Your Children after Separation,* by Stephanie Marston (New York: Pocket Books, 1994).

Your local library is an excellent place to find books that focus on different ages and divorce. Because divorce impacts so many of their young readers, most librarians make sure they have the latest books designed for young people.

Advocates for Kids

The custody mediation specialist is an advocate for kids. He or she is usually a proponent of mediation, because it allows parents to work out power struggles and other issues, including revenge, disappointment, and loss of self-esteem. A goal of the custody mediation expert is to empower parents as equally as possible so that they can determine what they really want to do for their children.

Most custody specialists will create an agreed-upon contract between you and your ex in dealing with each child. If it doesn't work, at least there is something to come back to and look at the baseline to see what needs to be changed. A primary objective is to keep the kids out of the court system.

When putting together a parenting agreement, focus on your childrens' needs, not yours. Identify the important dates and events in their lives, and what traditions

> • • • • •
> We believe that many times judges really don't know what is best for the kids; parents do. Be honest, drop your ego needs and get input from professionals, including teachers, as to what will best serve each child.
> • • • • •

you have. Both parents should sign the agreement, stipulating the name of the child or children, where they reside, when they will reside with each parent, what the addresses will be, and how individual parental responsibilities break down. Following are other things to include in the agreement:

- What decisions will be allocated directly to you and your ex
- What decisions you want to share
- How you and your spouse will exchange information
- Who pays for lessons, health care, vacations, camps, college needs, and transportation for visitations, if needed
- If the parent who has physical custody during a specific time has to be away, how the kids will be taken care of and if the other parent should be advised
- That if there are any illnesses or injury, each of you are notified immediately
- That it be the responsibility for both of you to keep yourselves advised of and available to the school or for special events and programs in which your kids participate
- Most important, if a decision can't be reached jointly, you both will be willing to submit the differences and have someone else arbitrate them, as well as identify professionals to be used for assistance with any disagreements

No matter what agreement you come to, it is critical to stress your love and the respect each of you have for your kids. You may be only able to focus on a short-term (three to four months) agreement, until you can see how things are going. Does your ex really come through with what was agreed upon? For that matter, do you?

Both of you are going to continue to be parents. If you are the parent with physical custody, you usually have a greater responsibility. The last thing you want to do is use your kids as a weapon. By working with someone who is a kid's advocate, you may learn plenty about your kid, as well as yourself.

Kids are an incredible joy within a marriage. They can also be when a divorce ends. Their whole sense of security, trust, and love will blossom if you are truthful and make a strong commitment to keep their other parent in the picture. Mom is Mom and Dad is Dad. Outside of an incredibly abusive parent figure, you will not change it. As Mom or Dad, you must assure them that you are there for them. Always.

13 Things the Noncustodial Parent Can Do to Stay in Touch with the Kids

• • • • •

1. **E-mail.** If your kids have access to a computer, get them their own e-mail addresses and send them encouragement, jokes, and overall sharing via cyberspace. Don't forget: Most libraries have computers if you or your kids don't—they usually have some restrictions on how long you can use their e-mail system, so check it out.

2. **Call regularly.** Ask the custodial parent if there are better times then others—i.e., whether he or she is trying to put into place specific homework and mealtime slots.

3. **Use tapes.** Kids are used to listening to audiotapes. Young ones love to hear Mom or Dad read stories to them. Tell jokes and riddles. Teens are into music—get a favorite group (assuming it's music that is OK with you), tape a lead introduction from you and then retape the actual music tape after your intro. Even if you only live a short distance from your kids, having your voice at their fingertips is a big plus.

4. **Show up.** Remember the movie *Liar Liar*? All the kid wanted was for his dad to stop making promises that he was going to pick him up, only to be a no-show. Make ongoing "show-up" times and dates with your kids, then follow through. The only valid excuse is death and dismemberment!

5. **Schedule nonevents.** This is time just for you and your kid. If you have more than one, this is one-on-one time. Listen, listen, listen.

6. **No-cost events.** Everyone hears of the Disneyland Mom or Dad. Sure, kids love the amusement park scene, but what they really love is time with you. That doesn't cost money. Fly a kite, pack a picnic, go

(continued)

to the park, even have a tea party. Enlist your kids and have them each design their "no-cost" day.

7. **Attend school events.** Kids go to school. If you live anywhere near them, so should you. Class activities, awards, sporting events, you name it—get involved. School is the single area where kids spend most of their time outside of sleeping. On the outside, they may act like it's hokey when you show up; on the inside, they are pleased.

8. **Become a soccer Mom or Dad.** Or baseball—whatever their sport or activity is. Slice the oranges for them, pack a thermos of coffee for you—it's another way to keep the connection going.

9. **Create their space.** Kids need to know that they have their own space at your place. This means sleeping and playing. Yep, this means duplicate toys, clothes, combs, and toothbrushes or any other items that are kept for their next stay. Not having to bring a suitcase means that they are not "just visiting."

10. **Bite your tongue.** No matter how ticked you are, don't knock the other parent when with or speaking on the phone. Kids shouldn't be the vent target. Period.

11. **Cheer them on and be generous with your bravos.** Victories come in small steps. Kids need ongoing encouragement from both parents.

12. **Keep up with schoolwork.** Be a research source for special projects; brainstorm with them on how to present them.

13. **Get a joke or riddle book.** Kids love to laugh, and so should you. They love jokes at their respective ages, even the corny ones.

• • • • •

16

Custody

Do What Makes Sense

Most parents want to believe that they are acting in their children's best interests. Sometimes it is a very hard thing to do because it is easy to get caught up in your own reactions to your spouse. There often is a tendency to want to get your spouse out of your life as soon as possible. When you have kids, that is difficult, if not impossible.

It's also tough not to identify your child with your spouse. When you look in your kid's face, you may be looking at a mirror image of your ex. You see the things that you loved about that person and the things that you hated. This can lead to some unexplained behavior on your part and create a terrible burden for your child.

> • • • • •
>
> The vast majority of kids need both parents. There are exceptions. If your child is being physically abused, contact law enforcement officials immediately.
>
> • • • • •

What Is Custody?

Try telling a kid that he or she is "owned" by someone, especially one of his parents. Custody is used to determine where the kids live legally, as well as some logistical issues, depending on the type of

> • • • • •
>
> Contrary to many parents' beliefs, custody does not mean that you own your kids. Kids aren't owned.
>
> • • • • •

custody arrangement: sole, split, or joint. It does not mean that you own the children, or that the children can be used as bargaining chips with your ex.

What You Should Do If You Want Custody

If you have children and want to stay in the home, and have not already done so, enroll them in neighborhood activities. Judges usually note a child's community ties and are reluctant to force a mother and child out of a home.

Ideally you would like to offer broad visitation and staying privileges to your ex. What you don't want to show is that you intend to cut off or prevent access to the kids. Be willing to draw up a detailed plan on how you will care for them as an ongoing operation, how you will have child care coverage if you have to be out, cover for any special problems, what kinds of schools the kids will attend, and any other activities that they will be involved in.

What you are addressing here are your children's needs on a day-to-day basis. Kids take a lot of time to raise. You need to show that the environment that you have or can move to will be safe and nurturing for their continued upbringing, that the friends and the relatives that will surround the child will be conducive to their continued development.

Sole Custody

Sole custody gives all decision-making power to one parent while taking it from the other one. The parent without custody will have only the right to visitation, the right to inherit from the child, the right to information, and possibly the right to custody of the child on the death of the parent who is granted custody.

Even if the parents agree to sole custody, they may want to negotiate an increase in the rights of the parent without custody. (Examples might include the right to be notified of specific types of facts, the right to participate in school or sports events, or the right to prevent a move out of state.) Of course, as you know by now from reading this book, these should be written into a court order or separation agreement.

Split Custody

Split custody means that each parent takes one or more kids. This may work in some cases. For example, this arrangement works if certain kids are strongly bonded to certain parents; where the kids have an unusually serious problem getting along with each other; or where one parent is unable to care for a particular kid as well as the other parent can. Again, the rights of each parent without custody may be expanded, and the kids' right to a relationship with both should be considered.

Joint Custody

As the name implies, joint custody is when custody is given to both parents jointly, subject to a written contract that defines the terms of their relationship. This is usually referred to as a "joint-parenting plan," and it explains how the child-rearing decisions will be made. This arrangement may avoid a custody battle, but the parents will still need to make many custody-related decisions in the preparation of the plan.

If you are seriously considering joint custody, set aside your ego and any thoughts of manipulation and getting even. We have seen parents use their kids as a wedge in preventing one parent from participating in a function at work or play, relocating, even participating in educational opportunities for one of the kids. Joint custody means that you will do, and want to do, what is in the best overall interest for the kids, not necessarily for yourself.

> • • • • •
> Joint custody should be for the mutual benefit of both parents and the kids.
> • • • • •

The bottom line when it comes to whether it will be joint custody or sole custody can be based primarily on what your relationship was with your ex prior to the initiation of divorce. If both of you always had your children's needs at heart and you can honestly say that you are not in a position to use your kids as pawns, then joint custody could work out very well. There are other times when it doesn't.

Sabrina agreed to joint custody of Sam. When their divorce first started, her ex threatened to try to take Sam away from her. Joint custody was a compromise. Initially she liked it a lot. She felt it was a real plus to be able to have some time to herself. "If I dated anyone, I didn't have to worry about child care. But there is another side. It is assumed when there is joint custody that it helps alleviate the power struggle. I think the opposite happened. It exaggerates it. It keeps it going longer."

Sabrina felt joint custody was an opportunity for a dominant husband to maintain control over his ex-wife. All in all, he may be more interested in controlling her than in caring for his child.

We have heard mixed reviews about joint custody from parents. Most of the negative comes from women. Initially, they were all for it. They liked the active involvement of the father and openly admitted that they liked the freedom and non-child caring time they each got with it. For Sabrina, snags would be encountered when there was a major decision to be made over her son's education. Sam was very bright and attentive in school but was also bored. During each of the school conferences held throughout the year, the parents were told that their child was quite bright and way ahead of the rest of the class.

After some testing, multiple discussions with the teacher, with the principal and aides from the class, it was recommended that her son skip a grade. The school was for it, the teacher was for it, the aides were for it, the counselor at school was for it, and so was Sabrina. The father wasn't. According to their joint custody agreement, if they couldn't agree, then nothing could or would happen. Clearly, this was a situation where the agreement needed a clause that would stipulate that if a joint decision could not be made, it would be passed or referred to someone else and that each party would abide by the third party's decision.

There are also other disadvantages. As a rule, joint custody restricts the mobility of parents in job or home relocation because of the need to be geographically closer to the kids. Now, if it has worked out that so many months are spent with the father and so many months with the mother, or summers with the father and schooltime with the mother, or any of the other arrangements that can be put together, it may not be a problem with today's transportation.

Children sometimes have secret hopes that their parents will reconcile. If you live close by and you are civil, even friendly, your children may not get or even want to understand why you are divorced. Keep in mind that most kids would prefer that their parents stay together even though they fought all the time.

> • • • • •
> If joint custody is going to be sought, both parents have to be equally dedicated to its success. If they aren't, it won't work.
> • • • • •

Joint physical custody can be expensive because of the need to maintain separate quarters for the child. It also can be emotionally expensive—some children find it stressful to be shuttled back and forth. You know your kids best, probably have a good idea about whether this arrangement will work. It's a good idea to include your kids in your discussions. They may feel that they need to be based permanently at one site because of school or some other involvement.

There are some financial benefits to joint custody. Once it has been agreed upon, parents are more likely to pay child support and are less likely to argue over amounts paid to the former spouse.

Inclusion in Your Parenting Agreement

Regardless of the arrangement chosen, there are many issues that should be included in a parenting plan, separation agreement, or court order. Some of these can be as important as the basic custody arrangement itself. To help you get started in your planning, here are a few areas to consider:

- Parenting time schedules
- Vacations and holidays
- Access to information, such as school and medical records
- Participation in child-related events
- Discipline
- Baby-sitting and day care
- Education
- Religious instruction and education
- Medical issues
- Moving out of state
- Parental disability (such as substance abuse or physical or emotional illness)
- Detrimental parental lifestyle
- Finances, such as child support, college costs, insurance, wills, school tuition, summer camp or other vacation activities, orthodontia, or other major medical and dental costs not reimbursed by insurance
- Modifications of custody or support
- How disputes will be resolved

Finally, it makes sense to settle on some rules of fair play for the custodial and noncustodial parent. Some of the rules you may not like. Some may seem very weak. Make sure they are logical and full of common sense. If they are not, you may find yourself back in court, a site that becomes a quick nonfavorite with most parents.

> • • • • •
> We strongly suggest that you really work hard to prepare a detailed agreement *now.* You have a better chance of keeping lawyers and judges out of your future life. That's a plus for you and your kids.
> • • • • •

What if Dad Has Custody?

Some dads make fantastic custodial parents. Some don't. If the father has been the primary caregiver and an active participant in his kids' upbringing, it may make sense for him to be the custodial parent. If it happens, it does not mean that the mother is a bad mother—there has been enough damage done to women by society wagging its finger implying such.

Recent custody decisions have gone against mothers who have chosen to improve themselves, e.g., by going to school. One that received a significant amount of publicity involved a college student, the mother, who was challenged by the baby's father. Since he lived at his parents' home, his reasoning was that his mother could provide day care. The judge agreed. The Michigan Supreme Court didn't and reversed the decision. Some mothers think that their kids would be better off with their father; some don't.

This is a decision that should be done with your child's best interests at heart. If you feel that your ex should be the primary parent because of time, parenting skills, and commitments, lay your ego aside and let it happen. If you need time to get additional skills, talk with your ex and determine if an agreement can be reached that meets both your needs and uses your strengths.

Contested Custody

It happens, and it is happening more today. In the old days it was assumed that the mother would have physical custody. No longer. More fathers are aggressively seeking custody, or at least joint custody, of their kids. When both parents have been actively involved with their kids, joint custody works well. When the father has been the primary provider and caregiver, his having custody has worked to the benefit of the kids. When the mother has been the primary caregiver, it usually works better for her to have custody. There are always exceptions.

If custody is contested, a judge will have to decide what is in the best interest of the child. While the statutes and case law vary, in general, here are some of the main considerations the judge will consider:

- The moral fitness of each parent insofar as it affects the child's welfare
- Who has been the primary caretaker
- The past relationship of the child with each parent
- The ability of each parent to provide continuing care for the child
- The stability of the home environment
- The mental and physical health of each parent
- The preference of the child, if the child is old enough to make an informed choice
- The willingness of each parent to make possible a continuing relationship of the child with the parent who does not have custody

Judges can be funny animals. Each one will interpret the best interests of the child in his or her own way. Our advice is that if you see a custody contest on the horizon, get consulting advice from an attorney who has expertise in custody disputes. This could be the one you are currently using as your divorce attorney, if he or she has expertise in this area. Be prepared to present evidence that is admissible and persuasive in court. A great deal of effort should be put into the preparation of this part of your case. This will involve a lot of work on your part to identify witnesses who will support your position.

We know of a case where it looked as if the father had no chance even at joint custody. He had not been involved with the kids while the marriage was intact, but he was in therapy and made a great deal of progress on some personal issues. His attitude toward his kids had changed dramatically.

His wife had hired a psychologist (not her husband's therapist) to interpret some of the psychological tests he had taken as part of his therapy. The report was quite negative.

The father said, "I want to have access to my kids and will fight for them, even if it looks hopeless. I want to be able to say to them when they ask, 'I did all I could within the law to try to get custody, and the judge would not let me have you.'"

He asked his therapist about the report and she said that the report was slanted against him. Several of the test areas were interpreted as negative where they could have been neutral or favorable to the father. The father discussed it with his lawyer, who, fortunately, understood the complexities of the use of psychological testing in child custody cases.

The lawyer then hired another psychologist to prepare a report. This time, some of the results were quite favorable to the father. In addition, the report pointed out the biases and weaknesses of the wife's report. To make a long story short, thanks to the tenacity of the father and the second report, joint custody was agreed on.

Others can help you by testifying firsthand about your parenting efforts. They could be your children's pediatrician, teachers, and baby-sitters, as well as neighbors and friends. Of course, your own testimony will be critical. Although your testimony may cover the most basic aspects of your daily life, you must remember that the judge must be given a complete picture of your life with your child.

For example, you probably will answer such questions as:

• Do you make breakfast for them every morning?
• Do you prepare or pack their lunches?
• Do you make dinner for them and eat it with them?

- Are you home when they return from school?
- Do you help with their homework?
- Do you take them to and from after-school activities?
- Do you bathe the younger children and put them to bed every night?

Children do well in a stable environment. You must show that you offer one and you must do whatever you can to strengthen your role in their day-to-day lives—everything from joining club activities at school in which they are involved to supervising extracurricular activities such as music lessons or soccer practice.

If you really want custody of the kids and haven't yet been a major factor in their upbringing, either in leisure or daily care, consider letting your spouse have temporary custody on a casual basis (i.e., not in writing or legally binding). Let your spouse realize the extent of activity that is involved in the day-to-day caring of the kids. Raising children is hard work. Your spouse may decide that it wasn't what it was thought to be. Don't make child care or household routines appear to be easy. They are not.

Custody Disputes and Child Snatching

One of the most complex areas of conflict in our mobile society is the subject of how conflicts are resolved between different state courts over the custody of children. In theory, all states are required under the U.S. Constitution to give full faith and credit to the valid judgments of other states. This is not true in custody disputes. Each state has jurisdiction over the children that reside within it. Not only are we a litigious society, we are definitely a mobile one. As families move from one state to another, circumstances change. That means that a custody judgment can be modified.

In an attempt to avoid these conflicts, all 50 states have now adopted the Uniform Child Custody Jurisdiction Act, which is designed primarily to discourage child snatching and to keep parents from moving from state to state to seek favorable custodial decisions or to avoid the orders of a prior home state. The act gives rules to determine which state has jurisdiction to decide a custody dispute. In addition, it has rules for the transfer between state courts of witnesses, social-service investigative reports, and other evidence. Most laws are complex. This one is no exception. You should always discuss any plans or questions you might have with your attorney.

Child snatching has become a national problem. When child snatching occurs, the police and other law enforcement agencies are usually reluctant to get involved. If there is a possibility of this, you need advice from an attorney on what your legal recourse will be. If your ex leaves with the kids, it is critical for you to act immediately. The longer your kids are gone, the more difficult it is to trace their physical whereabouts.

The Parental Kidnapping Prevention Act became effective in 1981. It requires all state courts to follow the jurisdictional standards of the Uniform Child Custody Jurisdiction Act. It also makes available a parent locator service to track down kidnapping parents and gives the Justice Department the power to assist in the apprehension of parents if they violate state felony laws in removing a child to another state.

Advice for the Custodial Parent

When support money is constantly late or doesn't appear, don't threaten or stop your ex from seeing the kids. Not only could you foul up your custody status if your spouse takes you back to court but you will put incredible pressure on your children. Unless the noncustodial parent is a raving lunatic and your kids' lives are threatened by being around him or her, they need contact both in person, on the telephone, and in writing. Don't think up reasons why your children can't see their other parent; that stomachache they complain about could be a result of the divorce action. Knowing that their parents are out there is an important security blanket. Be home when the children are to be returned.

Advice for the Noncustodial Parent

Call ahead if you would like to make an unscheduled visit. It makes sense to give fair warning; after all, your kids could have plans with friends or a special event already in the works. Don't keep them out too late and don't bring them back too early without clearing it with your ex. If, for whatever reason, you have to cancel a stay for a night, a weekend, a week, a month, or whatever, tell the truth. The last thing you should do is schedule time with them, then flake out. Remember the little boy in the movie *Liar Liar*—his only wish was for his dad to tell the truth and show up when he said he would.

> • • • • •
>
> It is critical at all times to let your kids know that they can rely on you.
>
> • • • • •

One of the worst things you can do is cancel at the last minute. If it becomes a habit, your kids' faith in you will drop to zip.

Savvy Words for Both Parents

Don't use your kids as aides to carry messages that their parents should be relating directly to each other. Don't probe and query your kids about what the other parent is doing, with whom, when, or why. Don't knock your ex, no matter how tempting it is. We know that this is one of the most difficult things you will ever do, but this person is your child's other parent. There has got to be something positive you can say. Be flexible. As your kids grow older, they are going to have different needs and different plans. At some time they are going to need and want to spend more time with the other parent. It is okay.

Grandparents Count, Too

Everyone loses something in a divorce, including the grandparents. Do yourself and your children a huge favor and keep communications open with all sets of grandparents. It's a special relationship and bond that is sometimes impossible to describe in words.

Some couples actually spell out some type of inclusion for either set of grandparents in their parental agreements. We think it's appropriate for you to let them know in the beginning that they are important to your kids and that you will not do anything to throw a wedge into their relationship. Tell them that you and your spouse are working hard to keep all channels open with the kids and that neither of you want to get into the "playing favorites" games that can happen in a divorce.

Make a verbal deal with them. You want to be on your kids' side. Even though you are divorcing their son or daughter, you are not divorcing them. Ask them to make a commitment with you that neither will say negative things. Encourage them to call the kids often and set up times when they can visit. Few of them want to be excluded from you or your children permanently. Keep the doors open; rarely will you regret it.

How Much?

All states now have child support guidelines that help the courts decide the amount of child support to be paid. The support obligation of each parent is often based on the ratio of each parent's income, the percentage of time the child spends with each parent, and the amount of alimony paid to the custodial parent.

To see what you might be paying in child support (or receiving), let's consider the example of Paul and Becky. They have two kids. Their joint gross income is $5,200 a month. Paul's is $4,300, Becky's $900 a month.

> Every parent is obligated to support his or her children, regardless of divorce. In a divorce situation, the noncustodial parent is usually ordered to pay some child support to the custodial parent. The remainder of the children's expenses are paid by the custodial parent.

Paul	$4,300	83%
Becky	900	17%
	$5,200	100%

Paul is earning 83 percent of the total and Becky is earning 17 percent. In their state, the child support guidelines for spouses with a gross income of $5,200 and two children is $983. According to the state guidelines, if Paul pays no alimony, he will be obligated to pay Becky $813 in monthly child support—83 percent of the suggested monthly payment of $983.

What if he pays alimony of $1,000 per month? At this point, you sharpen your pencil. Subtract the $1,000 from his income and add it to hers.

Paul	$4,300 − $1,000 =	$3,300	63%
Becky	900 + 1,000 =	$1,900	37%
	$5,200	$5,200	100%

The totals stay the same; the percentages change. Now, Paul's percentage is 63 percent of the total gross monthly income. Using the same Guidelines formula, multiply $983 by 63 percent. Paul's child support is reduced to $624 per month.

Paul and Becky present a very simplistic example. Other factors may enter in—for example, who pays for child care, health insurance, or education or school

> The rule of thumb is that as alimony increases, child support decreases.

expenses? If it's Paul, then it would be necessary to adjust the amount of child support he pays. In other cases, if custody is split, then the numbers get altered quite a bit.

The bottom line is that the guidelines are only *guidelines*. The key factors for you will be dependent on your personal and financial situation. It is not unusual for the amount of child support paid to be less than the actual amount realistically required to meet the needs of growing children. Many times the child support is not paid at all.

The payer of child support may harbor suspicion or anger against the custodial parent. He or she may think that the custodial parent is spending the money on himself or herself—not on the kids.

Be real. Child support is based on income. Obviously, it is based on some kind of lifestyle that was already established—when both parents were under the same roof. In an ideal world (we know ideal is a myth in most cases), the payer should think, "I want my kids to live in this kind of a house. I have to pay enough support that will make that kind of house payment possible. That means my ex is going to be there, too."

It's not unusual for the payer to be a tad ticked off when he or she has to pay child support and alimony. Or, if no alimony is due, there's a suspicion that the ex is living off the child support. If you are going to be the payer of child support or alimony, accept the common-sense fact that your ex is under the same roof as the kids.

Modifying Child Support

What happens when circumstances change after the divorce is final—say, one spouse loses his or her job; one becomes disabled; a settlement or judgment is awarded that was started when still married; or one of them wins the lottery?

Child support is usually modified for a substantial change of circumstances. How much of a change constitutes a "substantial" change in circumstance? Obviously, if the income changes, it would change the child support according to the child support guidelines.

Let's assume there are two children and child support is agreed upon. At some point, the older child decides to go live

Your property settlement is final and you usually cannot change anything about the property settlement unless you can prove fraud. Child support is different—it can be modified.

with Dad in the summertime. Since Dad is paying the full cost of supporting this child at his house (at least for several months), Dad thinks, "Now, I only have to pay half the child support," and he sends a check for half the amount. Because it was not changed by a court order, he still owes the whole amount and the ex-wife could force him to pay that back child support he did not pay.

Or, suppose that both kids go to live with Dad during the summer. He thinks, "I don't have to pay any child support during the summer, since both kids are living with me." Right? Wrong. The court order says that he must pay so much every month. It does not say "nine months out of the year." Unless the court order specifies nonpayments during certain months, he is liable for those payments, and his ex-wife could sue him for that money.

> • • • • •
> It is important to have all agreements in writing as circumstances change.
> • • • • •

Income Tax Considerations

Child support payments aren't deductible—ever. They are never included in the recipient's taxable income.

If there is only one child, he can be counted as an exemption by only one parent in a given year. Unless otherwise specified, the exemption usually goes to the parent who has physical custody of the child for the greater portion of the calendar year.

The exemption can be traded back and forth year to year between parents with a written waiver or IRS Form 8332. Once the custodial parent has executed the waiver, the noncustodial parent must attach the form to his or her income tax return. If the waiver is for more than one year, it must be attached each year.

With two or more children, the parents can divide up the exemptions, if they agree. The children's Social Security numbers must be listed on each parent's tax return.

For either parent to claim the exemption, the child must be in the custody of at least one parent for more than one-half of the calendar year. If the child lives with a grandparent or someone other than a parent for more than one-half of the calendar year, neither parent can claim the exemption.

> • • • • •
> Caution: Divorced parents who claim the same children on their tax returns are inviting an IRS audit.
> • • • • •

Child Care Credits

A custodial parent who pays child care expenses so that he or she can be gainfully employed may be eligible for a tax credit. To claim this credit, the parent must maintain a household that is the home of at least one child, and the day care expenses must be paid to someone who is not claimed as a dependent. Caution here. Our tax laws changing, and so is the amount allocated for child care. Make sure you check with your accountant or financial adviser as to what is currently allowed.

Only the custodial parent is entitled to claim both the child and the dependent care credit. This is true even if the custodial parent does not claim the dependency exemption for the child. A noncustodial parent may not claim a child care credit for expenses incurred even if that parent is entitled to claim the exemption for the child.

Here's an example. Carl and Mandy's son Bret, age 4, lives with Mandy four days a week and with Carl three days a week. Both Carl and Mandy work outside the home and each pays one-half of the $5,000 per year that it costs to have Bret in day care during the work week. Mandy gets to claim a child care credit for her share of the day care expenses. Although Carl and Mandy each have custody of Bret for a significant portion of the week, Mandy is considered the custodial parent because Bret spends a greater percentage of time with her than he does with Carl.

Head of Household

A head-of-household filing status is available to anyone divorced (single), who provides more than one-half the cost of maintaining the household, and who provides the primary home of at least one qualifying person for more than one-half of the year. A "qualifying person" is the taxpayer's child or any other person who qualifies as a dependent.

In determining whether the home is the principal home of the child for more than one-half of the year, do not count absences for vacation, sickness, school, or military service as time spent away from home if it is reasonable to assume that the child will return to the home.

Your kids are with you the rest of your life. What you do and say predivorce, during the divorce, and postdivorce will go with you to your grave—and theirs. You have a choice about which behavior guides you.

13 Thoughts from the Custodial Trenches
· · · · ·

1. If you are the mom, and you don't have physical custody of your kids, people will always think the worse. Don't let their misconceived attitudes affect you.

2. Kids are masters at playing parents off against each other. Create an alliance with your ex that delivers the message that although you are no longer married, you are still parents.

3. Joint custody doesn't always work. When it does, it's great. When it doesn't, parents ending up prolonging the war.

4. Create a parenting agreement that includes tradeoffs for holidays, vacations, illnesses, celebrations, religious instruction, discipline, financing for extra events, participation in school activities, and how disputes will be solved.

5. If custody is an ongoing issue, make sure your attorney has expertise in child custody cases.

6. Single parents are mother and father to their kids.

7. Be prepared to buy duplicates. Carrying toys, clothes, even toothbrushes back and forth gets old fast.

8. If you are not the parent with primary custody, it doesn't mean that you have lost your kids. Make sure you set up regular times to get together, have fun, and be silly with them. And always show up when you say you will. Only death and dismemberment are valid excuses.

(continued)

9. Joint custody works when both parents are equally committed to their kids.

10. Kids take time—lots of it.

11. Play "what-if" with your ex—before he or she officially *is* your ex. Look at situations that involve job relocation, more time commitments at work, even a significant other. How will you and your ex respond to changing circumstances?

12. Don't create a custody fight if your intent is to hurt your spouse and get even.

13. Don't forget to keep in touch with grandparents—on both sides. You and your kids need their love and support.

• • • • •

17

When It Still Isn't Working

The case is over, you are getting on with your life, and then it happens. Your ex is trying to weasel out of obeying a provision that you thought was crystal clear. It could be that your ex is just trying to make trouble for you and wear you down by testing your resolve, or it could be that there is a genuine ambiguity in the terms of the order or agreement. Let's look at each possibility.

Honest Differences

Sometimes nobody anticipated a circumstance that has come to pass, and the order or agreement is silent on that issue. Or it could be that there was a mistake and a key provision was left out. Finally, it could be that your ex is honestly confused about a provision that you thought was clear. You two could work out the problems with some informal solution. But understand that this will not be binding if there is a disagreement in the future. As much as you will not like to hear this, we suggest that you have a lawyer spell out the terms in a document that can be filed with the court so that there will not be a repeat later on.

But what if there is no good faith dispute? It could be that your ex is still in a power struggle, can't accept defeat, and is fighting over what has already been lost. (In one of our military cases, the wife of a general told Ed Schilling that she thought that he was the first person to ever tell her husband "no"—including his parents.)

Your ex may be pushing you to see how you will react if the child support payment is late, or what you will do, if anything, if child visitation is withheld or made very difficult. Your first step is to take a check of your emotional tank—is it empty or filling up? If you are running on fumes, then you need some support to see you through this.

We strongly urge you to see a lawyer about getting what you are entitled to. Our experience is that things will only get worse. Once your ex senses your weaknesses, you will be in for years of torment.

Sometimes your attempt to solve the matter yourself will only get you in trouble. This possibility arises in two common situations:

1. The parent who owes child support will stop payments because the custodial parent will not allow visitation.
2. The parent with custody withholds visitation if the other parent is not paying support.

You are not going to like the answer, but you need to know this anyway: You must continue to obey the existing court order. The right of visitation and the duty to pay support are completely separate issues. The court will enforce them independently. Some states have a statute that allows you to stop support if the custodial parent is willfully interfering with your visitation rights. Even with this statute, however, a court hearing must first be conducted to see if the visitation abuse is willful.

No matter how bad the situation is, do not put the children in the middle of your dispute. They already have enough stress in their young lives.

> • • • • •
> You cannot violate a court order to get back at the other parent who is violating an order.
> • • • • •

> • • • • •
> Do not pay support or discuss money in connection with picking up the children for visitation.
> • • • • •

Enforcement of Visitation or Child Support Clauses

As with the rest of your case, certain procedures must be followed to enforce visitation and support orders. You must file a petition for enforcement where your divorce decree was entered. If the custodial or support parent is living in another state, that state will also enforce your visitation or support order if you file a petition there.

If you are having trouble with the enforcement of child support orders, there are a variety of methods in addition to bringing an action in court to enforce the order.

The Uniform Reciprocal Enforcement Support Act

When the paying parent lives in another state, you can use the Uniform Reciprocal Enforcement Support Act (URESA), which is administered by your local district attorney. Since it is not a perfect world, there are pluses and minuses with this route. The big advantage of this method is that it is free to you (no lawyer's fee or court costs), and you don't have to go to the other state. Two big disadvantages are that child support is all you can ask for, and a new support order might be entered that may be less favorable than the one you have now.

If you have any questions, talk this over with someone at the agency. In our experience, these offices are often overworked and understaffed, and there different levels of skill of those on the staff of these offices.

Garnishment

Enforcement of orders for child support and alimony can be made through a process commonly referred to as a *garnishment*. This legal action is also called such things as a *wage assignment, income withholding order,* or *income deduction order.* This is an order that is directed to the employer of the paying parent requiring the employer to divert a portion of the employee's salary to the one due the payment. This is a common process and should be understood by any attorney who does even a few divorce cases.

> • • • • •
> Even the salary or retirement of a federal employee or retiree can be easily garnished.
> • • • • •

Many attorneys are surprised to learn that the salary or retirement of a federal employee or retiree can be easily garnished for alimony or child support. Also, attorney fees and court costs can be added to the amount taken out of the pay. If your attorney is not familiar with this process and has access to the Internet, have him or her log onto *www.qdro.net* and go to the Federal section of the site.

In some states, a garnishment order is done automatically as part of the initial court order process. In other states, the action is brought at a later time when there is a problem in missed or late payments. In the states where it is done automatically, the garnishment automatically goes into effect if the supporting parent falls behind for a certain number of days. After that, the current support and arrearages are automatically deducted until back payments are made up or there is a court order stopping the action.

Friend of the Court

Many states now provide for support enforcement at no charge through an office sometimes called the *friend of the court*. In these programs, the payments are sent directly to the court clerk, who records the payments and then sends them on to the recipient. The transactions are computerized and therefore it is easier to track arrearages and late payments.

In jurisdictions that have this setup, it is customary for the attorney representing the spouse who is to be paid to ask for a court order requiring payments through the clerk's office. And sometimes, this method is better for the paying spouse because there will be a good history of compliance with the court order. Using this system means that the receiving spouse will not be able to claim that the check was late or did not get there at all.

You may also be interested to know that nonsupport actions can also be brought in your local criminal court. You will have to weigh the likelihood of recovery through collection action alone before you decide to start a criminal prosecution. In addition, many states have laws that track deadbeat parents and keep them from getting such things as driver's or professional licenses and seize tax refund checks.

Taking Your Kids Out of State

As mentioned in Chapter 16, a common issue that arises in this mobile society is what happens if the parent with custody wants to leave (or, in cases such as the military, must leave) the state where the divorce took place and the noncustodial parent lives.

> • • • • •
> Check with your attorney before planning to move out of state.
> • • • • •

As always, the best result comes if this has been anticipated and provided for in a parenting agreement.

What if you did not deal with this in your agreement? If you are not permitted to leave the state under the terms of your parenting plan, agreement or court order, you must ask the court for permission or obtain the consent of your ex. If your ex agrees, have this in writing to avoid any confusion later on. Of course, new visitation arrangements must be made and support payments may also be adjusted in light of such things as the additional expense of transporting the kids for visitation.

If you have to go to court, the judge will look at the circumstances surrounding your desire to leave. The court will look more favorably on your request if it is because of such reasons as military orders, remarriage, employment opportunity, or a health condition. The court can find that it can be considered in the best interests of the child.

Does the court deny a request to leave the state? Sure, if the purpose of leaving is to keep the other parent from visiting or some other reason not in the child's interest. But the fact that the opportunity for visitation will be reduced is usually not a sufficient reason to deny the request.

Leaving without Permission

If there was no agreement about leaving the state with the kids and you find out that your ex has done so, or is thinking about leaving, see your attorney immediately.

If your kids have already been removed from the state, your attorney will file a petition in the court where the last custody order was entered. It will ask that the kids be returned and that a contempt citation be issued against the parent who removed them.

> • • • • •
> A delay in objecting to taking the children out of state may be looked at as consent.
> • • • • •

Time is of the essence when this happens. Any delay in objecting to your children being moved out of state might be seen as your approval of the removal. Also, if you delay in taking action, the parent with the kids may have time to set up a new home, making it more difficult to convince the court that they should be uprooted and brought back. You should know that a court will not automatically make your ex move back just because you did not give your consent. As always, the court will consider what is in the best interests of the kids.

Enforcing Orders to Bring the Children Back

This can really get messy, and you need a lawyer who knows the ins and outs of a law known as UCCJA, the Uniform Child Custody Jurisdiction Act. The UCCJA is a sort of universal law passed in each state that tells how disputes between state courts will be resolved. But it is not as simple as you might think. That's why you need a lawyer knowledgeable in child custody matters. Not all divorce lawyers understand this act, so ask probing questions or ask for a referral. This may be a good opportunity to try out your Internet skills in looking for a UCCJA attorney in your area.

In general terms, if the children are not promptly returned when you have a court order, and you are unable to go to where they are living and bring them back, you will file a petition for contempt of court. Your ex has *snatched* the kids and is subject to fine or imprisonment for a willful violation of the custody judgment. If your ex ignores this order, then you will have to go to the state where the children are and file an action.

This is where the UCCJA comes into play, especially if your ex has obtained an order in the new state permitting custody there. The law has rules to tell which state should properly have jurisdiction to decide a custody dispute and the transfer of evidence between state courts. In general, the rule is this: Where one state court has entered a final custody order, that state court retains jurisdiction over the children unless it transfers jurisdiction to the other court. But, again, have a knowledgeable attorney advise you on how the law applies in your case.

The 1981 federal Parental Kidnapping Prevention Act says that *all state courts* must follow the rules of the UCCJA. It also makes available a parent locator service to track down parents who have kidnapped their kids and requires the U.S. Justice Department to help in arresting the kidnapper.

13 Things to Know about Enforcing Orders

• • • • •

1. Be nice to your lawyer as you say goodbye. You may need one later on.

(continued)

2. The better drafted an order, the easier it will be to enforce if something goes wrong.

3. Check and double-check your agreement so that nothing important is left out.

4. You do not have the right to stop court-ordered child support because visitation is denied. Go back to court.

5. You do not have the right to stop court-ordered visitation if child support is cut off. Go back to court.

6. Amazingly, you do not have the right to stop child support if the children come to live with you. Go back to court.

7. If you are not getting what you are entitled to, see your lawyer immediately. Problems usually get worse the longer you wait.

8. Do not discuss enforcement problems in the presence of the children.

9. Paying child support to the registry of the court can protect the paying parent from allegations of missed payments.

10. If you are not receiving court-ordered child support, the district attorney's office may be able to help. Ask for the child support enforcement office.

11. Usually, a court can order that payments of child support or alimony be made directly from a person's salary.

12. See your attorney immediately if your ex is taking the children out of state and the agreement or order is silent on that issue or says the children cannot be taken out of state.

13. If your children are removed from your state without authority, find a lawyer who understands the Uniform Child Custody Jurisdiction Act.

• • • • •

18

Details, Details, Details
Are You Sure You Are Divorced?

So, you have had your day in court, and it's all over. Right? Not so fast. The fat lady has not sung yet, but she is waiting backstage for her cue. You may be wondering why she isn't on stage yet. This thing has gone on for too many months—why can't everyone get their acts together?

Once a divorce decree has been signed by the court, two major questions remain:

1. When does your marriage actually end? This can vary somewhat from state to state. In some states, the marriage is ended when the judge signs the decree. In other states, a certain period of time must pass before the marriage is ended. And in others, it may be ended when the judge rules in court, even before an order has been signed. It can all be confusing, so make sure your lawyer tells you exactly when the marriage is dissolved.

2. How and when will property be transferred? Your decree or agreement may require that certain personal property, such as furniture or jewelry, be physically transferred to the party to whom it has been awarded. And in the case of other assets, not only must the physical transfer take place, but the paperwork to transfer the title must also be accomplished.

> • • • • •
> Make sure you know when you are *legally* divorced.
> • • • • •

Complicated Property Transfers

Some property requires paperwork to complete the transfer:

Real Estate

The agreement or order may require that the title of real estate be changed to one party individually. In this case, a deed and other documents such as an appraisal or new title insurance may be needed. You may encounter a document called a quit-claim deed. This is a type of deed in which the person who transfers an interest does not guarantee that he has title. In essence, the deed says, "If I have any interest in this property, and I'm not saying I do, I transfer it to you." Discuss with your lawyer if this will be enough in your case. If rental property is involved, a new lease or insurance may also be necessary.

Vehicles

Titles for automobiles, boats, airplanes, or motorcycles may need to be changed. And don't forget to arrange for the transfer of insurance, which may mean finding a new company.

Insurance

For life insurance, it may be necessary to change a beneficiary, and new insurance may be part of the deal. Health insurance coverage may be critical as well. For example, if the nonemployed spouse was covered under the employed spouse's policy, steps must be taken with the employer to arrange for continued coverage after the divorce. Check this one carefully, because there may be strict time limits for the transfer.

> • • • • •
>
> If new policies are to be established or beneficiaries changed, then require written proof that this has been done.
>
> • • • • •

As we said earlier, if you are to be the beneficiary of a life insurance policy, it is far better for you to own the policy and pay the premiums than for the other party to do so and promise not to change the policy. An insurance company will not take on the burden of notifying you if there is a change from what the court ordered, so you could end up with no coverage and not know about it if the change was made since your last inquiry to the company.

> • • • • •
>
> Continued health care after the divorce for the nonemployee spouse is probably available, but strict time limits for conversion may apply.
>
> • • • • •

Stocks, Bonds, Mutual Funds, Bank Accounts, and Certificates of Deposit

A change of ownership of these accounts and money instruments may be necessary, or, at a minimum, the method of ownership and beneficiary designations need to be changed. For some cash instruments, such as so-called bearer bonds, it is only necessary to physically transfer possession. For savings bonds, other paperwork may be required.

Business

If there is to be a transfer of an interest in a business, certain formalities will be required, depending on the form of the business. If the business is a corporation and stock is owned, a transfer from one spouse to the other may be needed, or from both to one. If one spouse is an officer of the corporation, there will have to be a formal withdrawal from that office, and notices to the secretary of state of the state in which the business is incorporated. And if the business is operating under a trade name, notices also may be required to the secretary of state.

Debts

Creditors should be notified of new billing addresses, and new payment coupons might be needed. This is a great time to establish new lines of credit. You should destroy old credit cards and close all joint accounts if you have not already done so. Notify creditors who gave you joint credit that you are no longer married to that person and no longer responsible for his or her debts. And don't forget to notify the utility companies.

Wills

You will probably need to completely rewrite or significantly modify your existing will. At the least, review your will with an experienced estate attorney.

Also, ask an estate planning attorney about a living trust. A living trust retitles your assets and speeds up the process of transferring them to your heirs when you die. If you have access to the Internet, check out these Web sites. They offer information about wills and trusts, but reader beware: Their goal is to sell you something. Before you do anything that costs you money, consult your attorney.

- www.aias.com/romar.htm
- www.cyberstation.net/paralegal/ trust.htm
- www.willworks.com/samples.htm

> • • • • •
> If you do not have a will, get one now, even if you have no material assets. If you have assets, get advice from an estate planning attorney on living trusts now.
> • • • • •

Promissory Notes

Because of the terms of the agreement or order, one party may be required to execute a promissory note. For example, this may be needed if the court ordered one party to pay the other party a certain amount of money and the debtor party does not have that much cash on hand. We suggest that you either have notes collateralized (in case of a bankruptcy), backed by an insurance policy (in case of death), or both.

Trusts

You may need to change beneficiaries or terms of payment and management. A new trust may be needed to comply with terms of the agreement or order.

Income Taxes

At a minimum you need to clarify your filing status for your next tax return. There may also be a refund to deal with, and your agreement or order should say who it belongs to. And if your spouse was to cover you in case of a tax bill in the future, make sure the proper document has been prepared to protect you.

Retirement Accounts

Ideally, the retirement division order was prepared for signing at the time of the divorce. But if it was not, don't delay on this—the results of procrastination can be devastating. To reiterate, if no proper order is in place and the employee dies, the nonemployee spouse will end up with *nothing* from the retirement plan—and the retirement may have been the most valuable asset of the marriage. A particularly terrible result can take place if the employee remarries and then dies before an order is in place. In this case, the new spouse will receive all of the survivor benefits.

Social Security

If you were married for at least ten years and were the lower-earning spouse, you may be able to collect up to half of your spouse's benefits. It will not reduce your spouse's benefits. If you get remarried, are married for at least ten years, and get divorced from the second spouse, you can choose the benefit between ex-spouse #1, ex-spouse #2, or your own, whichever is higher. Again, it will not diminish their benefit.

The average length of marriage that ends in divorce is 9.6 years! Protect yourself. If you are considering signing those final papers after nine and a half years of marriage, you may want to hang in there another six months!

Tying Up Loose Ends

Taxes

What taxes may result from all of these transfers? The general rule is that the increased value of property transferred between spouses as part of a divorce is not taxable at the time of the transfer. The tax issue will arise when the property is later sold or transferred. (See the discussion in Chapter 12.)

The transfer of retirement accounts from one type of a retirement account into another is one of the exceptions. No taxes are due. Life guarantees us arthritis, death—and taxes. Tax laws change almost as often as the wind.

> • • • • •
> Seek the advice of a knowledgeable tax expert before you begin to transfer assets from one name to the other.
> • • • • •

Changing Your Name

A name change back to the woman's maiden name can be a part of the decree. (It can also be done later, but at more expense.) Some mothers prefer not to change their name so that the children will not have to explain a different name. Some keep their married name because they are professionally known by it, and some prefer it over their original maiden name. We have one friend who decided she didn't like any of the options, so she created her own chosen last name.

Back in Court Again? Ouch!

The court that dissolves the marriage will keep jurisdiction over the parties (that's you and your ex) and any children so that any orders or judgments can be enforced. Child support is the most common example of an order that is violated. If the required payments have not been made, then there are a number of methods that can be used to force the payments: garnishment of pay, seizing bank accounts or property, and imprisonment. We know of newspapers that publish a "most wanted" deadbeat parents list, including photos of parents who don't pay child support. (For more details, see Chapter 17.)

To Prenup or Not to Prenup

You may be wondering why we've included anything about agreements for another marriage. The simple fact is lots of people remarry and bring children to the new family unit. We've included several scenarios where a prenuptial agreement should be considered:

- *Two young people, with equal assets*—Young people in the early stages of promising careers, where each has some assets and wants to protect these, as well as their careers, as separate property
- *Two young people, with unequal assets*—People of middle age or younger, where one already has, or will probably acquire, substantial assets, and this one wants to protect these assets as separate property, while reasonably providing for the needs of the marriage, as well as the spouse and any children if there is a divorce

- *One young, one much older, with unequal assets*—A couple with large differences in age and wealth, where the older party has substantial wealth which he or she wants to preserve for his or her estate, and also wants to provide for disability or incapacity
- *Two older with unequal assets*—An elderly couple, where one party has substantially fewer assets than the other, and where both want to protect their separate property, provide for a comfortable lifestyle during the marriage, and reasonably provide for the spouse with fewer assets upon death or divorce
- *Two older, with equal assets*—For older parties with like assets who want to protect their property as separate, yet provide an arrangement by which they can live in line with their wealth.

13 Questions to Ask before You Leave Your Lawyer

• • • • •

1. When is the decree effective?

2. When will I get a copy of it?

3. If support payments are ordered, what is due and when? (And whether you are the one making payments or the one receiving them, set up a system for tracking payments.)

4. What documents will I receive showing that property transfers have been made?

5. Who is responsible for preparing and filing each document?

6. What am I required to do under the order?

7. What am I entitled to receive under the order?

8. How much do I owe? Will there be additional costs?

9. When can I pick up my personal property? or, When will it be delivered?

10. What should I do if the order is not followed? Will you still be available to help me?

11. Who will pay your fees if I have to sue for enforcement of the order?

12. Can you look at my will and tell me what I should do now, or can you refer me to someone who can?

13. Are there any limits on where I can take the children?

• • • • •

13 Topics for a Prenuptial Agreement*

• • • • •

1. How income will be used from the separate property of each spouse

2. How joint property will be acquired and used

3. Premarital and postmarital ownership by one party

4. How pensions will be paid out if one of the parties dies

5. What to do if one party becomes incapacitated or disabled

(continued)

6. Intentions of having children

7. Rearing of children from a prior marriage

8. Financial responsibilities toward parents

9. Responsibilities for debts acquired before and during the marriage

10. Filing status for income tax returns

11. Provisions in wills and trusts

12. Spousal support if there is a divorce

13. Property division if there is a divorce

*Exact contents will depend on circumstances of the parties.

• • • • •

19

The Divorce Ceremony
Acknowledging a New Beginning

If you and your ex are speaking, are reasonably pleasant to each other, have friends who are both mutual and exclusively your own, and want to move on with your lives and be amicable with each other, we propose that you have an "ending ceremony" or "divorce ceremony."

San Francisco Bay Area corporate consultant and therapist Jean Hollands, M.S., has performed hundreds of ending ceremonies. Her "divorce ceremony" was based on a ritual created by Robert E. Elliot, a professor at the Perkins School of Theology at Southern Methodist University in Dallas. She has generously agreed to share it with our readers. We have made some modifications to her original. Before you proceed, we would like to make a few suggestions:

- Divorcing couples who want to use the divorce ceremony should have had some type of couples' therapy.
- Timing is vital. Hollands has found that preparation for the ceremony is, in itself, therapeutic. It is not unusual for one member of a couple to be more reluctant to separate and divorce than the other.
- Use this divorce ceremony as a model—create the words and phrasing that fit your own situation.
- The couple can invite family members, close friends, parents, kids (from the marriage as well as stepchildren), and any friends who can assist in the good-bye. *Under no circumstances should new relationship partners of the couple be included.*

213

- Some couples prefer not to have family and friends with them. They may choose their therapist or clergy or to go it alone.
- If you have family and friends join you and the room in which you are conducting the ceremony allows it, have them encircle you and the therapist or clergy member who conducts the ceremony.
- The writing of the ceremony can be therapeutic by itself, even if you don't perform it. Some couples just read what they have written; some may merely substitute their names. They feel that it's beneficial for the emotional closing out of their marriage. You will note there is a reference to being released from the bonds of marriage. This is not a legal release in any matter, just emotional. Its purpose is to create closure.
- The ceremony is never intended to deepen the pain of the separating couple or family. It is designed to provide for time to openly express any repressed grief. If grief isn't acknowledged, then it can continue as a burden for untold years to come.
- If you want someone to lead the ceremony, it should be someone with whom you both are comfortable—a therapist, clergy member, or a close friend.
- What you do after the ceremony is your choice. Some couples go their separate ways, some leave with their friends, parents, or kids, some even go out to eat together.

The Divorce Ceremony

Therapist. We are gathered here to acknowledge the divorce of Susan and Michael. This is both a time of grief and a time of joy.

We grieve for the union of Susan and Michael and the good intentions that brought them together for these years. We also celebrate that Susan and Michael will continue to honor each other and that they have encouraged each other in the new paths each of them select.

We look back upon their marriage with thanks for what they have given to each other and with sadness for the difficult journey which brings their marriage to this closing.

Susan and Michael, we are here today to accept the decision that your marriage is ending. It is fitting, therefore, to stand before family, friends, and each other and declare to each other your release from your vows of marriage.

Susan. *Michael, I do release you as my husband.* I cannot be your wife any longer, but I do wish to be your friend. I thank you for the positive aspects of our life together. I would like to ask your forgiveness and offer you mine for the hurts we have done each other. Your path in life will always have meaning for me. I hope that your life will be filled with the joy and abundance that you deserve.

Michael. *Susan, I do release you as my wife.* I cannot be your husband any longer, but I do wish to be your friend. I thank you for the positive aspects of our life together. I would like to ask your forgiveness and offer you mine for the hurts we have done each other. Your path in life will always have meaning for me. I hope that your life will be filled with the joy and abundance that you deserve.

Therapist. I witness that you are released from your bonds of marriage and are no longer husband and wife. You are set free to face new futures as separate persons.

Carry no burdens of guilt or recrimination for what is past. It is past. *Accept grief as it may come,* but release the past into the past and receive the future as *a gift of new potentials and possibilities.*

[If there are children from the marriage or stepchildren, add] Though Michael and Susan are no longer husband and wife, they do remain father and mother. What began as a union of two people, Michael and Susan, became a family, as Jessica, Charissa, and Luke came into the lives of Michael and Susan. As the life Michael and Susan made together now comes to a close, important relationships remain: their children—Jessica, Charissa, and Luke.

Jessica, Charissa, and Luke, will you join us here?

It is appropriate that you are now standing here between your mother and father and that you will soon hear them speak to you and to each other.

Susan. Michael, I respect you and care about you as the father of our children. I will call upon you to continue to be the faithful father you have been. I trust you to love our children always, and to, with your finest ability, protect, guide, and care for Jessica, Charissa, and Luke as long as they shall need that from you.

Michael. Susan, I respect you and care about you as the mother of our children. I will call upon you to continue to be the faithful mother you have been. I trust you to love our children always, and to, with your finest ability, protect, guide, and care for Jessica, Charissa, and Luke as long as they shall need that from you.

Susan. I cherish you as my children, Jessica, Charissa, and Luke. I am thankful you are in my life. I pledge you my love always, and my protection and guidance and care as long as you need that from me.

Michael. I cherish you as my children, Jessica, Charissa, and Luke. I am thankful you are in my life. I pledge you my love always, and my protection and guidance and care as long as you need that from me.

Susan. We are sad for the pain that this divorce has caused you. You are not responsible for our decision to separate.

Michael. We ask you not to blame yourselves or worry about us. You are not the cause of our dissolution.

Susan. And we do not want you to blame yourselves for our inability to continue being married.

Susan. We both want you to be able to continue your lives, full of hope and abundance, even in the midst of your loss.

Michael. Yes, please forgive us when our problems seemed to shadow our parenting of you. We will look forward to peace for all of us now.

Susan. And to our friends, we give thanks for your faithful support.

Michael. Thank you all for your love. Please continue to care for us in the way you have.

Therapist. Some [or one] of your friends [or parents] have asked to represent the love and support from your friends with the following closing statement.

Parents. We pledge our love and support for each of you. Some of us will be more available perhaps to you, Susan, and others to you, Michael, but our hearts are full of compassion for the both of you.

We affirm our encouragement of you in your maintenance of the vows of parenthood, which you have reaffirmed here with us and to our grandchildren, Jessica, Charissa, and Luke today.

As your parents, we too *have been touched by the grief and pain that has come to you at the ending of your marriage.* However, we rejoice in you offering to include us and be friends with each other. To this end, we offer our loyalty, friendship, and love.

Friends. We pledge our love and support for each of you. Some of us will be more available perhaps to you, Susan, and others to you, Michael, but our hearts are full of compassion for the both of you.

We affirm our encouragement of you in your maintenance of the vows of parenthood which you have reaffirmed here with us and to your children, Jessica, Charissa, and Luke today.

We, too, *have been touched by the grief and pain that has come to you at the ending of your marriage.* However, we rejoice in you offering to include us and be friends with each other. To this end, we offer our loyalty, friendship, and love.

Therapist. Michael and Susan, your friendship may come in many stages. You may each feel denial, anger, grief, acceptance, and finally a letting go of each other and this closure.

Your maturity is an inspiration to all of us. Please call on any of us in times of need and discouragement. Your children will need all of your and our support as their home divides into two homes. Although it may be difficult for your friends and family to see you two on separate paths, we all wish you each and every happiness in your new and independent journeys. We are grateful for your courage. May that courage inspire us always.

20

Profiting after Your Divorce

Now that you know what you got or will get from the division of assets, you can start planning. This planning phase involves money—yours. You may have gotten a lump sum of money, you may receive it over a period of time, you may have to pay some out or you may (gulp!) have none, at least right now. If you are in the latter situation, with zip to your name, don't skip this chapter. It's as much for you as for someone with a deep pocket. In this chapter, we will discuss how to put together a viable financial plan.

You may be getting a check from one of the joint accounts representing your portion of the settlement. It may seem like a lot of money—a *huge* amount of money. You may be tempted to take that long-awaited vacation cruise, a reward for the stress and strain that you have been under. You may even think, "I might meet someone who *really* appreciates me!" Caution, caution, caution.

Take Sharon—she walked into Carol Ann's office and told this sad tale:

When I got divorced three years ago, I got a check for $356,000 in return for no alimony. I thought I had won the lottery—I had never seen so much money! Since then, I have traveled, bought jewelry and a new car, and have given money to friends. I had a great time. I didn't buy a house. I even took several friends to Europe with me. I've had a wonderful time but my money runs out next month—can you help me?

Sharon should have done some better planning at the beginning. She blew it. With just a little planning, Sharon could have been set for life—$356,000 is a lot of money, money that could have given her a nice trip or two, but better yet, it could have seeded multiple investments that would have created income and growth. A modern-day tragedy that is repeated way too often after the fallout of divorce. Your goal is not to clone Sharon's adventure.

Putting Together a Financial Plan

So what should be the first step in your postdivorce planning? Unless you are well-versed in the myriad choices available to you, start by talking to a financial planner, preferably a Certified Financial Planner. Look at our list of questions to ask a financial planner at the end of this chapter. This person can be your adviser and your guide. Your planner will help you put together a plan that will help you reach your financial goals.

Start by taking stock of your assets and liabilities. You've already done this in evaluating household properties, any investments that you might have, any cash in the bank or other types of accounts.

Then, ask yourself these questions:

- Do you need extra cash right now on a monthly basis to supplement your income?
- Do you need to use up some of your assets to pay off any debt?
- Do you want to buy a house, which will reposition liquid assets to an il-liquid asset? (By liquid assets, we mean you can get the money/cash within a few days; illiquid assets are the opposite—it could take months, even years to access the money.)
- Do you want to make that account grow as fast as possible to support your retirement?

If you told us that you wanted an extremely safe investment that creates extra income while growing fast, we would tell you to forget it. You are asking the impossible. You may be able to find a blend of two out of the three, but not all three.

The money triangle in Figure 20.1 represents three key areas of your money and investment strategies.

At the top of the triangle is *growth;* at the left, *income;* and at the right, *security.* (When we say *security,* we mean the amount of risk you are comfortable with to achieve the other two components.) The closer you move toward growth the further you move from income and security. If you were right in the middle of the triangle, you would have some income, some growth, and some security.

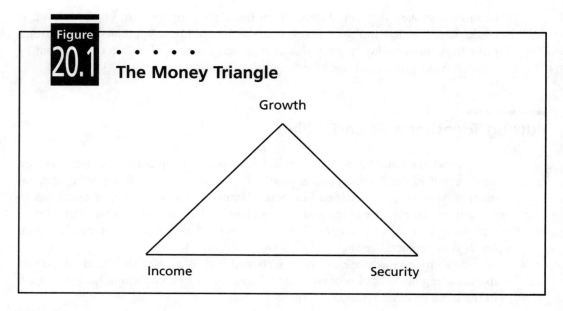

Figure 20.1

• • • • •

The Money Triangle

Growth

Income   Security

Security

Let's say that you are not willing to take risks with your money. When it comes to investing, you want your money to be safe. After all, you had an uncle who was wiped out during the Crash of '29. The only things that you would be willing to put your money in are checking accounts, savings accounts, certificates of deposit, money market funds, and Treasury bonds. Here are some ways to make these conservative vehicles work for you:

Checking accounts. Make sure your checking account pays interest. A non-interest-bearing checking account is the one place where there is a surprising amount of poorly used money. It's amazing how much money is left sitting in these accounts, not earning a penny in interest! Whatever funds you have, don't pooh-pooh interest on a few bucks. Every dime and dollar counts. Men rarely leave funds in noninterest-bearing accounts. If there is cash lying around doing very little, the odds are 95 percent that it will be a woman who is the owner of those funds.

Now, having money sitting around not doing anything is a problem that a lot of us would welcome quite happily. Let's be practical; there is no sense in throwing good money away. And to our way of thinking, this means money that is not earning any interest, even for a day.

Savings accounts and certificates of deposit. These two types of accounts have something in common. As the depositor, you have agreed to place your funds with these institutions for a specific period. And since they guarantee that you will get your money back with interest, the interest they offer you is much lower than what they charge someone for a loan. Oh, they pay more than a passbook savings account, but not a lot more. They then loan out your funds at a much higher rate. It can be anywhere from two to three percentage points above what you are currently receiving. Between loaning funds on deposit and credit card interest, the bulk of bank profits are made this way.

Money market funds. These are a good "parking place" for monies until you decide what you want to do with them. You can withdraw money from them like a checking account, but it typically will have certain restrictions such as only three withdrawals per month or a withdrawal must be for a minimum amount. It usually pays several percentage points higher than your typical passbook account.

Income

If you need your money to create extra cash each month, consider bonds or income mutual funds. (See the discussion on mutual funds later in this chapter.)

Bonds come in several flavors: *corporate, municipals,* and *Treasuries.* They promise you safety with interest. And, looking back at the money triangle, the safer the bond, the lower the interest. That means less income to you.

Are all bonds safe? Nope. There are some that promise to give your money back after so many years—but don't. Companies have problems and can't pay off their debts, just like people sometimes do.

You've heard a lot about stocks and bonds. There is a big difference between the two. Here's a simple way to compare them:

Bonds

- Principal is guaranteed (if it is still there).
- Rate of return is guaranteed (if funds are available).
- There will be no growth.
- You are loaning money to the company, a creditor.

Stocks

- Principal is not guaranteed.
- Rate of return is not guaranteed.
- Value will go up or down with the success of the company.
- You are an owner of the company, a shareholder.

Corporate bonds. These are usually rated from C to AAA. The higher the rating—AAA is the highest—the higher the level of safety, which is not a guarantee. There are bonds that are rated as "junk," meaning that their safety and ability to pay regular interest payments are in jeopardy. Usually, sticking with an A-rated or better bond will keep you in a margin of safety. If you absolutely need income and you are adamant about safety of your money, you may want to invest in bonds. Their return on investment has been disappointing over the years in comparison with what stocks have generated, but they can play a part in your having a balanced portfolio along with investments that feature growth.

Municipal bonds. These are federal tax–free and, if issued within your resident state, are also exempt from state taxes. They pay lower a interest rate than corporate bonds. The higher your tax bracket, the more valuable your return.

Treasury bonds. These are issued by and guaranteed by the U.S. government. Treasury bonds mature anywhere from ten years to 30 years, Treasury notes mature from one to ten years, and Treasury bills from 91 days to one year.

Bills, bonds, and notes are all conservative investments. The federal government's backing makes them fairly free of risk of default, but doesn't guarantee that they will not oscillate in price and market value. They will—not with the wide discounting range of other bonds, but with a slight variance depending on rates and maturity date. They are very liquid, are generally sold for modest fees, if any, and are free of state and local (but not federal) taxes.

What about Annuities?

Annuities are somewhat of a hybrid between security/income and growth investments. There are several types of annuities: *deferred, immediate,* and *variable.*

Deferred annuity. Owning a deferred annuity means that your money sits in a policy (created by an insurance company) accumulating interest over a period of time. Under current IRS rules, any increase in value, either from earnings, dividends, or interest will not be taxable until you withdraw funds at a later date. Then, you decide on how you want to receive your monies back: in a lump sum, monthly, annually, or some other option. It is also known as a TDA, a tax-deferred annuity.

Deferred annuities are fixed in their stated return. Their principal is guaranteed and you can get your money back within seven days.

Tax-sheltered annuity. This is purchased with pretax dollars. Participants include teachers, certain government employees, and those who work for tax-exempt organizations. They can place pretax dollars, up to a certain percentage of their income, on an annual basis. The net result is that their W-2s at the end of the year reflect a lesser amount for overall tax purposes.

Immediate annuity. This starts paying right away, possibly the month after you purchase it. This normally would be attractive to someone who is older and wants income now. Both the deferred and the immediate annuity are purchased with after-tax dollars. This means that not all of the revenue you receive with each payment will be taxable. A portion will be identified as a return of your original money that has already been taxed.

Variable annuity. This also is an insurance contract, but it differs from the fixed deferred annuity mentioned earlier. Neither the principal nor the rate of growth is guaranteed. It's similar to owning a mutual fund. Any taxes or gains are deferred until you withdraw them. The value will increase or decrease and is solely dependent upon the performance of the stock portfolio the insurance company is managing.

If you purchase a variable annuity, you are more of a risk-taker than the purchaser of a deferred annuity. Annuities enable you to build monies on a tax-deferred basis, and are often used in estate planning.

Growth

Investing your money for growth means that you are willing to leave the land of security and guarantees to look at higher risks with the hope of higher returns. Many products fit in this category. The most likely choices will be in *stocks* and *mutual funds.*

Stocks. Admittedly, the stock market can be a lucrative investment opportunity, but it can also be a bizarre circus, susceptible to daily whims and the emotions of participants. To invest and survive in the stock market, you must know and acknowledge both the risks and the remedies.

What is the market? Basically, it is a place where you can buy and sell ownership in a business. You are an owner, not a lender. Stock values change constantly. The price of a stock is determined by whatever someone else will pay for it. If a stock is listed on the New York Stock Exchange, or any of the other exchanges, prices will be negotiated on the floor of the exchange.

There are basically two types of stock: *growth* and *income*. A growth company pays little, if any, cash dividends. These companies tend to be newer or smaller and are likely to plow a large portion of earnings back into further growth opportunities, usually in research and development or expansion. Industries involving technology, communications, genetics, and health care offer classic examples.

Market prices of companies in these areas represent a substantial part of future prospects versus past performance. Stock value is expected to rise substantially over a period of time. The benefit to you is increased value, which is taxed at the time you elect to sell your shares.

Growth stocks are for growth, period. If you don't need cash income currently, but want to build a base where income can be generated at a later date, this becomes a viable option. On the other hand, if you need income now, high-yield income stocks and bonds become one of your options. Stocks that distribute a large portion of the profits to stockholders in the form of a cash dividend rarely offer much in growth possibility. There are, of course, exceptions.

Mutual funds. These investment options should be in every investor's portfolio. Even more, mutual funds can offer some significant benefits over individual stock purchases. A mutual fund is a pool of many companies. Some of the companies are similar, some invest in income type investments, some spread their money into multiple industries. The fund can be a stock fund with 75 to 100 different stocks in it that are bought and sold by the manager of the fund. Or it may be a bond fund with many different bonds in it. Or you could have a blend of stocks and bonds to create growth and income in the same fund.

There are more than 8,000 mutual funds today. It can be quite confusing in deciding which one(s) you should buy! Each fund has an objective that is stated clearly in its prospectus. It may be a group of high-tech companies for high growth. It may be a group of blue chip stocks for solid, steady, slower, less risky growth. It may be a group of Treasury bonds for income. Read carefully so that you understand what you buying.

The advantage of buying a stock mutual fund for growth or a bond mutual fund for income is that you are hedging your bets against having all your money in just one or two stocks or one or two bonds. With a large pool of stocks in a growth fund, if one stock fails, the others can hold up the fund. The fund manager's job is to watch

> • • • • •
>
> Mutual funds allow you to invest a small amount of money in a number of different stocks—something you couldn't do on your own with minimal dollars. Many funds even allow initial investments as low as $100.
>
> • • • • •

the market constantly and buy or sell as is prudent with meeting the objective of the fund.

Mutual funds offer many advantages. One is expertise. If you are swamped and don't have the time or the skill to study and pick your own stocks, mutual funds offer professional management. It is not only acceptable but smart to get help if you don't have the knowledge.

Mutual funds allow you to "dollar cost average" and reinvest dividends and gains. *Dollar cost averaging* means putting the same amount of money into the same fund on a regular basis (monthly, quarterly, etc.). One certainty of the stock market is that it will fluctuate. Instead of fighting or fearing this key fact, put it to work for you.

Let's say you decide to put in $100 per month. When the share price of your fund is up, your $100 doesn't buy as many shares. But when the share price is down, your $100 buys more shares. It's like getting them on sale! And then when the share price moves back up again, you have more shares growing for you. Most funds provide a bank draft authorization so that the bank can automatically deduct the $100 from your account each month. We think of it as tithing to yourself. It's a good way to place yourself into "automatic"—each month on a specific date, a set amount of money is transferred to your fund account. A forced type of investing/savings that becomes a habit!

Funds need to be watched like any other investment. Most follow consistent investment strategies based on extensive research, primarily done within the fund's management. The managers decide when and what securities to buy or sell; give you the option of regular disbursements or automatic reinvestment of gains, dividends, or interest; and take care of the paperwork for IRS purposes at the end of the year.

With that said, do people lose money in funds? Yes, they have and will. Mutual funds carry risk, just as other investments do. In considering investing in a fund, you would be wise to make sure that the manager has at least five years' experience with a positive track record.

> • • • • •
>
> You have the option of reinvesting dividends and capital gains or taking them in cash. We highly recommend that you reinvest all dividends and gains. This gives you the opportunity to speed up your compounding potential.
>
> • • • • •

Your Liquidity Fund

You may be tempted to put all your cash into some type of investment, thinking that's the best way to get growth. Don't. Life is quite good at delivering the unexpected. You need a slush fund for any possible emergencies. Emergencies come in the form of new tires, medical care that insurance doesn't cover, cutbacks or layoffs at work, Mother Nature's destruction, flying somewhere for a funeral, or (heaven forbid) bailing someone out of jail.

> • • • • •
> Everyone needs a liquidity fund, monies that you can access within seven days.
> • • • • •

We strongly suggest that you have from three to six months' fixed expenses in your liquidity fund—your backup emergency fund. That way, if you have to take time to get another job, get well, grieve, or fix the roof, you'll be able to cover those expenses plus your everyday fixed ones (utilities, housing, food, and any ongoing bills) for a few months. It does not mean eating out, getting spiffy new clothes, or taking vacations.

13 Questions to Ask a Financial Adviser

• • • • •

1.   Do you have the CFP (Certified Financial Planner) or ChFC (Chartered Financial Consultant) designations?
This ensures that he or she has had specialized training in the field of financial planning.

2. Do you have specialized training in the area of divorce?
A CDP (Certified Divorce Planner) is a financial professional who has had additional training in the specifics of the financial issues in divorce.

(continued)

3. **Do you work alone, or in an office with other professionals such as financial planners, accountants, attorneys, etc.?**
   No one person can know all the aspects of financial issues, tax laws, retirement issues, etc. When they have other professionals to bounce ideas off of, you are the winner.

4. **Do you continue with your education and keep up with the changing trends?**
   Countless classes, conferences, and educational meetings are available for those who are truly interested in keeping up.

5. **How is your personal portfolio doing?**
   It is tricky to ask someone about his or her personal investments, but wouldn't you be more comfortable with someone who had a successful investment history? Someone who scrambles to pay the rent each month probably won't make you wealthy.

6. **Can you give me the names of some of your clients?**
   Ask for referrals who have worked with them for a minimum of three years.

7. **Are you service-oriented?**
   You want to hear from your financial adviser more than once a year. You want someone who will explain the statements you get and review your portfolio with you once in a while to see if you are reaching your goals.

8. **How do you charge?**
   There are typically three ways of charging:
   - *Fee only.* The adviser charges for the time spent with you and for his or her advice. The adviser does not make any commissions on products that you buy.
   - *Commission only.* This adviser does not charge for his or her time or for a financial plan that he or she prepares. This adviser earns a commission on any investments that you make. These are typically in-house products. In return, the adviser should give you service.
   - *Fee plus commission.* Typically, this adviser doesn't charge for a first marketing appointment. If comprehensive work is done later, such

as a full financial plan, he or she will charge for time spent on that. In addition, the adviser will receive a commission on any product that you purchase through him or her. In return, the adviser should give you service.

9. **Have you made errors in advising clients in the past?**
    Everyone makes mistakes, including financial advisers. Anyone who says, "No, I've never made any errors," is lying. Use someone else. If the adviser 'fesses up, ask what the mistakes were and what the adviser learned. Then you be the judge.

10. **Have any complaints been filed against you?**
    You can check with the National Association of Security Dealers (NASD—1735 K St., N.W., Washington, DC 20006; 202-778-8000; www.nasd.com) or the Securities and Exchange Commission (SEC—405 Fifth St., N.W., Washington, DC 20549; 202-942-7040; www.sec.gov) for securities complaints. For real estate and insurance, check with your state departments that cover those areas.

11. **Where do you get your financial advice?**
    A terrific question, and one that will surprise them. Some rely solely on information generated from their company, others aggressively seek other sources. Find out where and what.

12. **What publications do you read on a regular basis?**
    Let's hope it's more than *Time* and *Newsweek.* Magazines such as *Money, Fortune,* and newspapers including the *Wall Street Journal* should head the list. Depending on which associations the adviser belongs to, there will be a professional trade journal with the memberships.

13. **What professional associations do you belong to and how long have you been advising clients?**
    Active professionals should belong to associations that enhance their skills and education. Your should hear names such as the International Association of Financial Planners or the Institute of Certified Financial Planners.

• • • • •

Afterword

Going through a divorce is like experiencing the perfect storm. In a perfect storm, it can't get any worse; it's an incredible display of nature's violent moods. During your divorce, you have experienced times when your seas felt fairly calm and times when you felt as though you would be toppled by hundred-foot waves. Forces come at you from all sides. It doesn't matter if it's emotional, legal, financial, or strategic. They just come at you. If you had your druthers, you would stay out of the storm, to make it stop or go away.

Our goal in this book was to become your quasi-partner—to help you with the game-play of what we, in our collective experiences, have garnered in the four areas of emotional feelings, legal issues, financial tactics, and strategic planning and then identify tactics that you could use to implement our advice.

From our previous books on the topic of divorce, each of us have had numerous calls and meetings with men and women who have read them. It is always exciting for an author and adviser to hear that a recommendation helped them. We are confident that you will be able to use a great deal of what we have written in the preceding pages to your advantage.

Our objective was to inform you, show you where to look for help, and yes, we admit, entertain you in the process. We trust we succeeded.

Appendix

Tables of State-by-State Divorce Statistics

The following tables are reprinted with permission from the American Bar Association, *Family Law Quarterly* 30, no. 4 (Winter 1997). These tables are for illustration only. Laws change often. Always check with your attorney for up-to-date rules.

Alimony/Spousal Support Factors

STATE	Statutory List	Marital Fault Not Considered	Marital Fault Relevant	Standard of Living	Status as Custodial Parent
Alabama			x	x	
Alaska	x	x		x	x
Arizona	x	x	x	x	x
Arkansas		x			
California	x	x		x	
Colorado	x	x		x	x
Connecticut	x		x	x	x
Delaware	x	x		x	x
D.C.			x	x	
Florida	x		x	x	
Georgia	x		x	x	
Hawaii	x	x		x	x
Idaho	x		x		
Illinois	x	x		x	x
Indiana	x	x		x	x
Iowa	x	x		x	x
Kansas		x			
Kentucky	x	x		x	
Louisiana	x		x		x
Maine	x	x			
Maryland	x		x	x	
Massachusetts	x		x	x	x
Michigan			x	x	
Minnesota	x	x		x	x
Mississippi			x		
Missouri	x		x	x	x
Montana	x	x		x	x
Nebraska		x			
Nevada			x	x	x
New Hampshire	x		x	x	x
New Jersey	x		x	x	x
New Mexico	x	x		x	
New York	x		x	x	x
North Carolina	x	x		x	
North Dakota			x	x	
Ohio	x	x			
Oklahoma		x		x	x
Oregon	x	x		x	x
Pennsylvania	x		x	x	
Rhode Island	x		x	x	x
South Carolina	x		x	x	x
South Dakota			x	x	
Tennessee	x		x	x	x
Texas	x		x	x	x
Utah	x		x	x	
Vermont	x	x		x	x
Virginia	x		x	x	
Washington	x	x		x	
West Virginia			x		
Wisconsin	x	x		x	x
Wyoming			x		

Custody Criteria

STATE	Statutory Guidelines	Children's Wishes	Joint Custody	Cooperative Parent	Domestic Violence	Health	Attorney or GAL
Alabama	x		x		x		
Alaska	x	x	x	x	x	x	x
Arizona	x	x	x	x	x	x	x
Arkansas							
California	x	x			x		x
Colorado	x	x	x	x	x	x	x
Connecticut		x	x				x
Delaware	x	x				x	x
D.C.	x	x	x	x	x	x	x
Florida	x	x	x	x	x	x	x
Georgia	x	x	x				x
Hawaii	x	x			x		x
Idaho	x	x	x		x	x	
Illinois	x	x	x	x	x	x	x
Indiana	x	x	x	x	x	x	x
Iowa	x	x	x	x	x	x	x
Kansas	x	x	x	x	x	x	
Kentucky	x	x	x	x	x	x	x
Louisiana	x	x	x		x		
Maine	x				x		x
Maryland			x		x		x
Massachusetts			x		x		x
Michigan	x	x	x	x	x	x	x
Minnesota	x	x	x		x		x
Mississippi	x		x				
Missouri	x	x	x	x	x	x	x
Montana	x	x	x		x		x
Nebraska	x	x	x			x	x
Nevada	x	x	x	x	x		x
New Hampshire	x	x	x		x		x
New Jersey	x	x	x	x	x		x
New Mexico	x	x	x	x	x	x	x
New York		x					x
North Carolina		x			x	x	
North Dakota	x	x			x	x	
Ohio	x	x	x		x	x	x
Oklahoma	x	x		x	x		
Oregon	x	x	x		x		
Pennsylvania	x	x	x	x	x	x	x
Rhode Island		x	x	x	x	x	x
South Carolina		x	x	x	x	x	x
South Dakota		x	x	x			
Tennessee	x	x	x		x	x	x
Texas	x	x	x	x	x	x	x
Utah	x	x	x	x			x
Vermont	x		x		x		x
Virginia	x	x	x	x	x	x	x
Washington	x	x			x	x	x
West Virginia		x	x		x		
Wisconsin	x	x	x	x	x	x	x
Wyoming		x	x		x		

Child Support Guidelines

STATE	Income Share	Percent of Income	Extraordinary Medical Add On*	Child-Care Add On*	College Support	UIFSA
Alabama	x		x	x	x	
Alaska		x	x			x
Arizona	x		x	x		x
Arkansas		x				x
California	x		x	x		
Colorado	x			x	x	x
Connecticut	x					
Delaware			x	x		x
D.C.		x		x	x	x
Florida	x		x	x		x
Georgia		x	x			
Hawaii				x	x	
Idaho	x		x	x		x
Illinois		x			x	x
Indiana	x		x	x	x	x
Iowa	x				x	
Kansas	x		x	x		x
Kentucky	x		x	x		
Louisiana	x		x	x		x
Maine	x		x	x		x
Maryland	x		x	x		x
Massachusetts		x	x		x	x
Michigan	x		x	x	x	x
Minnesota		x		x		x
Mississippi		x				
Missouri	x		x	x	x	x
Montana			x	x		x
Nebraska	x			x		x
Nevada		x	x			
New Hampshire		x			x	
New Jersey	x		x	x	x	
New Mexico	x		x	x		x
New York	x		x	x	x	
North Carolina	x		x	x		x
North Dakota		x				x
Ohio	x			x		
Oklahoma	x		x	x		x
Oregon	x		x	x	x	x
Pennsylvania	x		x	x		x
Rhode Island	x			x		x
South Carolina	x		x	x	x	x
South Dakota	x	x	x			x
Tennessee		x				
Texas		x	x			x
Utah	x		x	x		x
Vermont	x		x	x		
Virginia	x		x	x		x
Washington	x		x	x	x	x
West Virginia	x		x	x		
Wisconsin		x	x			x
Wyoming	x	x				x

*Source: Laura W. Morgan, Child Support Guidelines (1996).

Grounds for Divorce and Residency Requirements

STATE	No Fault Sole Ground	No Fault Added to Traditional	Incompatibility	Living Separate and Apart	Judicial Separation	Durational Requirements
Alabama		x	x	2 years	x	6 months
Alaska		x	x		x	None
Arizona	x				x	90 days
Arkansas		x		18 months	x	60 days
California	x				x	6 months
Colorado	x				x	90 days
Connecticut		x		18 months	x	1 year
Delaware	x					6 months
D.C.	x			1 year	x	6 months
Florida	x					6 months
Georgia		x				6 months
Hawaii	x			2 years	x	6 months
Idaho		x			x	6 weeks
Illinois		x		2 years	x	90 days
Indiana		x			x	60 days
Iowa	x				x	None
Kansas			x			60 days
Kentucky	x				x	180 days
Louisiana		x		6 months	x	None
Maine		x			x	6 months
Maryland		x		2 years	x	1 year
Massachusetts		x			x	None
Michigan	x				x	6 months
Minnesota	x			60 days	x	180 days
Mississippi		x				6 months
Missouri		x		1-2 years	x	90 days
Montana	x		x	180 days	x	90 days
Nebraska	x				x	1 year
Nevada			x	1 year	x	6 weeks
New Hampshire		x		2 years		1 year
New Jersey		x		18 months		1 year
New Mexico		x	x		x	6 months
New York		x		1 year	x	1 year
North Carolina		x		1 year	x	6 months
North Dakota		x			x	6 months
Ohio		x	x	1 year		6 months
Oklahoma		x	x		x	6 months
Oregon	x				x	6 months
Pennsylvania		x		2 years		6 months
Rhode Island		x		3 years	x	1 year
South Carolina		x		1 year	x	3 months (both residents)
South Dakota		x			x	None
Tennessee		x		2 years	x	6 months
Texas		x		3 years		6 months
Utah		x		3 years	x	90 days
Vermont		x		6 months		6 months
Virginia		x		1 year	x	6 months
Washington	x				x	1 year
West Virginia		x		1 year	x	1 year
Wisconsin	x				x	6 months
Wyoming	x		x		x	60 days

Property Division

STATE	Community Property	Only Marital Divided	Statutory List of Factors	Nonmonetary Contributions	Economic Misconduct	Contribution to Education
Alabama		x		x		x
Alaska			x	x	x	x
Arizona	x		x		x	x
Arkansas		x	x	x		
California	x		x	x	x	x
Colorado		x	x	x	x	
Connecticut			x	x	x	x
Delaware			x	x	x	
D.C.		x	x	x	x	
Florida		x	x	x		x
Georgia		x				
Hawaii			x	x	x	
Idaho	x		x			
Illinois		x	x	x	x	
Indiana		x	x	x	x	x
Iowa		x	x	x		
Kansas			x		x	
Kentucky		x	x	x	x	x
Louisiana	x					
Maine		x	x	x		
Maryland		x	x	x		
Massachusetts			x	x	x	
Michigan		x		x	x	x
Minnesota		x	x	x	x	
Mississippi						
Missouri		x	x	x	x	x
Montana		x		x	x	
Nebraska		x		x		
Nevada	x	x		x	x	x
New Hampshire			x	x	x	x
New Jersey		x	x	x	x	x
New Mexico	x					
New York		x	x	x	x	x
North Carolina		x	x	x	x	x
North Dakota				x	x	x
Ohio		x	x	x	x	x
Oklahoma		x		x	x	
Oregon				x		x
Pennsylvania		x	x	x	x	x
Rhode Island		x	x	x	x	x
South Carolina		x	x	x	x	x
South Dakota				x	x	
Tennessee		x	x	x	x	x
Texas	x				x	
Utah					x	
Vermont			x	x	x	x
Virginia		x	x	x	x	
Washington	x		x			
West Virginia		x	x	x	x	x
Wisconsin	x	x	x	x	x	x
Wyoming		x	x			

Third-Party Visitation

STATE	Stepparents	Grandparents—Death of Their Child	Grandparents—Child Divorce	Out of Wedlock	Any Interested Party
Alabama		x	x		
Alaska	x	x	x	x	x
Arizona		x	x	x	
Arkansas		x	x		
California	x	x	x		x
Colorado		x	x	x	
Connecticut	x	x	x	x	x
Delaware	x		x		
D.C.					
Florida		x	x	x	
Georgia		x	x		
Hawaii	x		x		
Idaho			x	x	
Illinois		x	x	x	
Indiana	x	x	x	x	
Iowa		x	x		
Kansas	x	x	x	x	
Kentucky		x	x	x	
Louisiana		x	x		
Maine	x	x	x	x	
Maryland		x	x		
Massachusetts		x	x		
Michigan	x	x	x		
Minnesota	x	x	x	x	
Mississippi		x	x		
Missouri		x	x	x	
Montana		x	x	x	
Nebraska	x	x	x		
Nevada		x	x	x	
New Hampshire	x	x	x		
New Jersey	x	x	x	x	
New Mexico	x	x	x	x	x
New York	x	x	x	x	
North Carolina			x		
North Dakota	x	x	x		
Ohio	x	x	x		x
Oklahoma		x	x	x	
Oregon	x	x	x	x	x
Pennsylvania		x	x		
Rhode Island		x	x		
South Carolina		x	x	x	
South Dakota		x	x	x	
Tennessee	x		x		
Texas	x	x	x	x	x
Utah	x	x	x		
Vermont		x	x		
Virginia	x		x		x
Washington	x		x		
West Virginia		x	x	x	
Wisconsin		x	x		
Wyoming	x	x	x		x

Divorce Resource Center

Associations and Organizations

Legal and Mediation Associations

American Academy of Family Mediators
4 Militia Drive
Lexington, MA 02173
617-674-2663
This organization can refer you to trained mediators in your area.

American Academy of Matrimonial Lawyers
150 North Michigan Avenue, Suite 2040
Chicago, IL 60601
312-263-6477; Fax: 312-263-7682
This organization can refer you to attorneys who specialize in family law matters.

American Bar Association
750 North Lake Shore Drive
Chicago, IL 60611
312-988-5000; 800-621-6159; Fax: 312-988-6281
The ABA has more than 400,000 members. Contact it for a listing of state bar associations and referrals within your state.

237

Association of Family and Conciliation Courts
329 West Wilson Street
Madison, WI 53703
602-251-4001; Fax: 602-251-2231; E-mail: afcc@igc.apc.org
This international association of judges, attorneys, counselors, custody evaluators, and mediators has a library of material on custody and visitation issues, child support, mediation, and more. Parent education programs and conferences on child welfare issues are sponsored on an ongoing basis. Their membership directory is available to nonmembers for $15.

Support Organizations

There are thousands of self-help groups and organizations that you can turn to for help. We've listed a few of them for you.

AMEND (Abusive Men Exploring New Directions)
777 Grant Street, Suite 600
Denver, CO 80203
303-832-6363; Fax: 303-832-6364
AMEND provides therapy for abusive men along with information on help resources for women in abusive relationships.

Association for Children for Enforcement of Support (ACES)
2260 Upton Avenue
Toledo, OH 43606
419-472-6609; 800-537-7072; Fax: 419-472-6295
If you are having problems collecting child support, ACES is good place to start. Contact them for a chapter near you.

Find the Children
11811 West Olympic Boulevard
Los Angeles, CA 90064
310-477-6721; Fax: 310-477-7166
A national nonprofit organization dedicated to the prevention, location, and recovery of missing children. Missing children are registered, and photographs and information about missing children are distributed. All services are free.

National Center for Missing and Exploited Children
2101 Wilson Boulevard, Suite 550
Arlington, VA 22201-3052
703-235-3900; 800-826-7653; Fax: 703-235-4067
800-843-5678 (24-hour hotline to report missing children)
This organization offers legal and technical assistance in parental abduction cases. The string attached is that the parent reporting the abduction must have legal custody before the abducted child will be entered into their computer system as a missing child. NCMEC tracks other groups that assist in recovering missing children. Contact them for a group near you.

National Foundation for Consumer Credit
8611 2nd Avenue, Suite 100
Silver Spring, MD 20910
301-589-5600; 800-388-2227; Fax: 301-495-5623;
Spanish assistance: 800-682-9832
This organization offers free or low-cost professional money management counseling and educational services to consumers nationwide. Its purpose is to educate, counsel, and promote the wise use of credit.

Older Women's League
666 11th Street, Suite 700
Washington, DC 20001
202-783-6686
Support and information on issues are provided to midlife and older women.

Parents Sharing Custody Network International
420 South Beverly Drive, Suite 100
Beverly Hills, CA 90212
310-286-9171
This national membership network is designed to assist those involved in the cooperative raising of children. A good resource for parents seeking information and solutions. It publishes a newsletter, *Do It with Love.*

Parents without Partners
401 North Michigan Avenue
Chicago, IL 60611-4267
312-644-6610; 800-637-7974
PWP provides information on child support and custody issues for custodial and noncustodial parents. Chapters are available nationwide.

Pension Rights Center
918 16th Street, NW, Suite 704
Washington, DC 20006
202-296-3776
Karen W. Ferguson, Director
Information is provided on how divorce affects pensions.

Stepfamily Association of America
215 Centennial Mall South, Suite 212
Lincoln, NE 68508
402-477-7837; Fax: 402-477-8317
Chapters are located throughout the United States and one in Canada. Provides education and support for anyone in a stepfamily.

Index

About the Authors

Judith Briles, Ph.D., is the founder of The Briles Group, Inc., a Colorado-based research and consulting firm. She is internationally acclaimed as a speaker and recognized as an expert in solutions to workplace and women's issues. Her audiences range from 50 to 5,000. More than 20,000 women and men hear Briles speak each year.

Briles is an award-winning author of 17 other books: *Becoming a Woman of Confidence; GenderTraps; Woman to Woman: From Sabotage to Support; The Confidence Factor; The Briles Report on Women in Healthcare; When God Says No; Money Sense; The Money Maze; The Workplace: Questions Women Ask; Raising Money-Wise Kids; Financial Savvy for Women; Money Guide; Faith and Savvy, Too!; Money Phases; Big Bucks Don't Grow on Trees; 10 Smart Moves for Women;* and *The Woman's Guide to Financial Savvy.*

She is featured regularly on Denver's KNUS radio and the Internet magazine *www.coloradotrends.com.* Her work has been featured in the *Wall Street Journal, Time, People, USA Today, Self, McCalls, Working Woman, Family Circle,* and the *New York Times.* She is a frequent guest on national television and radio and has appeared on CNN and CNNfn, as well as *Oprah, Leeza,* the *Geraldo Rivera Show, Sally Jessy Raphael,* the *Joan Rivers Show, HOME,* and *Good Morning America.*

For information on Briles's availability for speeches and workshops, participation in her annual "Confidence Working Cruise" designed for working professionals, or to obtain her quarterly newsletter, *The Woman's Voice,* please contact her at: The Briles Group, Inc., 14160 East Bellewood Drive, Aurora, CO 80015; 303-

627-9179, fax 303-627-9184; e-mail DrJBriles@aol.com; Web site www.briles.com.

The law offices of **Edwin C. Schilling III, JD, CFP,** concentrate in advising domestic relations lawyers nationwide on the division and valuation of federal and corporate pensions incident to divorce. He has assisted in more than 1,600 cases in all 50 states. As assistant staff judge advocate of the Air Force Accounting and Finance office, he approved or denied more than 6,000 cases involving the division or garnishment of military retired pay and civil service pay.

Schilling has given more than 100 presentations nationwide on dividing and valuing pensions. He also has testified as an expert witness in numerous cases across the nation, and his valuations have been used by counsel in over 30 states. He is the coauthor of the books *The Survival Manual for Women in Divorce* and *The Survival Manual for Men in Divorce* and the videotape and manual *How to Successfully Manage Military Divorce.*

Schilling is a member of the Family Law sections of the Alaska, Colorado, and Louisiana bar associations. He served as an executive member of the Federal Legislation and Procedures Committee of the ABA Family Law Section, and chairman of the Military Retired Pay Subcommittee. He is a graduate of the College for Financial Planning and a licensed Certified Financial Planner. He can be reached at: 2767 South Parker Road, #230, Aurora, CO 80014; 303-755-5121, fax 303-755-9217; Web sites www.federaldivorces.com, www.wld.com/lawyer/schilling.edwin/aurora, or on the "Divorce Military Style" section of divorcenet.com.

Carol Ann Wilson, CFP, CDP, is a recognized specialist in marital financial issues and a pioneer in the field of divorce financial planning. Her Divorce Plan™ software is widely used by attorneys and financial planners to calculate financially equitable settlements. She also has served as an expert witness in court in more than 100 divorce cases nationwide. In 1993, she founded the Institute for Certified Divorce Planners to train attorneys, CPAs, and financial professionals in the financial issues of divorce.

Wilson is the author of *The Financial Advisor's Guide to Divorce Settlement* and coauthor of *The Survival Manual for Women in Divorce* and *The Survival Manual for Men in Divorce.* She frequently serves as a speaker and faculty member of high-ranking legal and financial organizations, including the Colorado Bar Association, the Chicago Bar Association, the International Association for Financial Planning, and the Institute of Certified Financial Planners. She has been published in *Trial Talk, The Colorado Lawyer,* and the *Journal of Financial Planning,* and has been featured in publications such as *Financial Advisor, Accounting Today, Glamour, Savvy,* and others.

Wilson has served as delegate to the White House Small Business Conference and is a member of the International Association for Financial Planning and the Institute for Certified Financial Planners. For information about her books, the Institute for Certified Divorce Planners, or the name of a Certified Divorce Planner, please contact her at: The Institute for Certified Divorce Planners, 2724 Winding Trail Place, Boulder, CO 80304; 800-875-1760; e-mail InstCDP@aol.com; Web site www.InstituteCDP.com.